MANY A CLOSE
RUN THING

MANY A CLOSE RUN THING

Tales from Kiwi aviator
TOM ENRIGHT

HarperCollinsPublishers

HarperCollinsPublishers
First published in 2019
by HarperCollinsPublishers (New Zealand) Limited
Unit D1, 63 Apollo Drive, Rosedale, Auckland 0632, New Zealand
harpercollins.co.nz

Copyright © Thomas Enright 2019

Tom Enright asserts the moral right to be identified as the author of this work. This work is copyright. All rights reserved. No part of this publication may be reproduced, copied, scanned, stored in a retrieval system, recorded, or transmitted, in any form or by any means, without the prior written permission of the publisher.

HarperCollinsPublishers
Unit D1, 63 Apollo Drive, Rosedale, Auckland 0632, New Zealand
Level 13, 201 Elizabeth Street, Sydney NSW 2000, Australia
A 53, Sector 57, Noida, UP, India
1 London Bridge Street, London, SE1 9GF, United Kingdom
Bay Adelaide Centre, East Tower, 22 Adelaide Street West, 41st floor, Toronto,
   Ontario M5H 4E3, Canada
195 Broadway, New York NY 10007, USA

A catalogue record for this book is available from the National Library of New Zealand.

ISBN 978 1 7755 4143 1 (pbk)
ISBN 978 1 7754 9174 3 (ebook)

Cover design by Darren Holt, HarperCollins Design Studio
Typeset in Bembo by Kirby Jones
Front cover image: from the author's collection
Back cover image: Creative Commons/Tyler Brenot
Printed and bound in Australia by McPherson's Printing Group
The papers used by HarperCollins in the manufacture of this book are a natural, recyclable product made from wood grown in sustainable plantation forests. The fibre source and manufacturing processes meet recognised international environmental standards, and carry certification.

I began to write this book not long after tragically losing my dear wife, June. Just two days after the joyful celebration of the 50th anniversary of our marriage, she fell down stairs and died shortly thereafter. Left lamenting were five sons and their spouses, nine grandchildren and me. With sadness, we interred her ashes beneath a lacy Japanese maple in Auckland's beautiful Mt Eden Gardens.

I dedicate this book to my darling June.

And I am honoured to add also
14/75 and 5 Squadrons, RNZAF,
and the wonderful staff and companions
I met at the RAF College at Cranwell.

'As between me and death, it's been a close-run thing.'

The Duke of Wellington,
on his return from the Peninsular Wars

*'In military aviation, I had more than my fair share
of close-run things.'*

Tom Enright

CONTENTS

Introduction	3

MILITARY DAYS — 5

1	An Otago Upbringing	7
2	Off to England, Aged 17	16
3	Becoming a Pilot at Cranwell	24
4	Opening Night, Cranwell South New Airfield	34
5	Cranwell's Lessons for Life	43
6	Ohakea and a Wild Ride	57
7	Timaru Air Show	73
8	Wellington Airport Opening, 1959	80
9	Displays, Birdstrike and Bone Domes	95
10	It's Your Best Pupil Who'll Kill You	101
11	Trouble in the Mountains	115
12	The Sunderland	121
13	Around the Pacific	129
14	A Night to Remember	172
15	Sir Tim Wallis, a Great Kiwi	181
16	The Mighty Hunter, the Orion	189

AIRLINE TALES — 201

17	Off to the Airline World	203
18	A Day at the Office	232
19	Ensuring Air Crew Remain Competent	243
20	Singapore Airlines	253
21	Boys and Girls	271
22	Flying Still	274
23	Malaysian Airlines Flight 370	279
24	Looking Back	306

INTRODUCTION

Aviation has given me a great life. From my earliest days I have had an endless fascination with all things to do with flying. My enchantment began during my childhood in Central Otago, New Zealand. Horses were then in common use, few people owned motor cars and aeroplanes were a rarity. When a plane flew through our alpine skies, it was an event. People in nearby valleys would ring up – cranking on the old party-line telephone – to bring us the news that an aeroplane was headed our way. We children would rush outside and wait patiently until the mysterious buzzing object appeared in our patch of sky. The roar, muted by distance, of what seemed so powerful an engine was music to my ears. From my first distant encounter with an aeroplane I wanted to make flying my life.

Fast forward from the two room, one teacher school of St Bathans to secondary schooling in the City of Dunedin. There I joined the Air Training Corps of the Royal New Zealand Air Force (RNZAF). I overcame a terrifying first flight and soaked up everything to do with aviation which came my way. Schooling done, I joined the RNZAF as an engineering apprentice, choosing to study the trade of aircraft instruments. The RNZAF sent me to England at the age of 16. Leaving my parents and brothers and sisters behind was a wrench but there were many exciting things to look forward to.

On graduation, I was recommended for a cadetship with the Royal Air Force College at Cranwell, England (the RAF is the British air force) where I was awarded the coveted pilot's wings.

My first 20 years flying was in a variety of military aircraft in which I had most interesting and thrilling experiences, including rather more than my fair share of close-run things. Then fortune smiled on me and I spent 25 years as an airline pilot.

When I talked about my experiences to people, both in and out of aviation, I was frequently exhorted to write about things which had happened to me. For a long time I remained diffident and perhaps a little shy about parading my life before the world. But gradually I have come to see that the lessons I have learned are of value to young people setting out on a flying career. I have also realised that interest in aviation and flying is quite widespread. I have enjoyed letting the memories spring onto paper. I hope there will be pleasure and interest in my words.

MILITARY JAYS

MILITARY DAYS

I

AN OTAGO UPBRINGING

My first flight was in a Tiger Moth. It was so terrifying that it is a wonder I ever flew again. But I overcame that experience and enjoyed 45 years of enthralling life in the air.

I was born into a farming family at Ranfurly, Otago Central, New Zealand in 1934 – one of nine children – and spent my early life in the district of St Bathans.

St Bathans is a famed gold mining district. The precious metal was discovered there in 1862. The lure of easy money attracted the usual horde of pick and shovel wielding fortune hunters but the primitive methods used by these rough men were not very productive. However, St Bathans was fortunate to attract the attentions of an enterprising Scotsman, one John Ewing. Of limited formal education, John had an active brain and excellent organisational abilities. He introduced to the New Zealand goldfields new methods from California which required large quantities of water to sluice away topsoil and uncover the gold. The water from rivers and streams plunging through the ancient hills was brought to the mines via hundreds of kilometres of water races. Building the races through rocky mountains and hills required herculean efforts. Surveyed with homemade equipment, they were laboriously hacked out with hand tools. Even vertical faces on some hills did not deter these resourceful men. They built up rock walls lying against the faces to the level required to transport the water across the face.

There were two major goldfields in this district: the Blue Lake and the Grey Lake. Each contained quantities of gold in deep folds in the earth. The Blue Lake started out as a large hillock but the miners sluiced it all away and managed to excavate the rich gravels and quartz beds to deep levels. Now filled with water, the ancient excavation has flooded to form a picturesque lake, which attracts tourists, swimmers and boaties from far afield.

My grandfather, an Irishman, had come to New Zealand with the initial rush of miners in the 1880s and arrived in St Bathans. He had the wisdom to recognise that the fifty thousand odd miners working in the district needed to be supplied with food and he became a farmer. He was also a successful gold miner and company director. My father, second youngest of six healthy children, ran one of Grandfather's operations, a coal mine. This thriving business supplied the village and surrounding areas. As a young man, my father had lots of gumption and go, riding to the hares and hounds, enlisting as a reservist in the New Zealand Territorial Army and attending annual army camps.

In 1914, my uncle Jack, the St Bathans postmaster, was first in the district to receive the news that Great Britain had accepted the New Zealand Government's offer of a fighting force to oppose the Germans. He immediately informed my father, who promptly volunteered. Dad was the first man in Central Otago to volunteer for active service in the army on the outbreak of World War I. As a country man with his own mounts, he was welcomed into the First Otago Mounted Rifles.

His War Service Certificate, which graces my office, records four years and 123 days' war service, of which three years and 358 days were spent overseas. The theatres in which he served were Egypt (as part of the Egyptian Expeditionary Force), the Balkans and Western Europe. In Europe he was a trench mortarman, specialising in short range attacks on enemy trenches. His unit was popular as their mortar shells could shred the rolls of razor-sharp wire the Germans put up as barriers. On several occasions, he was loaned to the British army to assist in getting their wagons through the mud. He was gassed and shot in the foot and spent at least two periods in hospital.

We know that he had been wounded in Gallipoli and was sent to an English hospital. On discharge on sick leave, before rejoining his battalion, he visited County Wicklow, Ireland, his mother's birthplace. At a remote spot in the Irish countryside, his stagecoach driver said, 'This is as far as we go. Walk 25 miles that way.' That distance being no problem to a fit young soldier he was soon knocking on the relatives' door. Consternation! This was 1916 and Ireland was in rebellion. Runners were immediately despatched around the district to warn the more hot-headed republican sympathisers that this was not a British soldier and was to be left unharmed.

Amazingly, Dad survived the long years of slaughter and hellish battles. He was a brave and honourable man.

To my deep regret, it was only after his death that I learned how his life had been gutted by the trauma of something that happened to him in the battles at Gallipoli. Dad was always reluctant to talk about the war but my elder brother coaxed this dreadful story out of him. He'd been sheltering in a shell hole with all his mates and went on a toilet call. On his return he found the sanctuary had taken a direct hit. All his friends were killed and he saw their remains pitchforked into sugar bags. Dad said he could never think of the war without bursting into tears.

In those days, no one wanted to talk about the British failure against the Turks and there was little understanding of trauma, so those old soldiers never received treatment for disabling states of mind. Dad simply lost his drive. On his return from the war he was content to just drift along and live on pocket money doled out by his mother. In recognition of his war service, he was granted valuable land near the village of St Bathans by the government. Had he followed his father's example he would have built upon this base to carve out a family estate. But because of its association with the war and the loss of his friends, he virtually gave the land away and was content to work for wages for the rest of his life – to my mother's chagrin.

My mother, Violet, was a champion. She was of English Norfolk yeoman stock whose family name was Youngman. The family were strictly Presbyterian so when my young mother, influenced by a friend who was a Catholic prelate, converted to Catholicism, mortal offence was taken and Violet was cast out. She managed to find a position on the Hawkdun Station at St Bathans. This property adjoined my grandfather's land and so she met my father Thomas and they married. After the wedding she discovered that Dad's savings amounted to only five pounds. He had been content to work his father's coal operation without wages. My mother told me if she had known this she would never have married him. But, champion that she was, she faced up to the situation in which she found herself, purchased a house and brought up and educated me and my four brothers and four sisters. Mum was of a generation whose parents regarded education of girls as unimportant but she was absolutely determined that her daughters would have the best education possible. My four sisters were taught by the best, and subsequently each one became a qualified teacher herself and a talented artist. I am proud of all of them. When, finally, the youngest children finished schooling, Mum started a career in real estate, working with energy and skill. Everyone in the family was devastated when she was killed in a motor accident.

My mother was a valiant woman.

My early education started in the infants' room of the two-room St Bathans school, a stone structure without framing. In 1943, it succumbed to an earthquake that caused extensive damage throughout New Zealand. I well remember the moment it struck. My elder brother Jack and I were trying to find our milking cow. I was standing at the top of an old cliff created by miners sluicing away earth in their quest for gold. Suddenly this cliff collapsed, almost at our feet, with a thunderous roar. Jack and I turned and ran, vaulting an eight-strand fence 100 yards back from the cliff edge. Such is the power of adrenaline. We ran home to tell Mum and were promptly despatched back to find the cow.

In 1943, when I was nine, I had a brief career in the army. An army major appeared in St Bathans and directed the digging of trenches by the old men and boys of the district (all the young men were in uniform fighting overseas). We were expected to get in the trenches and fight invading Japanese, who were at that very moment on the high seas heading for Fiji. The suppression of Fiji would be followed by Samoa then New Zealand, in preparation for the invasion of Australia. The Japanese 'co-prosperity sphere' was to be directed on the axis Toyko–Wellington. A special currency had been created and supplies were aboard the war fleet.

But, abruptly, work on the trenches stopped and the major disappeared. I now realise this was because the invading Japanese fleet had been destroyed at the Battle of the Coral Sea; the Americans were reading the Japanese code and sank the enemy ships.

Thank you, mighty United States Navy! You saved us. Today I won't hear a word said against you.

Schooldays in Dunedin

At the end of the war, my family shifted to the city of Dunedin. This move enabled us to have educational opportunities but we missed the country life. We retained our old house at St Bathans and returned every school holidays, embarking on the Central Otago rail line, travelling in ancient carriages drawn by a steam engine billowing clouds of smoke and steam. This line, through the spectacular Taieri River Gorge, is now a tourist rail experience as far as Middlemarch. The railroad bed from then on has been converted into the Central Otago Rail Trail. Our old sun-dried brick house remains in the family to this day and continues to delight generations of children.

The line runs past the airfield at Taieri which, in my schooldays, was the air base for the RNZAF's fleet of Tiger Moths. As the train approached the airfield, we children would crowd around the windows in the hope of seeing aircraft flying at low level and even – joy of joys – swooping over our train and landing. Every time I saw one of the airborne machines, I imagined myself in the cockpit and longed for the day when I might fly. Long after my siblings had ceased to talk about the marvellous machines I would remember the thrill of seeing an aircraft in flight.

In Dunedin, I attended a school run by the Christian Brothers order. Fine and honourable men, the Brothers were strict disciplinarians and demanding taskmasters. They taught me Latin declensions and a love of boxing. The boxing master was a large Australian man nicknamed 'Big Dig' ('Dig/Digger' is slang for 'Australian'). He also taught Latin. If dissatisfied with class performance, he would line us all up around the walls of the room, reach into the pocket of his gown for his strap ('the cuts', carried by all Brothers) and deliver a stinging blow on the hand to each third boy.

The Air Training Corps experience furthered my

knowledge of aviation and each week included one afternoon at school and Friday evening at the city unit hall, training with regular and reservist Air Force officers and NCOs.

The physical training sessions allowed me opportunities to practise my boxing techniques. During one memorable sparring match, I took my instructor, a PTI (physical training instructor), by surprise. My knockout punch wasn't the usual right uppercut but a powerful straight left to the jaw. I had surprised several boxers with this and caught out the PTI with a hard blow. He went down like a poleaxed steer.

On his regaining his feet I could see that he was really angry and steeled myself for a hiding. Instead he visibly controlled his anger and went calmly on with the lesson. He was really disciplined and I admired him for it.

I was lucky to have cousins who farmed near Timaru. They were great fun and invited me to work for them during school holidays and were like my second family. They recognised I was a natural with horses – I had the reputation of being a horse whisperer – and my principal job was driving their teams of up to eight horses. A teamster's life was hard work. I'd be up at 5.30 in the cracking frost to bring in the horses, groom them, feed them, feed myself – 10 minutes for breakfast – harness them and, if lucky, start ploughing or whatever by 8.30. At 4 pm the work stopped, and the horses were taken to the stables to be washed, groomed and fed. In the early evening, they were driven out to the paddocks to graze. There the beasts would trample fences all night. It was a relief when my cousins were able to afford a crawler tractor for their steep pastures.

My first flight

On weekends, we Air Training Corps cadets were sometimes invited to the base at Taieri, where there were often opportunities to go flying. After several visits, my number came up, and I was thrilled to contemplate my impending first flight. Kitted out with woolly boots, a jacket and a parachute, I was strapped in to the front seat of a DH.82 Tiger Moth. We taxied out over the grass field, and soon I was airborne for the first flight of my life. We climbed steadily to about 6000 feet*, and I was enthralled with the splendid views of the Taieri River and surrounding farmland. Then, without warning, we dove straight down at the earth below.

It was terrifying!

The pilot, who thought I'd been on several flights in the Tiger Moth, then pulled up out of the dive into a vertical climb and continued into a 30-minute aerobatic routine. We looped, we rolled, we spun down out of the sky and did all manner of things until I scarcely knew which way was up anymore. The world seemed to be spinning and rotating as I clung desperately to the wing struts — if you could find them today they would still bear my fingerprints! The violent manoeuvring seemed to go on forever but at last it was over. We returned to blessed Mother Earth. I was ashen faced.

It is a wonder that I ever flew again.

The pilot was aghast. He'd confused me with another cadet, who had had several flights and had asked to do aerobatics; he apologised handsomely. However, I soon calmed down and wanted to try again, hopefully with a more sedate flight. My mother was alarmed at my still ashen appearance on my return home.

I resolved that if I ever became a pilot I would never frighten anyone if I could avoid it.

---

* Or about 1830 metres. The worlds of both military and civil aviation have largely resisted the metric system, a convention reflected in the text of this book. To convert: 1 foot = 0.305 metres; 1 nautical mile = 1.85 kilometres; and 1 knot = 1.85 km/h.

Enlistment in the Air Force

My life continued with crowded schooldays and intervals on the farm until, at the end of 1950, I was ready to leave school. The RNZAF were recruiting trainee engineers and sent me to Wellington for a series of searching tests.

My return to the South Island on the interisland ferry was memorable as we sailed through a sudden, severe storm. In a multi-bunk cabin perched just above the propeller, my fellow applicants and I clung on throughout the night. The propeller would come out of the water as the ship crested each wave, race at high speed then drop back into the water in each trough with a shuddering crash. No one got any sleep. Several yachts racing from Wellington to Christchurch were lost in the stormy conditions that night.

Memories of the storm faded fast when I received word that the RNZAF had accepted me for a three-year engineering course. The RNZAF accepted that training facilities in Royal Air Force establishments were more highly developed than anything available in New Zealand. It was decided to send 12 apprentices to England to evaluate the benefit of better training at the Number 1 School Of Technical Training, RAF Halton, in Buckinghamshire. Ours was the first intake in this scheme; several other courses were sent in the years following, until the RNZAF decided its own facilities were adequate for the training of engineers.

There I was aged 16, barely past my first kiss, facing the prospect of saying goodbye to my parents and brothers and sisters for three years. I accepted the air force's offer gladly, secure in the knowledge that an aviation career was what I wanted. I enlisted in the RNZAF in early 1951.

2

OFF TO ENGLAND, AGED 17

Things moved fast. The infamous 1951 Wharf Strike was looming and the vessel on which we were to sail to England was scheduled to be one of the last to depart New Zealand before that conflict brought military personnel onto the wharves to replace the strikers. So we were rushed through pre-departure procedures and training. My first inoculation against smallpox did not take so I was given a big dose 'to make sure'. A few days later I turned bright red over most of my body and had to be taken to the departing vessel in an ambulance.

About thirty days of relaxed shipboard life led to our arrival in the awesome city of London.

Royal Air Force Halton

Halton was located in the wooded countryside of Buckinghamshire, an hour or so by rail from London. The Officers' Mess building was an impressive country house gifted to the Royal Air Force by one of the Rothschild family, famed financiers. The donor was a bit of a showman and once entertained – and alarmed – members of the royal family by driving them in a coach drawn by zebras – notoriously stubborn beasts.

There were about 3000 persons resident at Halton, so it was a large establishment. We apprentices were accommodated in three-storey blocks. It could be quite a rough place. Sometimes in the night hours, senior apprentices from one block would stage raids on another block. If your block was under attack by several dozen young men, it was essential to repel them to prevent beds being tipped over, belongings scattered about and a mess created that would take hours to clean up before the following morning's inspection. This meant the battles, especially on the stairs, were willing. Defenders would drop things from floors above onto attackers. It wasn't unusual for several apprentices to be taken to sick quarters to be patched up after a raid. The authorities tolerated the goings on but did keep an eye on things to prevent extreme behaviour. The RAF encouraged 'spirit', and raids were thought to encourage spirited behaviour.

One day, a party of trainees was at Farnborough, the national aviation research and development facility, for the annual air show. A prototype DH.110 fighter aircraft, flown by John Derry – widely regarded as the first British pilot to break the sound barrier – disintegrated during a display flight. Engines crashed into the crowd. Twenty-seven people were killed. The Halton party was highly commended for assisting in the grisly task of gathering up the killed and wounded. At a late hour, they arrived home to find a kindly chef had prepared supper for them. The problem was he'd chosen corned beef sandwiches, the sight of which sent practically all of them running for the toilets.

Halton days were full of interest. Practical training in the workshops was matched with engineering studies which, on graduation, led to the award of the British National Certificate in Mechanical Engineering. I was taught useful skills and the discipline of working to fine limits. Aircraft instrument engineers must demonstrate fine precision, for example limits on some surfaces of a trade test job were to one tenth of a 'thou' (one thousandth of an inch). Military studies and sports filled out the curriculum.

We Kiwis were sought after by the various rugby coaches and my boxing prowess continued to improve.

Leave came around regularly and I visited first my mother's family. Ancestors had left the farming life of Norfolk and settled in Godalming, Surrey, a tailoring and clothing centre. There they prospered and set up the first Jaeger mill to produce fine woollen garments. That mill was still in operation when I visited.

There were two elderly brothers in the family. One was a very proper English gentleman. He told me he found Australians odd. 'Why' I asked, and he related a wartime story. During the war, an Australian bomber squadron flew from a nearby airfield. One evening, the high-spirited airmen were given leave and selected Godalming for their festivities. There was no shortage of beer but no food was available for the hungry fellows without ration cards. A little scouting round town yielded an unlucky jumbuck ('Strine' for sheep), which was slaughtered and hung over a fire in short order. Not only was the slaughtering a crime in wartime Britain, but the fire got out of hand and drew the firefighters and local constabulary. Godalming gaol bulged with Australians.

Next morning, my elderly relative, a Justice of the Peace, was called in to deal with them. He was assisted by another JP, even more elderly. A 23-year-old wing commander from the airmen's base came to plead for the brave airmen, fighting for England, asking that they be spared the stigma of a criminal conviction. The two JPs conferred and agreed a lecture would suffice. The older JP marshalled his thoughts but made a most ill-considered beginning. 'You men must realise,' he said, 'that less than a hundred years ago, people were deported for this sort of thing.' A stunned silence greeted these words. But only for a moment. Every Australian was outraged by this slur on his ancestors. Yelling in fury, the airmen advanced on the lawgivers, throwing courtroom furniture about. Then they stormed out of the court. Good British sense prevailed. The charges were voided, the considerable bill for the fire damage, the jumbuck and the courtroom furniture was paid and everybody forgot about it. And that, said my relative, was why he thought Australians were odd.

I did not spend all my leave with these relatives. I made contact with a patriotic organisation set up to offer hospitality to young commonwealth servicemen visiting the United Kingdom. Called the Dominions Fellowship Trust, it was ruled by a Lady Macdonald of the Isles, a redoubtable Scot whom no one crossed a second time. The hosts were subject to much more rigorous selection than the guests. Lady Macdonald told me that two Australian navy officers asked to go to a castle with a butler. They were sent to a castle with a butler. But to the butler's consternation when he came to lay out their clothes for dinner, he found only spare pairs of socks.

Through the trust I stayed with some charming and interesting people. One Scottish family who hosted me sold pedigree cattle, often to South American buyers. Brought by chauffeured Bentley from Glasgow airport, the prospective buyers were greeted with a globule of whisky. The animals, kept inside for three days prior, always looked magnificent. They'd had their teeth cleaned, their hooves polished and their coats brushed to a rosy glow (which was, no doubt, enhanced by the whisky.) Sales were in guineas, of course. This expert salesmanship could most profitably be transferred to the rough paddocks of New Zealand, where the bull for sale is likely to be shown standing in mud.

That same Scottish farmer took me fishing. He rented three pools of a salmon river for three thousand pounds a year. He said that if he wanted, he could re-let one pool to a local club for double that.

The British people showed me tremendous kindness and I retain a high regard for them.

At infrequent intervals, I was taken aloft for flying experience. Sometimes I travelled in large aircraft to sporting events. Each experience made me more aware of the beauty of flight, up in the air where all is clean and bright and earthly worries have dropped away. I joined the gliding club. I loved the quiet whisper of air through which we flew at modest speeds and the glorious views of the wooded countryside. It was through this gliding that I gained my first experience of guiding a craft throughout a flight. We used winches to pull ourselves up to start the long glide. When the tow rope had dropped away, all was quiet and peaceful, with just a whisper of air as we sailed along, ever on the lookout for a thermal to gain more height. Superb views of the beautiful Buckinghamshire countryside, with its farms, woods and villages and small towns, were visible from our lofty perches.

The gliding made me realise how badly I wanted to become a pilot. In order to switch from engineering to flying, I reasoned, my best chance was to distinguish myself at Halton and work hard to achieve a respected reputation My hope was to be considered for a flying course at the RAF college at Cranwell. Gradually, I moved up the trainee ranks – corporal, sergeant, finally the flight sergeant (this was the head trainee position with only one occupant). Being the flight sergeant carried considerable prestige and conferred authority over all the many apprentices.

***

The three years of the course at Halton flew by. A parade was reviewed by the newly crowned Queen Elizabeth herself. We were honoured. One moment had all the ladies gasping: a gust of wind blew the royal dress right up over Her Majesty's head. With aplomb, she smoothed the dress back and carried on as if nothing had happened. She was a classic lady.

I commanded the passing out parade of my entry. At the graduation ceremony, I received a large number of prizes. There was a surprising amount of publicity of the event in New Zealand, which delighted my parents. More importantly, my hard work paid off. I was recommended for a cadetship at the Royal Air Force College at Cranwell, Lincolnshire. My dream of becoming a pilot was coming within reach.

Farewell to Halton

After much deliberation, the New Zealand Government decided to accept the unbudgeted expense of my pilot training. Prior to starting the course, I returned to New Zealand on leave and had a joyous reunion with my family. After suitable leave, I was sent on a flight grading course at the RNZAF base at Taieri, where the training unit flew the historic DH.82, the Tiger Moth.

Taieri is a cold and frosty place in winter. Before the first flight of the day, engines had to be tested by being run to full power. To ensure against the aircraft pitching over, two engineers had to sit on the tail. Despite their greatcoats, the poor fellows would turn blue with cold in the frigid gale of the propwash. I sympathised.

I simply loved the flying and shrugged off the cold. Even though the old Tiger Moths were pretty basic, with primitive instrumentation and things flapping in the slipstream a bit, I soon learned to love the way aircraft can be smoothly guided in accurate flypaths. I adjusted to aerobatics, quickly forgetting any fears engineered by my first flight – what a difference when you know what is going on and are controlling the manoeuvres!

After about seven hours' instruction, following a prolonged session of takeoffs and landings under supervision, my instructor climbed out of the aircraft and waved me off on my first solo flight. The thrill of being aloft alone will always be with me. With no one else up there to guide you, you are totally responsible for everything that happens. After an immaculate circuit, I made my first solo landing, a smooth three-pointer. No one in New Zealand could have been as happy as I was on that wonderful day.

Of the many training exercises we were taught, I especially remember inverted spins and recoveries. In a spin, the aircraft is in a stalled condition of flight, invariably steeply nose down, rolling and twisting, with high gravity forces acting on the pilot's body. Obviously, one needs to know and apply the recovery actions or the spin will continue into the ground. For a normal spin they are full opposite rudder, stick slowly and centrally forward, spin stops, centralise, nose brought back above the horizon, power up, recover to straight and level flight. Then there were inverted spins, which I found thrilling. An inverted spin is entered from upside-down flight; the spin is induced by booting in full rudder while pushing forward on the stick to create an inverted stall – rough stuff that, requiring force and determination. Once the spin was established, the pilot's safety harness – four straps over a central metal boss – used to creak alarmingly as the negative gravity (G) generated by the bucketing aircraft propelled the pilot outside the open cockpit against the restraint of the straps.

Practising inverted spins in an open cockpit needs some nerve and discipline and isn't to everyone's taste.

During our training, there was one accident. An instructor, wearing the usual heavy fleece-lined boots, applied full rudder to enter a spin rather too enthusiastically. His boot jammed between the end of the rudder and the cockpit wall. He couldn't pull his foot back, so with rudder still applied the aircraft continued its spin into the ground. The student pilot bailed out and parachuted to earth unharmed, but the instructor continued in the cockpit till ground impact. Happily, he survived without serious injury.

Having now demonstrated that I had ability as a pilot, I once again bade farewell to kith and kin and was soon on my way back to England.

3

BECOMING A PILOT AT CRANWELL

The journey was in a four-engine piston Hastings, then the backbone of the RNZAF's transport fleet. Overnight and refuelling stops extended the journey to several days. I saw much of the world that was new to me. At one Middle East station, the locals told us about a recent incident involving a visiting navigator of a British aircraft. Apparently, the unfortunate man had suffered a nervous breakdown. He seemed to get upset when he saw a local Arab riding an overburdened donkey, a common sight in those lands. Shrieking, the navigator seized a knife from the kitchen and set off in hot pursuit. The startled Arab dug in his heels and made a speedy departure. The poor navigator was taken off by men in white coats. I suppose the lesson is to keep an eye on your crew members.

On arrival in England, I travelled to Lincolnshire to start three enthralling years at Cranwell. The college at Cranwell occupies a striking building dominated by its dome, a magnificent landmark in the flat country surrounding the now thriving town of Sleaford.

The Royal Air Force was established in 1918 to be a force separate from the British Army and the Royal Navy. On the advice of the South African Field Marshal Jan Smuts, commissioned by the British Government to render advice, two basic establishments were set up to train officers and engineers – Cranwell and my old school, Halton. Field Marshal Smuts has pride of place among the rich collections of portraits and aviation scenes in the college hall.

For the first two terms of my course, of four months each, we cadets lived in the Junior Entry Huts, spartan accommodation designed to teach future officers what barrack life was like for ordinary airmen. It was also an introduction to Cranwell life. Frequent raids on the newly arrived by the next-up Entry were a Cranwell tradition, designed to mould the recruits into a cohesive team. It worked: after a week of night raids, it was the Entry against the world. A favourite ordeal to be inflicted on a new cadet hustled from his warm bed was flying the 'Messerschmitt', a bath with a broomstick for a control column. Willing hands lifted and swung the bath while buckets of water were thrown over the new cadet, shivering in the cold air. This was quite a trial on a frosty night, but it was done in a good-natured way – on completion of a 'flight' the victim was taken in to a warm shower. I survived the raids better than most, thanks to my Halton experiences.

Boxing helped me get off to a good start. Immediately after arrival, newcomers had to enter the boxing ring before the eagle eyes of the commandant, his staff and all the senior cadets for the Junior Entries Boxing Tournament. No one was interested in boxing expertise – this relic of wartime pilot selection processes was designed to discover spirit and toughness. Physical training staff matched the new cadets to similar opponents. Observing that I knew what I was doing in the ring, they matched me with another experienced boxer. The pair of us agreed to give this audience what they wanted by standing toe to toe and slugging it out till one of us dropped.

We did precisely this to resounding cheers from an audience looking for blood. I dropped first and won the competition, the cup being awarded to the best loser! This 'victory' marked me out as a man to watch.

Living conditions improved. After the two-term stint in the Junior Entry Huts I moved to the college building and began to enjoy officer's privileges, including the services of a batman to bring me a morning cup of tea and clean my shoes. Life was fun, with flying, good friends and the delights of the City of Lincoln half an hour down the road. Frequent socials and formal dining-in nights helped us retain the interest of the local feminine community. Many were from the 'bulk stores' of nearby nursing and teaching colleges.

Flying training started with navigation exercises in old twin engine aircraft, Ansons, piloted by elderly contract pilots. These knowledgeable aviators had much to teach us. Navigation is a particularly interesting facet of aviation which I have always enjoyed but I was impatient for my own pilot flying training to begin.

Pilot training begins at last

Flying training commenced with the *ab initio,* or *from the beginning* phase. Flying is a unique discipline, and one quickly learns there is one right way, and many wrong ways, to do everything. There are lots of pitfalls, and each trainee has to be taught to avoid them. Once instructed in basic manoeuvres such as turning, climbing and descending, the new pilot enters the circuit to practise takeoffs and landings until considered fit for the great day of first solo flight. From then on, flying is normally a dual detail, with the instructor demonstrating new techniques, followed by a solo detail in which the student practises what has just been taught.

The responsibility of being in command when solo is not for everyone – some pilots become frightened and give up. But for me, each flight was a new adventure and delight. I set myself the highest standards in every exercise. It seemed to me that the instructors recognised and respected my desire to excel. Systematically and painstakingly they imparted skills in instrument flying, aerobatics, navigation and all aspects of accurately controlling aircraft. I knew how fortunate I was to be learning these superb arts and was extremely happy.

It is said that flying isn't inherently dangerous but, like the sea, is terribly unforgiving of any incapacity, neglect or negligence. Some of our companions made errors and died in accidents during training. They were buried in the beautiful and historic churchyard of the village at Cranwell. These sobering examples made us take enormous care in everything we did.

The ab initio trainer used then was the piston-engine Provost, on which one learned the basics of flying. Every flight was a thrill in itself. The Provost had an unusual engine-starting device. One pulled up a lever to fire a cartridge, there was a loud bang and a cloud of smoke, and the engine caught with a throaty roar. Sometimes it was necessary to repeat the procedure with another cartridge – one trainee used 16 one morning until ordered to desist and have the engine serviced.

After taxiing to the duty runway, I would open the throttle and roar off to do what always made me happy: flying. After mastering the basic handling and circuit-training exercises, I progressed to more advanced lessons. I particularly enjoyed doing solo aerobatics, loops, barrel rolls, slow rolls, stall turns and inverted flying. Authorised low flying, conducted in strictly defined areas so as to avoid nuisance to the public, was pure joy as trees, fields, houses and farmers on tractors flashed by just below me.

Learning the disciplines of all-weather instrument flying was utterly absorbing. The Provost is equipped with amber cockpit screens, and the trainee pilot wears blue goggles. The trainee can see only inside the cockpit as the amber–blue combination cuts off outside light and so, deprived of a natural horizon, must interpret attitudes solely by reference to the aircraft instruments. The basic instruments are a turn indicator, an airspeed indicator and an altimeter. If the turn indicator is centralised, the airspeed remains constant and the altimeter shows a constant height, one is flying straight and level. A slip indicator is kept central by the correct positioning of the rudder to prevent 'yaw', or flying sideways through the air.

An artificial horizon, an instrument stabilised by gyroscopes, is a comforting presence but it may be 'toppled' (spinning wildly) by manoeuvring beyond certain limits. When it isn't working and the flight is controlled by basic instruments, flight is said to be 'on limited panel'. All instrument flight requires a systematic scan of the whole instrument panel every ten seconds or so, but this scan needs to be faster for flight on limited panel.

The recovery from unusual positions, which may be induced by weather or mishandling, is taught by the instructor flying the aircraft into a steep diving or climbing turn, then handing over control for the trainee to recover to straight and level flight, using limited panel instruments only.

Navigation and landing approach instruments and procedures must be mastered to complete the acquisition of skills necessary for full instrument flight. Such flights are conducted under Instrument Flight Rules (IFR) as distinct from Visual Flight Rules (VFR). Abilities must be demonstrated regularly before an Instrument Rating Examiner under the strict rules of an instrument rating test. Flight in conditions below those specified for VFR may be conducted only by pilots with a current instrument rating. Instrument ratings are issued in various grades, the higher grades permitting the holder to operate to lower levels of cloudbase and visibility.

This phase of flying training is the most difficult but also the most satisfying. The ability to operate in all weathers is the mark of the professional pilot. Those who falter in their training and 'get the chop' commonly do so during their introduction to instrument flying.

College life

Cranwell is very well appointed. Quarters were comfortable and well maintained. The library was, and remains, magnificent. Collections of *The Times* and other prominent newspapers stretch back through decades. Squash and tennis courts, swimming pools and all manner of facilities abound. An aircraft museum displays V1 bombs, early German jet aircraft and World War II fighters.

After being appointed the leader of the college rifle team, I was frequently on the rifle ranges. Our rifle team had the good fortune to have as an armourer a Mr Collins, a famous shot. At the start of World War II, he was called upon to demonstrate the firepower of the ordinary .303 rifle to a collection of admirals and generals. From a standing start on the 300-yard (274-metre) range, he was given 60 seconds and fired 23 bulls and 7 inners. He was a tremendous asset and with his advice we did well in inter-service competitions and also at the well known civil rifle ranges at Bisley, southwest of London.

A feature of the college is the dining room, with its huge collection of candelabra and silver. Visiting girls were always impressed. The collection was bought with the RAF's share of prize money from World War II operations. Prize money originated in ancient times in the Royal Navy. If an enemy ship was brought safely to a navy base, its value was determined by a special court and fixed percentages of that value were paid to all who contributed to the victory. After the end of World War II, the RAF received its share for the assistance provided in various successful operations, including the capture of enemy ships. The Air Board decided to spend this money on the silver collection at Cranwell.

Dining-in nights were always lively affairs. Spirited mess games (silly things rather fuelled by alcohol, often involving rugby-type tackles, or racing teams with one member clinging to a bedframe, or burning pianos – outside of course) were played in manly fashion. Afterwards participants sometimes needed to be stitched up by medical staff. One *was* expected to show spirit and join in games with gusto. Spirit was valued in the RAF.

When a birthday coincided with a dining-in night, after dinner the birthday cadet was de-bagged (trousers removed) and then tossed high in the air on a carpet manned on all sides by cheering cadets. Our lady guests loved it.

There were three squadrons in the cadet wing, and at formal functions each cadet sat at his squadron table. The scene was magnificent. Three long table rows groaning with polished silverware, gleaming linens and good things, smart cadets and staff in their formal evening dress uniforms, visitors often in exotic uniforms and the college band playing from a discreet balcony.

A long foot-bar ran the length of the tables. A favourite prank was for a cadet to crawl under the tablecloths and tie visitors' shoe laces to the bar. Royal Navy and United States Navy officers were a favourite target. When, at the conclusion of dinner, the PMC (President of the Mess Committee) called on a junior officer to propose the Royal Toast and everyone rose to their feet with a glass of port in hand, the hapless victim would sprawl on his back. His extreme embarrassment at his inability to join the formal salute to the Queen would entertain the entire cadet force.

In the last term of each Entry, a senior under officer and two under officers were promoted in each of the three squadrons. I was honoured by promotion to senior under officer of my squadron. The appointment carried the privileges of my own suite and batman. Never again do I expect to have a manservant laying out my clothes for a formal dinner and standing by to assist with my bow tie. St Bathans seemed a long way off.

On formal dining in nights the senior under officer of the duty squadron was the official host of the mess, under the scrutiny of the commandant. I had the privilege of hosting some outstanding people, among them visiting royalty – both overseas and British – senior military figures, leading academics and other notables. From my brief associations with those VIPs, I learned a lot. Invariably they were polite and charming to every person they met. Each had distinctive mannerisms, elan and supreme confidence in themselves and their respective institutions.

On one occasion, I was the official host at a dinner for cadets from the United States Air Academy, Colorado Springs. The academy had been formed only about two years before, and this was the first overseas visit by United States Air Force (USAF) cadets. At dinner, both sets of cadets were on their best behaviour before the watchful eyes of their respective staffs. The atmosphere was proper, perhaps a little strained. Now, I had approved the musical program played by the college band and had in all innocence selected 'Way Down South in Dixie' as a cheerful number to relax everyone. Unbeknown to me it was a sort of battle hymn to the Good Old Boys of the Southern States still smarting from their defeat by the God-damned Yankees. As the first notes sounded, stunned silence fell and our guests froze. Then a tall, fine-looking American leaped to his feet and, brandishing our silver, let out a stentorian yell – a real battle cry of the South. Immediately, every northern cadet leaped to his feet and roared back an answer. I don't think the old hall had ever seen anything like it. Laughing, the commandant looked at me. I could only join in his laughter at this riotous scene. As did all the Cranwellians, who enthusiastically joined in the tumult. Gradually, the uproar subsided, and all settled to one of the happiest and most convivial evenings ever, the usual formalities gone with the wind.

Another outstanding memory from Cranwell was the rehearsal for an airshow that was to be broadcast live internationally. Television was then in its infancy and the international broadcast was to be a world first. The BBC had chosen the RAF to be the subject, and filming was taking place in Germany and at Cranwell. The Cranwell contribution was an air show by college and visiting aircraft. Wisely, the commandant ordered a practice flypast by all participants. On the day before the actual filming, the entire cadet wing was lined up to watch the aircraft being put through their paces.

Included in the show was a Blackburn Beverley, a huge freight aircraft designed to drop heavy army tanks onto battlefields. As the Beverley flew past with its cavernous rear doors open in flight, a parachute deployed to the rear and pulled out a massive armoured vehicle. As this load descended, four large parachutes – one attached to each corner of the vehicle – were pulled from their sockets as 'Roman Candles', the initial stage of deployment before the slipstream billows out the canopy into the familiar shape. Unfortunately, the captain had neglected to allow for the height of Cranwell above sea level and dropped too low. There was insufficient time for the parachutes to open fully and slow the vehicle before it struck the ground. To the amusement of the cadets, the massive vehicle struck with a mighty crash and bounced back into the air in four pieces, with a now deployed parachute attached to each piece. The cadets cheered. But the show wasn't over yet. Figures, tiny in the distance, ran to one of the billowing chutes and started folding it into their arms. However, the wind gusted and lifted the parachute about 100 feet into the air, the small kicking figures of the soldiers, who were too slow to let go, borne aloft. The cadets were delighted – no one had expected anything like this. Slowly the wind gust expired and the relieved soldiers gently returned to the ground.

4

OPENING NIGHT, CRANWELL SOUTH NEW AIRFIELD

The flat terrain of Lincolnshire is ideal for flying training, and airfields are dotted about the largely agricultural countryside. Here and there are abandoned runways, relics of wartime bases. The RAF college was serviced by two airfields: Cranwell North and Cranwell South. The larger Cranwell South has always hosted the more advanced training aircraft plus visitors and regular flying displays open to the general public. Until the early 1950s, Cranwell North was used by ab initio trainers and glider and aeroclub aircraft. Today, it is largely a wonderful wooded area interspersed with tracks for runners, horse riders and dog walkers, secure for all within the guarded perimeters of the military area. My son and granddaughter run and ride there today.

The old Cranwell South runway was deemed to be too limited for modern aircraft, so a new runway was constructed. During this activity, ab initio training on Provost aircraft was moved to a small airfield, Barkston Heath, a few miles from Cranwell. This was where I was delightedly learning to fly.

After many months of construction to replace the old

runway, all the work was completed on the new Cranwell South airfield and it was declared available for operations. Its first use was to be for night flying from Barkston Heath. This was during my third term at Cranwell when we were on Provost aircraft and was my first experience of night flying. My instructor was relatively junior and, as it happened, it was his first night of instructing a pupil in the arts of flying in the dark.

A total of 12 aircraft were detailed to take part in the night's program. Four aircraft were planned to practise night takeoffs and landings in the Barkston Heath circuit; four were to go to Cranwell South; and four were to practise upper-air work. My aircraft was to be one of the four to go to Cranwell South. The meteorologist's briefing included nothing out of the ordinary. Twelve aircraft were airborne in short order.

The transit time from Barkston Heath to Cranwell South was only a few minutes but even in that short time we began to sense trouble ahead. A cloud base had formed and was lowering, and a moderate wind was rising. Unfortunately, the new radio equipment at Cranwell South was extremely noisy, and we were unable to communicate with the controller in the airfield control tower. The four aircraft now present in the circuit were forced into ever lower circuits by the descending cloud base, and nasty patches of fog began appearing and drifting about. None of these phenomena had been foretold by the meteorologist. Conditions were deteriorating fast. My instructor was concerned.

The sudden onset of bad weather from the north-east was unusual. A powerful area of high pressure, an anticyclone, had formed over Siberia, and as a secondary effect, cold air laden with moisture picked up over the North Sea poured over the United Kingdom. Wet north-easterlies soon covered eastern England, and their speed rose quickly. Advection fog began to form along the English eastern seaboard and then move inland as the wind speed rose to gale force.

Fog is generally classified as advection fog or radiation fog. Radiation fog commonly forms in the dawn hours as the air temperature decreases to the point where moisture droplets coalesce. The air is still, and the fog doesn't move. Advection fog is formed by the wind as moisture-laden air moves over a cooler land mass. Conditions at any point affected by it can fluctuate rapidly, and areas of virtually zero visibility can form, fade, re-form and move about with speed.

As fog banks in the Cranwell South circuit area began to appear, calls from the four aircraft attempting to establish contact with the control tower became more urgent. Ominously, calls from one aircraft suddenly ceased. My instructor and I were able to discern the outline of Cranwell North airfield and in the centre of it a fire was blazing fiercely. We discussed the height above sea level of the college dome and agreed it was 310 feet. Cautiously we then descended to 400 feet to investigate the fire. Sadly, it proved to be the silent fourth aircraft. Two persons were killed. This was the first accident of the night's flying.

Having established that emergency services were making their way to the crash scene, my instructor decided to go back to Barkston Heath. Simultaneously, a broadcast on emergency frequency 121.5 megahertz ordered all aircraft to return there. Barkston Heath circuit training had been suspended because a fog bank had formed on the approach to the duty runway. Eleven aircraft remained airborne and soon all were flying neat, disciplined left-hand circuits. It was a crowded piece of airspace and strict discipline was observed.

The commanding officer of Barkston Heath, rapidly summoned to the control tower, pondered what to do. It was by then apparent that a major storm was rising over the whole of the United Kingdom, with extensive areas of advection fog. The CO decided that the least risk was to continue landing the aircraft, rather than divert them to another airfield, despite the difficulties at Barkston Heath. He gave orders for landings to continue. By now, I was painfully aware that this wasn't going to be a conventional introduction to night flying and I could see my instructor was becoming anxious.

From the downwind position in the Barkston Heath circuit, the first of the 11 aircraft was cleared to land and commenced its landing pattern. The pilot entered a timed instrument turn through 180 degrees as he entered the fog bank in the approach area. He made a nice job of it and emerged from the fog bank at about 100 feet pretty well lined up with the runway. However in rounding out, he became disorientated – probably by the bright runway lights and fluctuating patches of fog – raised his nose too high, stalled and crashed. With sideways drift as the aircraft contacted the ground, the undercarriage wasn't up to the strain and collapsed, leaving the aircraft to skid along the concrete in a shower of sparks. The crew were uninjured.

Landings were again suspended. Once more, the CO debated diverting all aircraft.

By now though, it was apparent many aircraft throughout the country were in difficulties in the rising storm that had hit without warning.

The CO elected to change to the standby runway and continue landings. The problem was that the standby runway didn't have electric runway lights but was illuminated by gooseneck flares, dim kerosene-burning lights. These lights were difficult to see in the drifting fog. Aircraft flying in a circuit maintain safety and avoid collisions by following a strictly defined path anchored to the runway in use (the circuit) and keeping to defined altitudes. That night, to keep to the circuit pattern, it was necessary to maintain visual contact with the runway. But the fog was compromising visibility and therefore safety; on top of that the pilots now had to compensate for the inability to see the flares continuously. Consequently, the chances of the pilots becoming disorientated and straying from the all-important pattern were becoming dangerously high. The difficulty in the Barkston Heath circuit that night was greatly compounded by the requirement to re-orient to the dim standby flares runway from the brightly lit main runway.

It was disappointing that the CO and senior air traffic control officer didn't intervene more forcefully. Each aircraft could, for example, have been allocated its own altitude, separated from every other aircraft's altitude, and instructed to remain at that altitude until summoned for its landing approach. Perhaps the officers were unable to appreciate the developing situation because of the visibility restrictions.

In the absence of instructions to the contrary, the remaining ten aircraft were obligated to maintain the same altitude. But pilots became thoroughly disorientated in attempting to fly the new circuit pattern and strayed into different flight paths. Never before nor since, in 20,000-plus hours flying, did I experience an aviation situation that deteriorated into chaos, but chaos this was. Unexpectedly out of the murk a red light (the port, or left, navigation light on an aircraft's wing-tip) would flash across our bows from right to left as a collision was barely averted. Seconds later, a green light (starboard or right navigation light) would flash from left to right. Circuit discipline had broken down. It was terrifying as aircraft bore down on us from all directions. Our guardian angels were busy that night!

A bank of fog had established itself on the approach to the standby runway, so several aircraft attempted an approach by the difficult manoeuvre of a timed instrument turn. However on breaking out of the fog at low altitude, they were not sufficiently aligned with the runway lights to complete a landing. They then had to go around to rejoin the circus at circuit height. Finally, one pilot, displaying immense skill, burst out of the fog in line with the runway and commenced his round-out for landing. An unexpected gust of wind hit him from sideways, the downwind wing struck the concrete, and the aircraft cartwheeled down the runway. Luckily the crew suffered minor injuries only.

Landings were once again suspended while an increasingly desperate CO weighed his options. After the crew were evacuated he ordered the wreckage bulldozed to the side of the runway by the big fire engines with their heavy bull bars in front. Then landings attempts were resumed. The fog bank shifted a bit and several aircraft landed safely, but the fog re-formed before we could land.

My instructor managed to position himself positively at the upwind end of the circuit and said, 'This time we are going to land.' Dangerous words. He then, to his great credit, flew an immaculate circuit and burst out of the fog exactly aligned with the runway centre and at good distance for landing. Superb flying. But before I could take a breath of relief, I looked down and there, mere feet below us, was a red navigation light. A Provost was immediately below us and we were about to land on top of it. I screamed, 'Aircraft below. Emergency go-round.' Immensely startled, my instructor (who, recall, was on his first night-flying instructional duty) simply lost it. He jerked back on the control column to enter a steep climb but didn't advance the throttle to bring the engine to full power. I noted the altimeter reading at 400 feet above ground level. From our steep nose-up attitude and near-zero airspeed our Provost hammerhead-stalled.

A hammerhead stall is usually encountered only in training when, in clear conditions at a height which permits a safe recovery, the aircraft is deliberately flown vertically upwards until forward airspeed is lost. The nose, weighted by the heavy engine, pitches down with sickening force, and the aircraft invariably enters a vertical dive. Pilots calmly execute this manoeuvre and recovery to normal flight at, say, 10,000 feet. But to find oneself in a vertical dive at 400 feet on a foggy night is to have an exceptionally short life expectancy.

Frantically, I seized the control column and drove it full forward. As the airspeed crept up, I applied emergency power. We pulled out of the dive at very low altitude – must have been cutting the daisies. I set the aircraft into a climb and we left the circuit. I didn't look at my instructor or say anything but I sensed him staring at me. He knew I had just saved his life – and my own, of course. Thereafter, that man always treated me with respect.

The instructor told air traffic control that we were climbing to 3000 feet and would wait for the situation to improve. Two other pilots elected to join us, and we circled for some time. The remaining aircraft managed to land, with only one more accident resulting in minor damage.

'Aircraft circling Barkston Heath, divert to Marham. Surface wind 50 knots rising,' came the unmistakable voice of the CO. I calculated the course and we set heading. RAF Marham was a large master airfield, equipped with special facilities designed to get aircraft safely down when normal facilities were insufficient. Fog dispersal equipment was installed. Unfortunately, fog dispersal equipment ('FIDO') is effective only on radiation fog; fuel burning in trenches besides the runway heats the fog and disperses it, but the method is ineffective in advection fog, where new moisture-laden air is continuously arriving with the wind.

At that time, the closure of a master airfield was almost unheard of. Consequently, we were quite unprepared for the dread words of the next radio instruction: 'Marham closed, divert to Gaydon. Surface wind 65 knots.' We looked at one another askance in the dimly lit cockpit.

The next few minutes were busy as we established the location of Gaydon, northwest of London. RAF Gaydon is another master airfield. We set heading for it. By now we were thoroughly alarmed, for if the weather was so bad that Marham could be closed, then Gaydon could be closed too.

Our fuel situation was good. Continuing to Gaydon, we discussed our situation, particularly what to do if it closed. We could see little alternative to bailing out (we were equipped with parachutes, of course). A night parachute descent in 65 knots of wind would be certain to result in serious injury at the least. The speed of touchdown on land would be likely to cause arm and leg fractures and if one were dashed against a tree or other obstruction, injuries could easily be fatal. So we decided to parachute over a substantial body of water if we could arrange rescue facilities there. But even that wasn't a welcome prospect.

On our arrival at Gaydon, the approach radio controller advised a 30-minute delay before we commenced a GCA, or ground-controlled approach. A skilled controller uses ground radar to achieve the specified track over the Earth and a vertical profile. He issues advice such as 'Three degrees right' and 'Increase rate of descent to 1100 feet per minute.' The delay was to be to the limit of our safe fuel endurance and was highly unusual. The cause was multiple aircraft approaching Gaydon having declared a state of distress due to low fuel. It seemed half the RAF and lots of the USAF were inbound.

In our allocated holding pattern, we were far from relaxed as landing conditions were advised as wind 50–70 knots with 25-knot crosswind, some ice on the runway, visibility 100 yards in blowing fog. Had an alternative been available Gaydon also would have been closed.

Eventually, it was our turn to switch to GCA frequency. What a marvellous man that controller was! I will never forget his calm and measured voice. Despite the huge strain he must have been under, he spoke unhurriedly, as if welcoming us to Gaydon on a sunny day. My instructor closely followed his clear instructions as we fought the elements all the way down the GCA slope and smacked down in extremely rough conditions. We slithered off the runway and looked at one another! Down! Phew!

But we weren't yet done. Following ground control instructions, we taxied to the dispersal area. Despite the intense activity there, conditions were so bad that we actually motored right through the back of the dispersal area without seeing anything. Thus, we found ourselves on an unlit taxiway on the far side of the dispersal area. Almost immediately, a bright light appeared, a few feet ahead of us and off the taxiway; this proved to be the wing light of a Canberra bomber, also lost, coming the other way and about to collide with us. Enough! We pulled off the taxiway, shut down and radioed to the ground crew that we wouldn't move from there and would they please come to get us. They did.

Few pilots can have had such an experience as their introduction to night flying.

The next day, the storm continued and so we returned to Cranwell by train. Passengers were mightily astonished at the sight of six pilots in flying suits, with parachutes slung over their shoulders, travelling to Grantham Station.

And that is why, on its opening night, not a single aircraft landed at new Cranwell South.

5

CRANWELL'S LESSONS FOR LIFE

Returning to Cranwell rather the wiser for my introduction to night flying, I continued my flying, academic and military training. The lesson I learned from that night's experiences is to always be ready for the unexpected in the air and, in the last resort, to depend on yourself to act positively in an emergency. I was touched to learn that my batman, reporting at 6.30 am the morning after the night diversion, on learning there had been an accident was distressed to find my bed empty.

I continued my boxing activities and progressed steadily. Representing the college, our teams travelled extensively to matches throughout the United Kingdom, boxing against military and civil opponents. At a match against Oxford University we encountered a hostile student crowd. They cheered every blow landed by their man and booed my hits. My opponent had apparently not heard of the Queensberry rules and caught me a crippling blow below the belt when the referee was not looking. I was saved by the bell and dragged myself to my corner. But I was so angry! That low blow and the jeering from the audience made me so mad that when the bell rang for the next round I had recovered somewhat. Springing to my feet I sped across the ring. My opponent was still rising and open to my attack, defenceless. Driven by fury, my straight left to his jaw was my strongest ever punch. He went down for the count and then some. The screaming and noise from the audience was deafening – I'd never experienced anything like it. As my opponent was being assisted groggily from the ring, I made two circuits of the ropes giving the V-sign; while my glove concealed the two fingers, the students were in no doubt as to the meaning of my gestures. The screaming and shouting rose to levels which seemed enough to lift the roof right off the hall.

That was my most satisfying win ever and the story enhanced my reputation at Cranwell. But then, alas, a signal arrived from Wellington to order Flight Cadet Enright to stop boxing: it was against RNZAF policy for pilots to box. There was much muttering among the college staff, but I had no choice but to obey. So ended my boxing career. Perhaps it was just as well. No punch-drunk individual is ever going to pass a pilot medical exam. Boxing was one of many ways cadets were encouraged to show spirit. This was an attitude surviving from the war, when on some nights dozens of people from one squadron might be killed in operations over Germany. In hindsight I probably got carried away by the idea of spirit and was guilty of undisciplined conduct in the air. My friend Pete, a Scotsman, and I performed formation aerobatics together after only a few hours of solo time. We also had a bet as to the first to touch wheels on the ground in a practice forced landing. One day I did this on a field that had been rolled smooth after ploughing The aircraft was mud-splattered and I was very lucky on return to the airfield to get it checked and washed down by a sergeant who saved my career by keeping his mouth shut. These escapades were pretty stupid.

Not all close calls were of my own making however. After radioing for a radar steer to return to Barkstone Heath, I was given a true bearing (the opposite of a course for home) and held this until I came to the sea! I belatedly realised the error and turned for home but was down to a dangerously low fuel state on my priority arrival.

One day in the air, I chanced across another Provost. After he made a pass at me, we entered into a dogfight, the objective being to see which pilot could get onto the other's tail (in a position from which you could shoot down an opponent in a war situation). Dogfighting was strictly forbidden, so I had assumed the other aircraft was manned by a solo pupil. After a spirited battle of high-G turns, snap rolls and vertical climbs and descents, I managed to nail him by flying right behind him. Aaaah! There were two heads in the cockpit, not one; I had been duelling with an instructor! Summoned by my instructor on return to base, I could only confess to my behaviour, and truly expected to be sent back to New Zealand. But I wasn't.

Some months later, at a mess function, I was told that the instructor involved in the dogfight, an experienced fighter pilot, was so impressed by my getting on his tail that he'd argued that the Air Force didn't want to lose such a spirited pilot! Again, I was lucky but resolved to be properly disciplined in the future.

Soon, I passed all basic-phase flying tests of my course and moved on to the much-anticipated advanced phase, where I was to learn to fly jet aircraft.

Jet flying

It was a bitingly cold Lincolnshire day when I stood beside a dual control Vampire T.11 for my first jet training flight. My new instructor and I were sizing each other up but any awkwardness was soon dispelled by the excitement of strapping myself into the awesome ejection seat. With the seat safety pins withdrawn by the attending engineer, we completed the prestart drills and the engine came up to speed. No more rattling and spluttering from a piston engine – the only noise from the jet engine was a smooth whine. The skirl of rising revolutions as I applied taxi power was pure joy. After smoothly advancing the throttle to takeoff power when aligned with the runway I was thrilled by the thunderous roar as we accelerated fast down the runway. After the undercarriage was retracted I experienced the smooth, responsive reaction to the slightest change of pressure on the controls: a lovely sensation. As we went faster and faster I knew I had found my element. After turns, climbs, descents and manoeuvres the instructor watched approvingly as I set maximum power and we sped through the sky. I was reluctant to turn for home.

After the flight I was embarrassed when in the tearoom I overheard my instructor saying to the other instructors, 'Bloody Enright! He got his hands on the controls, and there was no way I was going to prise him off them till we got back in the circuit!' But later, he said he was pleased that I wasn't afraid to take the aircraft up to high speed.

The advanced phase flying was of absorbing interest. After a few hours mastering basic skills in the fast jet – such as accurate straight and level flight, turning, circuit discipline and landings – I moved on to aerobatics, formation flying, night flying and advanced navigation. Each dual lesson under the supervision of my instructor was followed by a solo detail practising the new lessons. With the passage of each regular check, my instructors became more senior until (a bit nervously) I sat beside the Wing Commander Flying – he assured me I was doing all right and taught me some of the finer points of smooth aerobatics.

A couple of months into the advanced flying phase, I learnt a sobering lesson. I found the theory of flight interesting and always paid close attention during aerodynamics classes. We covered the theory of flight at speeds in the vicinity of the local speed of sound ('Mach 1', popularly known as the sound barrier). Airflow over the wing is accelerated to produce lift, which keeps the aircraft airborne. When the airflow reaches Mach 1 it creates a turbulent wake in which the elevator controls are not able to control aircraft attitude. At this and higher speeds the pilot cannot control the aircraft until the speed/mach number has been reduced, usually by descending to lower altitudes where the local speed of sound increases. The instructor postulated that if, for example, a Vampire T.11 was put into a vertical dive above 40,000 feet it would be uncontrollable and unable to pull out of the dive until control gradually returned, probably about 25,000 feet. On a solo flight I decided to test this theory. I flew carefully up to 43,000 feet, rolled over on to my back and with full power applied dived vertically. Everything happened just as the aerodynamicist had predicted and after a turbulent ride straight down I gradually resumed control by 20,000 feet.

I did not say anything to anyone about my experiment but two weeks later two pilots were injured on ejection at high speed from a T.11 which could not be slowed from a dive. When the hood was jettisoned prior to use of the ejection seats, both pilots suffered flailing arms in the high-speed slipstream. A week after that another T.11 could not be recovered from a high-speed run; the pupil ejected safely but the instructor was killed. Rumours began to circulate that the Vampire could develop rogue characteristics at high speed.

Hmm I thought to myself, there's a lesson there for you Thomas. I did not conduct any further experiments.

In those days navigation was tricky as the air over the United Kingdom was polluted to the extent that the visibility was commonly reduced to less than a mile. Even in the home circuit it wasn't unknown for trainee pilots to become disorientated and get lost.

The British made a determined effort to clean up the air. Their success was proven by the predominance of white moths of a certain species; when the air was cleansed, trees emerged from the grime, and the white moths were able to hide from the birds. Records from previous centuries showed the predominance of black moths on dirty trees. In the new clean air, orientation was much simpler, and the number of pilots calling for assistance when uncertain of position diminished. Even experienced pilots could be disorientated; a visiting American test pilot once remarked, 'You haven't been lost till you've been lost at Mach 3.' Mach 3 is very fast and I didn't doubt that it would be dismaying to be at that speed when not knowing where you were going.

High performance in training was expected. The most awful thing imaginable was to be labelled 'LMF' (lacking in moral fibre) through lack of courage in difficult situations. One experience was a salutary lesson in what was expected in those rather daring days when pilots were expected to show spirit. (Things have changed since then and probably just as well.) I was about to get airborne for an instrument training detail under the supervision of an instructor in a T.11 Vampire which was equipped with ejection seats. Calling for takeoff clearance from a position lined up beside the runway, we were instructed to hold for Red Formation to land. The number two in this formation was a cadet who was just completing a sentence of 14 days punishment for arriving back late on a Saturday night. The punishment routine at Cranwell was severe, and the cadet pilot, I'd noticed, was exhausted. He should not have been flying, and what happened was the result of poor supervision. During a formation break and landing, the aircraft approach the runway in line astern at close intervals. Following aircraft must not descend below the preceding aircraft's height or they risk flying into that aircraft's wake, which may cause loss of control. From my position at the runway line-up point, I could see that the tired pilot had got low, dangerously low, on his approach.

Sure enough, he flicked to a wings-vertical attitude at about 100 feet and came straight at us. I reached for the ejection-seat handle as my only hope, despite knowing that ejection from a stationary aircraft would result in serious injuries. But, at the last possible moment, the out-of-control pilot flicked to the opposite wings-vertical attitude and he turned away from us – perhaps he did it to save us. His wingtip contacted the ground and he smashed to a stop upside-down right in front of us. Obviously, he'd been killed.

In the calmest voice, my instructor said, 'Enright, he is too close for us to taxi past. We will have to wait until the ground crew can push us backwards, then we will have a cup of coffee and then do the detail. All right, Enright?'

'Y– y– yes, sir,' I replied. And that is what we did.

A close-run thing there! And I avoided being labelled as LMF.

Today, most authorities would give up flying for the day after such an accident, but then spirit counted more.

More misses and near misses

Pilots know that a lapse of judgment can create danger. Inevitably trainees had to learn to deal with the loss of colleagues and friends. A member of my Entry suffered engine failure and flew out to sea to avoid the risk of his aircraft crashing into a built-up area. A rescue helicopter located him in short order but due to rough sea conditions the single crewman couldn't secure him. The helicopter returned to its base then returned with augmented crew and soon had the downed pilot on board. But he was suffering from hypothermia after his prolonged immersion. Although he was still alive entering hospital, he succumbed.

The authorities decided that an exercise to restore the confidence of cadets in the rescue facilities was needed. Their solution was that each of us had to sit in a dinghy on the airfield until a helicopter hovering overhead winched down a crewman to attach rescue harness. We were then pulled up to the helicopter. The straps creaked alarmingly, and the thought of the helicopter having an engine failure was scary, so the restoration of confidence wasn't totally successful.

Fear is another emotion I had to get my head around. I did a parachute-jumping course at RAF Abingdon during a leave. The jump school motto was, 'Knowledge dispels fear.' We wondered if this was the wrong way round. The first week of rigorous training, learning to distribute the shock of landing over the whole body, included jumping from a hangar roof supported only by a single cord wound around a drum on an ordinary office fan. We progressed to the first jump from a tethered balloon at 800 feet. The signal to jump, once one was standing in the exit door, was supposed to be a tap on the shoulder. But if one hesitated, the tap was likely to be followed by a heavy boot to the bum – no one came back once in that door.

For the first hundred feet, falling free was absolutely exhilarating – a feeling described by a friend of mine as the second thrill in life. The course was completed with a further balloon jump and two aircraft jumps. I was glad to have this experience as I wouldn't have the fear of parachuting in my future career if the need arose.

Army parachutists carrying heavy loads used to let down their pack weighted with gear on a long line so that after the pack hit the ground, the parachutist would slow up. Now, in the Abingdon drop zone, there were two tall trees. One unlucky soldier had his pack catch in the top of the first tree and then the wind blew his parachute to catch in the second tree. What to do? The man remained suspended high above the ground while his supervisors pondered. Finally, the local fire brigade was summoned and arrived with a vehicle carrying a large extension ladder, up which a brave fireman climbed to cut free the hapless soldier. But the combined weight of the two men was too much and the ladder broke. The parachutist showed the value of his training by landing unharmed atop the fireman, but the latter broke his leg.

Finale

The parachute course completed, back I went to Cranwell. Flying continued to enthral me and life outside my studies was full. My boxing career having been curtailed, I had taken rugby rather more seriously; I regularly played in the college second XV and kept pretty fit.

There were other pursuits, some quite unexpected. The college had kept a pack of beagles for many years, absolutely beautiful little dogs; for fitness we cadets ran – not rode – behind them. Occasionally I enjoyed explorations with the speleology club. Some of these were in Berkshire, where it was sobering to crawl through old mines where in the past poor children dragged heavy ore trucks through the black tunnels. One expedition was to an old slate mine in Devon. According to the locals, in 1941 armed sailors arrived one day and kept everybody away from the vicinity. Rumour had it that crown jewels had been sent there for safekeeping in the event of a German invasion.

All too soon, final exams were upon us. Over five days we sat ten three hour papers. But that wasn't all we fitted in to that week. Because our night-flying program had been delayed by bad weather our superiors decreed that we would fly by night and sit exams by day. This left little time for sleep, and soon we were exhausted. We should never have been flying like that and it is fortuitous that no one had an accident.

Finally, the day of the graduation of Number 70 Entry arrived. I'd been selected from the three senior under officers to command the parade. We were honoured that the reviewing officer was Admiral of the Fleet the Earl Mountbatten of Burma, the First Sea Lord.

Lady Mountbatten accompanied her husband. She was a most charming lady whom I entertained at lunch. This day at Cranwell proved to be the last public function the Mountbattens attended together as shortly afterwards, during a visit to Borneo, Lady Mountbatten succumbed to an infection and died.

From long practice, the college presented an impeccable occasion. The passing-out parade was a grand affair, and the whole cadet wing was immaculately turned out, with shining boots, swords and rifles, parading in front of the college. The Band of the Royal Air Force was positioned behind the three squadrons, men and instruments in shining array. One needs a loud voice – I have one, fortunately – to carry to all participants in such a large parade and a lot of self-confidence is needed to be in command of such an assembly. The several score guests, proud parents, family and friends were housed in a covered grandstand facing the parade.

That day, I was awarded six prizes. To my knowledge, no one before or since has won six prizes on graduation – from not only Cranwell but also the equivalent British military and naval colleges. The three principal prizes – the trophy for the best pilot, the Queen's medal (for academic ability) and the Sword of Honour (for all round performance) were presented

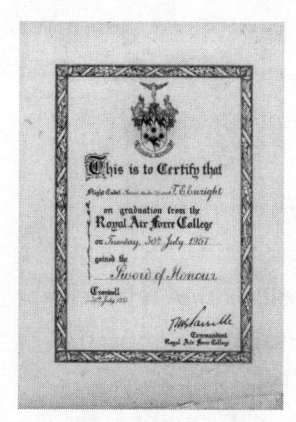

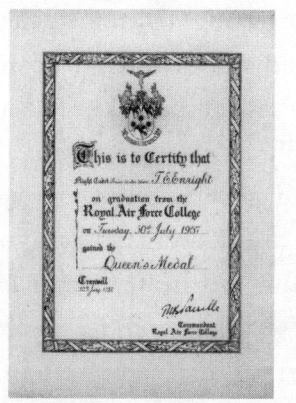

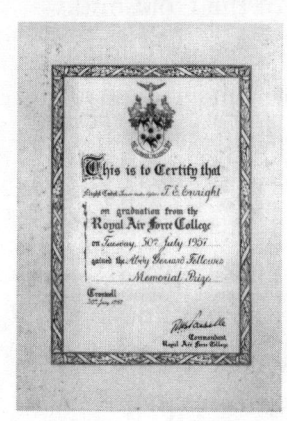

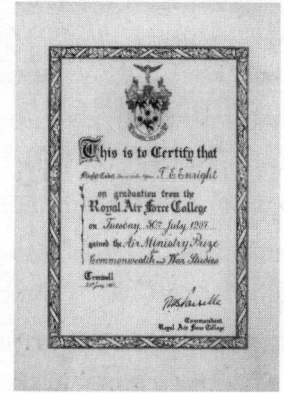

On graduation from the Royal Air Force College Cranwell in July 1957, I was awarded six prizes. These were:

The Abby Gerrard Fellowes Memorial Prize (for best flying abilities)

The Queen's Medal (for academic studies)

The Sword of Honour (for best all-rounder).

The other prizes were the R M Groves Memorial Prize, the J A Chance Memorial Prize and the Air Ministry Prize for Commonwealth and War Studies.

The reviewing officer for the passing out parade was Admiral of the Fleet the Earl Mountbatten of Burma, the First Sea Lord. Lord Mountbatten opened his address to the College staff and cadets with this statement, 'I must begin by expressing my absolute astonishment on hearing the same name read out three times for three such widely different prizes, and as far as I know I should think that must be a record for any College and I congratulate Senior Under Officer Enright very much indeed'.

(*College Journal*, December 1957, p.233)

on the graduation parade by the reviewing officer. Upon my being summoned the third time to receive the Sword of Honour, a visibly astonished Lord Mountbatten quipped 'What? You again?'

He then stepped forward and, in a charming manner, invited me to see his sword. This magnificent weapon had been awarded to him by the City and Guilds of London to commemorate his service in India at the formation of the independent countries India and Pakistan. Lord Mountbatten pointed out the inscribed shields, or motifs, of the Goldsmiths Guild, the Silversmiths Guild and several other prestigious organisations. I was so carried away by this wonderful man's presence and interest that I quite forgot the parade at my back until he said, 'Well, we better get on with it.' Which we did.

Friends in the viewing stand commented later that it was a quintessentially English occasion. In the visitors' stand, no one spoke, and no child cried. All waited patiently for Lord Mountbatten and me to finish our conversation.

I will always treasure the memory of this gracious man.

Farnborough, Boscombe Down, then homeward bound

Following my graduation from Cranwell, I had some time available before catching ship to New Zealand. I requested a visit to Farnborough and to Boscombe Down, the main experimental flying establishment of England. Permission was granted and, wearing my new pilot officer's uniform, I caught a train to Farnborough, where a chauffeur-driven car awaited me at the station. It was an especially large and shiny car, and I sensed the driver was a bit surprised to see me.

Arriving at the security gate at Farnborough, I was astonished to find a high-powered welcoming party – an air commodore, two group captains and a wing commander.

Carefully waiting until the chauffeur had walked around the car and opened my door, I stepped out and gave the officers a snappy salute. They were clearly astonished so I observed that there appeared to have been a foul-up. 'Yes,' they said, 'we were told to expect a representative of the New Zealand Government. But never mind, Tom. Can we use your car to get to the mess? We have a good morning tea.'

After that grand arrival, practically all of Farnborough was open to me and I had an engrossing time. Especially memorable were visits to the aviation medical unit and to the empire test pilot's school.

At the latter, the chief helicopter pilot took me for a flight in a Whirlwind Seven, a large navy helicopter, and invited me to take control. Attempting to hover, I made the common mistake of overcorrecting when the wind blew me downstream and ended up oscillating back and forth. Taking control from me the test pilot proceeded to demonstrate what this could build up to. He commenced a swing from about 100 degrees to the left to 100 degrees to the right in about ten seconds, at a height of 50 feet above the ground. Wow! That was some manoeuvre.

At Boscombe Down, I was also made welcome and filled in three days with well-organised activities. The highlight was being allowed to occupy the co-pilot's seat on a Valiant V-bomber. This was an extraordinary privilege as only the co-pilot had complete control of the fuel system and no one could supervise what I was doing.

The staff related an incident in which an engine fitter, who had been a fighter pilot during the war, was running up a Lightning, a supersonic fighter with two engines, one on top of the other. The aircraft was anchored to the ground by a substantial chain. By accident the fitter knocked on the afterburner switch when the engines were set at full power. Afterburners pour in additional fuel to greatly increase the power delivered by the engines and these engines roared. The anchoring chain broke under the strain, the brakes were totally unable to restrain the aircraft and the Lightning leaped forward and into the air, narrowly avoiding a passing bus full of workers. The cockpit hood was blown off so there could be no communication with anyone. Finding himself suddenly airborne, to his credit the fitter managed to fly the aircraft to Bristol airport and land safely. That was quite a feat for someone who hadn't flown anything for nearly 20 years.

* * *

My ship sailed from Portsmouth, and for the next month I enjoyed the luxury of lying about in the sun as we made our way to Auckland. My family was there waiting to welcome me back to New Zealand.

6

OHAKEA AND A WILD RIDE

Magic days

My achievements at Cranwell had once again stirred surprising media interest and I was interviewed a number of times. Asked what it was like to be a cadet at the college, I quoted the college warrant officer who, on our arrival years earlier, had explained the niceties of respectful address. 'You call me sir,' he said, 'and I call you sir. But the difference is … you mean it!'

After leave and some time relaxing with my family, I was posted to 14 Squadron (which later became 75 Squadron), a fighter squadron then equipped with Vampire aircraft. Our base was the RNZAF Station Ohakea, located in the North Island near Palmerston North.

After my years flying in the limited visibility of English skies (before they cleaned up the air), it was astonishing to find typical visibilities of 100 miles in New Zealand and wonderful vistas of our beautiful country. I was also delighted to find fishing, game shooting and skiing readily (and cheaply) available and spent most weekends at one or another of those three pursuits. Most fishing streams and rivers are open to all who pay a modest sum for a licence, and many landowners are pleased to have a few deer cleared off their property. About two hours' drive from Ohakea are the ski-fields of Mt Ruapehu and the famed trout-fishing area of Lake Taupo. So in no time I had settled in to my new home.

My happiness was greatly enhanced when I met the woman who was to become my wife of 50 years, June, a dietitian at Palmerston North Hospital and the daughter of a dairy farmer.

It was exciting being part of a fighter squadron. I particularly enjoyed weapons work, firing rockets and cannon and dropping bombs, where the name of the game was precision. Smooth accurate flying was needed to keep the sensitive gun and bomb sights working accurately. It was immensely satisfying to lay a weapon right on to the target. Air-to-air firing (with live ammunition) practice required especial care. A banner target was towed by another aircraft and it was essential to ensure all attacks were made from the side of the towline – a cannon round fired from dead astern might hit the towing aircraft, so all attacks had to be broken off in good time. We fired rockets which had 60-pound concrete heads rather than explosives and it was stimulating to hold the target steadily in the sight and push the firing button to see the rocket take off with a whoosh and streak to the target. One rocket I fired disintegrated just in front of my aircraft and debris severely damaged the engine. Despite severe vibration and just enough power to stay airborne, I was able to make an emergency landing back at Ohakea. For about ten minutes of this slow journey, I was unsure if I was going to make it and was grateful that I had the experience of a parachute course in case I had to go over the side.

Other magic days were spent with all the aircraft, about 15, in a long line astern and screaming through the Marlborough Sounds at the top of the South Island at 300 knots at authorised very low levels.

The aerobat

By this stage I was considered to be accomplished at aerobatics and soon was regularly selected to perform low-level displays before the public at air shows throughout the country. I was thrilled to be asked by the leader of the RNZAF aerobatic team to join as one of the pilots of the four aircraft. From then on, at various aerobatic displays, I first performed the solo aerobatic display and then joined the team for the formation aerobatics. I learned a lot from these exacting tasks and felt quite at home in the Vampire cockpit. We flew two versions: the two-seat T.11 equipped with ejection seats and the single-seat FB5, which didn't have an ejection seat.

Wild ride

One day, completing a training flight in an FB5 at Ohakea, I was downwind runway 15, number two for landing. Fuel at 15 minutes remaining was low but not concerning. Number one ahead of me in the circuit was a Devon, a rather slow piston-engine aircraft, so I extended the downwind leg of my circuit to allow time for the Devon to land and clear the runway. When I turned onto finals, however, the Devon was still on the runway. I was now starting to watch my fuel level closely and decided that if I had to go around, I'd need to ask for landing priority due to low fuel state. Sure enough, came the call from Ohakea Tower: 'Vampire on finals, go around. Runway obstructed.' I advanced the throttle fully forward, and the Goblin engine came screaming up to full power. I banked to the left to start a tight circuit.

Boom!

The explosion from my engine brought the whole station to its feet. Klaxons blared and emergency crews raced for their vehicles as the crash alarm echoed round the station.

Quickly, I had to decide what to do. My brain racing, I considered my options. Bail out? Far too low with no ejection seat. Turn back to land on the airfield? No, much too low. The only choice was a forced landing straight ahead. I made a hurried distress call: 'Mayday. Mayday. Mayday. Engine failure. Forced landing ahead.' Frantically, I searched the farmland ahead for the best landing path.

A recall of a lesson learned flashed through my mind: a Vampire's forced landing in which the aircraft went through several fences but did not sustain serious damage. I could select the best landing ground ignoring fences. No way was I going to stop in any field at the touch-down speed of a jet fighter. The best-looking ground lay to the south-east. Discounting the several fences on it, I selected a path. There were also two ditches to cross: unwelcome, but they looked survivable. A third ditch in the distance was too far away to be scrutinised. The direction selected was into wind.

Setting up an approach at 120 knots, I considered another lesson recently learned: according to a USAF publication, an all-wheels-down landing was the safest configuration for a tricycle-type undercarriage jet fighter in a forced landing. I therefore selected gear down (a decision which probably saved my life) and began furiously pumping the emergency hydraulic hand pump, knowing the failed engine wouldn't provide sufficient pressure to lower the gear. Next, jettison the cockpit hood – I snatched the black and yellow handle and the Perspex canopy sailed off over the tail. With the ground fast approaching, I steeled myself to fight every inch of the way in the wild ride ahead.

At 100 feet bleeding off speed, I chose my touch-down point. Flaps were selected but probably weren't extending due to low hydraulic pressure. Clearly I was going to impact three fences just ahead with two more in the background.

Crash! Bang! Clang! I flew through the first three fences and bounced through the first ditch, taking out hundreds of metres of fenceline. Wreckage was flying everywhere. On the ground and riding rough, I bounced through another ditch – crash! Going through the fourth fence I hit a totara post, a tough pole which fractured the mainspar of the starboard wing. The post broke into three pieces and one piece clipped my helmet as it hurtled by. Phew, close-run thing there.

Then I was through the fifth fence and skating on slippery newly mown hay, still doing about 80 knots, braking with all my might in the belief my main gear wheels were down (they weren't). But now I saw I was in deep trouble as the third ditch loomed up. Not apparent from where I made the forced landing decision, the ditch was deep with a solid, vertical far side. I couldn't see how I could possibly survive the coming impact and resigned myself – it was curtains for me! Well, I'd fought as hard as I could but because I was still moving at about 70 knots speed approaching this steep bank I could do no more. The closer the ditch came, the more the adrenaline pumped and the slower everything seemed to move.

I expected to die. Interestingly, I wasn't frightened. There was no flashback of past life, just an awareness that I was about to learn the mystery of the ages, what lies on the other side. Then came the heaviest imaginable impact as I struck the far ditch, and slowly, oh so slowly, slowly, a jet black curtain came down over my eyes. I lost consciousness. I guess that's what it must be like to die.

My decision to lower the undercarriage now paid off. The nose gear, locked down, struck violently and sheared off. The main gear, not locked down, was dragging on the ground. The fuselage was held in a nose-high attitude. Had it been in a nose down configuration it would have speared into the ditch far bank with fatal results. The nose gear's shearing off absorbed some of the kinetic energy of the crash.

Sitting on a parachute, I went through the bottom of the seat and the floor of the aircraft as well! This dissipated more energy as the airframe crumpled. Each of these factors absorbed energy, and amazingly I escaped a broken back. The aircraft had enough of a nose-high attitude to bounce out of the ditch, leaving a deep gouge.

I came to. Unbelievably, I was alive! I smelled smoke – a magnesium fire – and leaped out of the wrecked cockpit and ran! A local farmhand reckoned I did the first hundred yards away from the wreckage in 8.9 seconds. Marvelling at my luck, I watched the rescue vehicles crashing through the farmer's gates and across his fields.

Close-run thing? You bet!

In the end, the episode cost me money! In the bar at my celebratory party I said that approaching touchdown, I took one wire out of the first fence, three wires out of the second, and five wires out of the third, and I reckoned that was a pretty smooth let-down. At that a roar went up from the crowd, the 'Line Book' (in which outrageous statements are recorded) was called for and I had to shout the bar.

I was thankful to have walked away from that lot without a back injury and have taken care of my back ever since.

The Air Force paid me a nice compliment by classifying the forced landing as 'commendable' and, surprisingly, not holding a court of inquiry. It emerged that an impurity in the metal of a compression blade had caused a typical crystalline fracture line. Nine inches (23 centimetres) of the blade came away and jammed in the engine casing. There was a violent seizure, sufficient to fracture all four engine mountings front and rear, and the turbine was mashed by a mass of metal. A magnesium bearing caught fire – magnesium fires generate their own oxygen supply (good old de Havillands!).

Sometime later, I happened to be in the RAF Changi mess in Singapore when an old Cranwell friend walked in and saw me. He started back as if he'd seen a ghost – as indeed he thought he had. He'd attended a funeral service for me at Cranwell. A rumour about the crash had turned into a report of my death!

What a pity I wasn't at Cranwell that day. It would have been a hoot to be waiting in the bar when the churchgoers returned, to assure them the rumours of my death had been greatly exaggerated and to buy them all a drink!

Are you sure, Enright?

After my scary forced landing, life continued at Ohakea. I was aware that I was acquiring an awesome reputation as a display pilot. Mess parties, weekend fishing, hunting and skiing forays and delightful evenings with June filled my life. I was flying about 60 hours per month doing aerobatics, weapons work, displays and interesting navigation exercises around our beautiful land. Everything was sweet. Then suddenly I felt that I had became the station pariah! It all started with an aerobatic show practice.

Display pilots must never fly directly over public enclosures – the public must always be safeguarded against mishap. Manoeuvres must all be carried out over the runway or on the side of it opposite to the crowd. Display flying at low levels requires tight control so that the aircraft interests the crowd by staying close but the aircraft must not cross the line of the runway. I always carried out my low-level practices orientated to some feature representing a runway. My favourite practice ground near Ohakea was at Himitangi where a line of pine trees provided an excellent runway substitute.

The Vampire, conceived by the celebrated English firm of de Havillands, was designed at the end of World War II and was not the last word in single-engine aircraft. It has some tricky handling characteristics. At high wing loadings, when the aircraft is being manoeuvred tightly, there is a tendency to stall one wing, leaving the other wing generating high forces; this could lead to a 'flick roll', in which the aircraft rotates rapidly, quite out of control. This quirk can quickly bite the unsuspecting pilot. I'd learned to respect it and tried to leave a margin for error in every low-level manoeuvre.

One day I was rehearsing before my trees low-level aerobatic manoeuvres for a coming air show. One of the more spectacular manoeuvres in my repertoire was a maximum-rate roll. In the Vampire cockpit, if you progressively applied full aileron (which controls roll rate) and full rudder (which balances yaw), you could end up with a spectacular rate of roll and control your altitude by moving the control column fully forward to fully aft as the rolls went from right side up to upside down. This sequence requires strength and skill and a fine sense of timing. (Note to tyro aerobatic pilots: don't try this unless you know exactly what you are doing.) On this day, without any particular concern, I set up my max-rate roll, aligned before the pine trees.

One, two, three, four max-rate rolls. Superb! This is precision flying and I am filled with satisfaction, enjoying myself. Recover – in coordinated movements, centralise the rudder and ailerons and return the elevator to neutral.

Alarm! Alarm! Alarm! The ailerons were jammed and would not centralise. God Almighty! I'd started the series of rolls at 500 feet but was losing height rapidly as the roll continued while I was sorting things out. I was diving to the ground. With only seconds to recover, I wrenched the aileron with manic force and, with a loud clang, it came free. Dangerously low – I actually flew between two pine trees – a very close call! Back in control, I climbed away from this scene.

Amazed that I'd survived this, I called Ohakea to declare the emergency of jammed controls. I then climbed to 10,000 feet altitude, turned the aircraft upside down and shook the control column. This procedure was to discover if I had any loose objects floating about the cockpit – anything loose would have fallen into the canopy. Nothing appeared, so I returned to Ohakea.

The airframe sergeant investigating the incident, Buster Brown (BB) was a widely respected person and a master of the airframe trade. My aircraft was immediately turned over to him for examination and the fleet of Vampires was grounded as a precaution. Buster quickly nailed the problem. Good old de Havilland had routed the aileron control cables through a venturi-shaped channel (near the control column). Unwisely, a cable clamp was added at this point. De Havillands had recognised the danger of the clamp being jammed within the venturi channel and provided a fabric boot around the relevant area to keep out foreign objects. Unfortunately, the boot was secured by a knot on the underside of the fitting, requiring the tradesman fitter to tie the knot by feel from an awkward position. In my jammed aileron case, the knot had come undone, leaving the boot loose. The clamp picked up the boot, and the whole mess was dragged through the venturi channel on my initial aileron application. The clamp and boot then jammed in the channel on my attempted recovery.

Buster and his men quickly pinpointed the boot jam, but this didn't explain the loud mechanical clang that I'd reported. Hour after hour, BB and his men continued their investigation. My telephone rang.

BB: Are you quite sure, sir, there was a loud mechanical clang?

Me: Yes.

BB: Okay, sir. We'll keep looking.

Later my flight commander called. 'Are you sure there was a loud mechanical clang?'

'Yes, sir.' I was beginning to wonder – am I becoming the station pariah?

Next the squadron commander: 'Are you sure there was a loud mechanical clang?'

'Yes, sir.'

The wing commander: 'Are you sure there was a loud mechanical clang?'

'Yes, sir.'

Finally, the group captain himself: 'Enright, are you sure there was a loud mechanical clang?'

'Yes, sir. A loud one.'

Sigh! Harrumph! 'All right, Enright, we'll keep the fleet grounded and keep looking.' I was gratified the group captain accepted my word.

A day later, I was telephoned by BB, he and his crew having worked without respite for about 72 hours.

BB: Sir, could you come down to the hangar please?

Me: Of course.

At the hangar, BB and his crew eyed me expectantly.

'Sir, please sit in the cockpit.'

'Done.'

'Sir, please close your eyes.'

A movement of the hand in the cockpit. Clang!

'Yes, yes, that's it exactly – but it was a lot louder.'

The exhausted BB and his crew exploded in mad laughter, falling all over the hangar floor. I waited patiently until they had overcome the hysterics, induced by exhaustion I think.

'Okay, what was it?'

BB suppressed a last hysterical laugh. 'We finally realised what it was – it was you hitting the stops on the other side as the aileron came free!'

The fleet was released to its tasks, and I was no longer a pariah.

A stint at Woodbourne

On another occasion, I was certainly a station pariah. I was temporarily posted as adjutant to RNZAF Woodbourne, near Blenheim. My commanding officer was a well-known bomber pilot who had flown many missions against Germany when based in England in World War II. It was difficult being his adjutant as his handwriting was almost impossible to read. His wartime experiences had induced a permanent nervous system defect and he was unable to hold a pen firmly. Of course, everyone sympathised.

I had several jobs there and was always busy. Nevertheless, I found time to fly the station Harvard aircraft whenever possible. I was frequently asked to fly a passenger to Wigram Air Base, near Christchurch. To save time, I usually set off early in the morning.

On track from Woodbourne to Wigram are two high mountain ranges, the Landward and Seaward Kaikouras. The prevailing winds in this area are westerly, and often strong. One has to be careful mountain-flying in strong winds as there is often severe turbulence and strong downwash (air masses flowing downwards after passing over the tops of the mountains) on the lee (eastern) side of the ranges.

Early one morning en route to Wigram, as I was passing over the first range in gale winds, I wasn't surprised to develop a sharp rate of descent – 2000 feet per minute – into the steep Clarence River valley between the two ranges. I applied climb power to counter this but wasn't too concerned. Invariably, the downwash on the lee side of one range turns into an updraft on the windward side of the range on the other side of the valley. Generally one develops a smart rate of climb in this updraft and easily clears the second lot of mountain tops. The usual technique is to press on and sail up the updraft and over the second range. But on this occasion, where I expected to enter an updraft I found instead an increase in the strength of the downdraft. All of a sudden, I was below the mountain tops and descending at nearly 4000 feet per minute, an alarming rate. I was forced to continue downwards and turned to follow the Clarence River towards its mouth to the north-east, the only escape route I had. When I reached about 500 feet above the river, finally the downwash, reflected off the valley floor, petered out and height was stabilised. There was no way I could climb out of the valley and had to continue to follow the river to its mouth, where I could turn southwards towards Wigram again, now over the sea.

On arrival at Wigram, my passenger was white. He'd had a big fright. I explained to him that we'd struck freak conditions where the air, instead of being forced up the mountainside, had developed a circular motion, like being on the outside of a tube, and caused our unexpected descent.

Later in this flight, when flying over the sea near Kaikoura, I saw a strange sight. Lying dead in the water was an enormous sperm whale. Facing in the opposite direction were three sharks apparently nibbling away at its lips.

Aerobatics and the perils of passengers

The Harvard aircraft at Woodbourne bore the crest of a large unit based there, Number One Repair Depot. It was a matter of pride to them that their aircraft was always in immaculate order. When parked among the dozens of training aircraft at Wigram, it was a standout, shining and bright, not a blob of grease anywhere.

At Woodbourne, there was always a lengthy list of people asking for a flight on the Harvard, and I took a passenger whenever I could, usually on my weekly training exercises flight. One morning, an attractive and popular WAAF from the accounts section was waiting at the aircraft. She said she would very much like to do some aerobatics. Of course I was willing.

Since my own terror on my first flight I'd always taken care to stop if a passenger was frightened. On arrival at a safe height, I told the lass to speak up if she wanted to stop. Then I did a leisurely loop and a barrel roll before checking with her that it was all OK. She enthusiastically asked for more. Happy to oblige I wound things up a bit for about five minutes, then again asked if she was still enjoying it. She was and asked for more, more, more. 'All right,' I said. 'I'll wind it up but you tell me if you want to stop'. We communicated through radio headsets.

All right, I thought, we'll really go for it! A hammerhead stall, tight maximum-rate turns, a spin and an Immelmann turn – a tactic developed in World War I air battles, where a turn is reversed by rolling upside down rather than right-side up. Still not a word.

All of a sudden I froze. Something wasn't right. I adjusted my mirror to check on my passenger but there was no one in sight in the rear cockpit. Aghast, I realised what had happened – her radio lead had pulled out of its socket in the high-G situations and she'd been unable to speak to me. The poor thing had slumped to the bottom of the seat and was now being violently ill. I felt terrible – people who have been tossed around while airsick have told me that it's so awful all you want to do is die!

Naturally, we landed immediately and taxied to dispersal. The shocked, disapproving looks I got from the engineers who met us were unambiguous. Not only was the station's favourite WAAF slumped over and needing assistance to get out of the cockpit, but Number One Repair Depot's immaculate aircraft was sprayed with vomit.

Wordlessly I went to my locker, retrieved two pounds and handed them over to the engineers. I was indeed a pariah. But I was saved – the heroic girl made sure everyone knew she wanted to fly with me again.

I returned to Ohakea with my reputation intact.

Nearly done in by the Queen Mum

The next memorable event in my life at Ohakea occurred when the Queen Mother, then touring New Zealand, presented the Queen's Colour standard to my then squadron, the renowned Number 75.

During the First World War, 75 Squadron was formed by the British Army in 1916 in the midst of desperate fighting in France. It is believed to have shot down the first 'Hun', introducing the world to the new version of battle, aerial combat. It was also tasked with Home Defence, shooting down German Zeppelin airships which were dropping bombs on London. During World War II, the squadron was equipped with Lancasters engaged in the bombing of Germany. It suffered the highest casualty rate of all bomber squadrons. This is quite something considering Bomber Command had the highest casualty rate of any military unit.

At a recent commemorative function in Auckland, a delightful tale of World War II wartime days was told about 75. The squadron was then equipped with Blenheim aircraft, and a number of them were frequently queued up on a taxiway awaiting their turn to take off for a bombing raid on Germany. The taxiway was adjacent to a small village. One night, a man ran out of the village, clambered over the airfield fence and knocked on the door of one of the idling aircraft. The crew opened the door and the man pitched in two bricks saying, 'Drop those on the bastards in Germany, from me and Mum.'

And so, in accepting the honour of the Queen's Colour, we were remembering illustrious forebears. During World War II, so many New Zealanders were posted to the squadron that the British told the New Zealand Government that they might as well take it, and 75 became an RNZAF squadron.

The presentation of the Colours was at the showgrounds, Palmerston North. I was selected for the honour of receiving the Colours and duly appeared on parade before a large audience, including my parents and the faithful June and her parents. I wished for a trouble-free ceremony, which called for the Queen Mother to insert the base of the Colour shaft into a small cup, suspended from a band around my neck, hanging between my legs. Normally, the Colour bearer awaits the Royal Personage kneeling with one leg on a little dais. He is instructed to grasp the Colour, furled around the shaft, when it is presented to him in a particular manner well understood by Royal Personages. The drill is established. Usually no problem!

But it was a windy day. The Queen Mum, who wasn't a muscular person, had an obvious problem in controlling the heavy Colour in the gusts buffeting the showgrounds. As wind changes hit from side to side, the furled Colour and its heavy shaft whipped about. I could see the Queen Mum's suppressed mirth but she appeared to be concerned she might do me an injury. Perhaps she was picturing the scene of her trusty and beloved servant (me) being struck by the flailing shaft and rolling about the parade ground clutching himself – with number one girlfriend looking on. And her mother too. And my mum and dad.

The Queen Mother and I looked at each other and grinned. Swish, swish went the pole. The Queen Mum stepped back to a safe distance. We grinned at one another some more. The wind quietened, and the Queen Mum stepped forward and neatly placed the shaft in the cup. Bull's-eye!

'Got it?' she asked. 'Got it?'

I nodded. We both smiled.

7

TIMARU AIR SHOW

Continuing my career flying Vampires, I did solo aerobatic displays and flew in the formation aerobatic team, sometimes performing solo and team displays at the same show. The Vampire was a crowd pleaser – noisy, low, right there in front of the crowd. My eight consecutive rolls were an unusual and thrilling feature of my display routine – those were the days before aircraft were equipped with powered controls. Tightly flown, this roll series was quite safe. However, if there was rough handling, the Vampire was prone to flick rolls. Once a flick roll started, it usually continued extremely rapidly. It was disorientating and hard to stop, and entry to a flick roll at low altitude had often proved fatal.

In gunnery practice, for instance, it was easy for the pilot to develop intense concentration on the target and this could result in the flight being allowed to descend below a safe level. The likely response is a frantic high-G pull-out, a procedure fraught with the danger of entry to a flick roll. This sequence has killed a number of pilots worldwide.

I loved display flying. Recently, a Boeing 777 captain told me he decided to become a pilot on seeing a Vampire arrive at 390 knots upside down at 100 feet. The aircraft was bunted up into an outside loop to the vertical, held to 4000 feet then pulled through into a normal loop and on with the show. I recognised my trademark start from his description.

One year a major air display was scheduled at Timaru. The Timaru airport terminal building is dedicated to Richard Pearse. Some New Zealand aviation historians claim that he was the first man in the world to achieve powered flight and that he'd flown in New Zealand before the Wright brothers made their historic flight in the USA.

I knew Timaru well, having spent most of my school holidays working for my cousins on their farm in the district. I regarded these farmers as my second family and so was determined to put on a polished flying display for them and the Timaru crowd.

All the display participants assembled at RNZAF Wigram, Christchurch, for final practice and briefing. It was immediately apparent to me that the southern air traffic controllers were unused to high-speed aircraft. They proposed a signal of a red Very light to abort any aircraft's initial run-in to start the display if for any reason there was an interruption. I explained that a Very light wasn't suitable for my high-speed inverted arrival. After discussion, it was agreed a time slot would be reserved for me, irrespective of any other activities. I undertook to arrive at my scheduled time plus or minus 30 seconds.

At that time, the RNZAF had a squadron of Canberra aircraft in Singapore. One of these aircraft had come to visit New Zealand and was to be flown at the Timaru Air Show. At a late stage, a staff officer in Wellington decided it would make a fine spectacle if the 'old and the new' jet aircraft were to fly past together in formation, and this request was conveyed to us at Wigram. The Canberra captain and I needed to get together to plan this, particularly as I was under an obligation to air traffic control to arrive within 30 seconds of my scheduled time. I tried to discuss slotting in a combined formation flypast but was fobbed off by the Canberra captain, who was busy with other things. He was of superior rank to me, so I said nothing – he had a reputation for brusqueness. But I realised it was important to have an agreed plan and resolved to speak at the pre-flight briefing that we two crews would attend on the day of the display.

Meanwhile, following my practice display, the officer commanding the flying wing of Wigram took me aside. He complimented me on the standard of my flying display and said he was surprised at what a Vampire could be made to do. But, he said, he was worried that my inverted arrival was at 100 feet. Could you consider upping it to 300 feet he asked? He was such a gentleman, asking when he could have ordered, and of course I agreed at once. This was fortuitous. As events turned out, I was to need that extra 200 feet!

The display was on the next day. I planned the departure from Wigram and the route with care. My run-in was to start crossing the village of Pleasant Point, north-west of Timaru airport, which happened to be exactly in line with the extended runway. I was determined to be at that point exactly on time. The Canberra captain and I were briefed by the operations officer together. As it was obvious – to me at least – that I should be the formation leader, I started into a standard fighter squadron briefing. It was immediately communicated that mighty Canberra captains were not in need of the wisdom of upstart fighter pilots. I was told acidly: 'Get on with your own business.'

The briefing officer and I looked at one another in astonishment. I was shocked and worried but could hardly argue with a wing commander (I was a flight lieutenant then). It seemed as if the coordination would need to be effected by radio in the air. I was well aware this was unsatisfactory and likely to prejudice flight safety. But what could I do?

Prior to our becoming airborne, there was quite some excitement at Timaru. A large formation of the Wigram training aircraft – some 12 Harvards and four Devons, from memory – was assembled in a tight formation at the takeoff point. The Harvard in the middle of the bunch caught fire and there was considerable toing and froing as the fire tenders tried to get to it. Thankfully, the fire was extinguished before it spread to other aircraft.

At Wigram, the Canberra departed ahead of me and disappeared to the south. I took off exactly on time and set heading for Pleasant Point. Arriving inverted at high speed for a display, you don't have the opportunity to see the airfield until you cross the boundary, so pre-planning the correct direction of arrival is vital, given that you must never, never fly directly above the crowd.

About halfway to Timaru, I saw the Canberra about 40 miles ahead. Clearly the pilot couldn't see me. I thought it high time we discussed our joint flypast so advised him of my relative position. I was rudely told to stop nattering on the busy frequency. Well, up you, I thought, and concentrated on my own task. It remained unresolved how we were to join up for our flypast.

Pleasant Point flashed by right on time. I advised Timaru air traffic control that I was commencing my run-in on schedule and looked ahead for my next checkpoint, a small village. Passing over this proved I was on the correct path on the runway extended centreline and would arrive at the correct place on the airfield boundary. This was also where I'd planned to commence my roll to inverted flight and my inverted descent to 300 feet above the ground. Passing this point, I commenced the roll and descent. I was now committed to the planned arrival.

Out of the blue, there came a slightly panicked radio call from the Canberra. 'Which direction are you coming from?'

'North-west,' I snapped, alarmed, and wondering what was coming next. Nearly established in inverted flight, I suddenly spotted the Canberra. He was coming at me from 90 degrees left and pulling into a very tight turn in an attempt to join formation. This insane manoeuvre caused him to go belly up to me, and so he was unable to see me, as he was crossing ahead. Being upside down, I had to take tricky avoiding action to prevent a collision and was thankful to be at 300 feet rather than my usual 100. A collision between the two aircraft would likely have scattered wreckage into the crowd. Very close-run thing there!

Although I was absolutely appalled, there was no time to think as almost immediately I swooped across the airfield boundary and began my routine by pushing up in an outside loop to a vertical climb.

At the start of a display, the adrenaline is usually coursing with the effort of holding to tight limits. But it was flowing especially strongly after the Canberra's foolish attempt to join formation had brought us so close to a collision. Later, with more experience, I realised that any interruption to a routine is cause to abort the display and leave the circuit. I should have done that immediately after the incident. But I didn't have time to think it through right there. I didn't feel too overstressed and continued, as always giving complete attention to my routine. That turned out to be a big mistake.

The pièce de résistance in my routine was to straighten up on my display line in front of the crowd to enter a maximum-rate roll and hold it for eight rolls. In the Vampire, you need to rapidly but smoothly apply full aileron and full rudder and control altitude by moving the elevator forward and backwards as you go right side up – inverted – through each roll. This was regarded as spectacular in the days before power controls; but it needed strength and sure handling and I took pride in my performance.

Nearing the end of the display and breathing hard with the exertion, I entered a tight wingover turn, pulling high G loading to position for the eight rolls. There was no word on the radio from either the Canberra or air traffic control. Next thing I caught sight of the Canberra, again foolishly trying to join me in formation. He was on my left, inside the radius of my turn and again belly up to me and closing fast. Really, trying to join formation in the middle of a display and without any idea of what I was going to do next! The bastard must be mad, I thought. Was he trying to ram me? Again?

I still don't know quite how I avoided him in my high-G turn; certainly, we avoided a collision by only a narrow margin. It was up to me to do the manoeuvring to miss hitting him as he couldn't see me. I was forced into a dangerously tight manoeuvre and was one highly stressed pilot on straightening up on the display line ready to start the eight maximum-rate rolls. I should have quit right there. But did not. Moments later, with full rudder and full aileron applied, I was established in the maximum-rate roll routine, in this case rolling to the left. I was conscious of being overstressed and was trying to avoid rough handling of the controls. Rolls 1, 2, 3, 4 were completed successfully. And then the Vampire bit back! I must have wrenched the elevator back too sharply. With unbelievable rapidity I flick-rolled. From rolling to the left, I was instantaneously rolling rapidly to the right. Luck was on my side and I didn't keep flick-rolling into the ground but managed to regain control by easing off the G load. I had the sense to reverse the controls and, to my own amazement, established myself in maximum-rate rolls to the right! I completed four more rolls and continued until I'd finished my display. Without any further thought of a combined flypast with the Canberra, I departed Timaru for Wigram as planned.

The weather deteriorated, and I had to find my way through driving rain to land at Wigram. I reported to Operations and then decided to refuel and fly back to Ohakea, forgoing the big party at Timaru. I would have dropped the Canberra pilot in his tracks if I'd met him that day. With bitterness I reflected on the disaster we'd nearly brought to Timaru and the fact that only pure luck had saved me in the flick roll. I resolved that I would never again continue a display that had been interrupted by a serious incident.

To my dying day, I will remain astonished. Not one person commented on the reversal of my rapid-rate rolls. The performance was watched by my squadron commander, squadron pilots and numerous others. Yet no one spoke of the feat of an instantaneous roll-reversal! Did they think Tom had invented a new heretofore impossible manoeuvre? Remarkable!

As I sit and write all these years later, I am still consumed by deep anger at the Canberra pilot. Idiot, think what you nearly did, not once but twice, to the people of Timaru. Stupidly and recklessly, you made two ham-fisted attempts from an impossible angle of 90 degrees to join me in formation during my aerobatic routine. No thanks to you, two collisions were narrowly avoided. Had we collided, with your 90-degree angle of approach and my forward speed, the wreckage would likely have impacted the densely packed crowd – it would have been a John Derry at Farnborough all over again. If you hadn't been so snooty, it would have been easy to arrange to join up for a combined flypast after my display was finished. Instead, we had this madness.

Close-run things? Plenty that day.

8

WELLINGTON AIRPORT OPENING, 1959

Shoehorned in

Wellington is a compact, hilly city, well known for boisterous weather. During the fairly frequent strong southerlies, gales whip through the harbour and streets of the city. Northerlies are also gusty and turbulent. It is said that in Wellington, if you lose your hat, put up your hand and grab another one going by.

The siting of Wellington airport was a contentious issue. Most opponents argued for the development of Paraparaumu airport over an hour north-west of Wellington; proponents decried the travel time to that location. Eventually, the runway was built between hills, with the northern end in the harbour and the southern end projecting into Cook Strait. Certainly, having an airport within a few minutes' drive of the city centre is an asset. One appreciates this after arrival on a calm day. But the convenience is forgotten if you are bucketing about on the approach in a southerly or strong northerly wind, desperately hoping your pilot's skill is up to the white-knuckle arrival.

Construction was completed in 1959, and a massive contingent of military and civil aircraft from New Zealand and overseas was assembled for the opening display. Included in the armada was a great white Vulcan bomber of the RAF, one of the largest of aircraft in those days. The Wellington runway was of barely sufficient length to accommodate the big visitor. However, recognising the public relations triumph of having the pride of their military fleet arrive at the opening of the new airport at New Zealand's capital, the British decided the Vulcan would land at Wellington, despite the difficulties. An unusual sequence was planned to assist the pilot in his difficult task. The aircraft, on arrival with just enough fuel to divert to Ohakea if necessary, would do two touch-and-go landings before a final approach and landing.

Reservations about the wisdom of this plan were expressed by members of the RNZAF. They were mindful that, in the Vulcan, only the pilots had ejection seats. The absence of this survival aid for all crew, in the Vulcan and other British V-bombers, had been the cause of numerous protests from the RAF Aviation Medicine Unit. But the New Zealanders recognised that the decision to participate was the prerogative of the British, and the Vulcan arrival plan remained unchanged.

Close to the big day, at Ohakea, the airfield was busy. Our tarmacs were crowded with visiting aircraft. There were also many visiting crews to entertain. A USAF Centuries Series supersonic fighter arrived, and I was fortunate to be invited to take a flight with the laconic American pilot. To my amusement, during the pre-flight safety briefing I was told, 'Son, on this takeoff, if I say, "Eject", and you say, "What did you say?", you'll be talking to yourself.' Our takeoff, rotating to a near vertical climb just after lift-off, was truly spectacular. I enjoyed the high-speed flight very much.

RNZAF Woodbourne and Wellington airport itself shared the burden of accommodating the rest of the armada.

My part in the occasion was flying in the Vampire aerobatic team. We were the act everybody wanted to see and last on the day's program, to follow immediately after the Vulcan's landing. I'd sunburnt my face quite severely skiing the previous weekend and to prevent the oxygen mask chafing was wearing a surgical mask underneath. This allowed the ground crew to have fun with bystanders by pointing me out as their flying doctor.

Our team was led by a legendary flier, a great leader whose flying was always smooth and accurate. His radio instructions to the team were always measured and unhurried, as regular as a metronome.

For the Wellington opening, we tried adding a fifth aircraft to join in our display. The culmination of the team show was a downwards bomb burst. Four aircraft pull over the top of a loop and enter a vertical dive, in close formation. The leader calls, 'Break, break, *go.*' Numbers two and three in the formation rapidly roll through 90 degrees, and number four through 180 degrees. Each aircraft then pulls through to give a thrilling demonstration of near contact with the ground. The four aircraft, each trailing smoke, thus recover to level flight, one heading to each quarter of the compass. Exciting stuff, but we wanted to do more. For this occasion, we'd sought the approval of the group captain, CO Ohakea, for the fifth aircraft to do a head-on pass through our downburst. This aircraft was to do a solo routine and then wait about until bomb-burst time. Four aircraft breaking vertically downwards passing head on another aircraft climbing vertically, with all aircraft trailing smoke, was truly spectacular. The sequence wasn't as risky as it might seem at first sight: if the solo aircraft realised he was too early to pull up, he could abort the manoeuvre and fly away in low-level flight. We performed this routine three times in rehearsals at Ohakea, but after due deliberation the group captain decided not to authorise this sequence at the opening of Wellington display.

Considering how events played out, this was probably fortuitous.

On the day planned for the display, a Saturday, a stiff northerly was blowing, with low cloud, strong winds, heavy showers and turbulence. Reluctantly, a decision was made to cancel the display, which was then rescheduled for the Sunday following.

After the decision to abort the display on the Saturday, the aerobatic team was instructed to position to Wellington. Thus, we set off, with our spare aircraft, as a formation of six Vampires. I happened to be number six, at the tail end of the formation. Following our leader, the six-plane formation made it as far as Paraparaumu before being thwarted by low visibility; we were unable to proceed to Wellington via the west coast route. The formation leader decided to back-track through the Manawatu Gorge, a steep, narrow, winding river valley, and from there fly down the centre of the island via Masterton to Wellington. Mountains lie on the right-hand side of this route after leaving the gorge. The flight time with this diversion was towards the limit of our safe fuel endurance after the turnback from Paraparaumu. On arrival at the Manawatu Gorge, we found low cloud and poor visibility and flew through this steep, restricted valley twisting and turning continuously through all the quite sharp corners, a task of some difficulty. As each aircraft followed the one ahead, the turns became tighter and tighter and as number six in the formation I was starting to pull some real G in those narrow confines.

At last, we arrived at the eastern end of the gorge and our leader turned south to head for Wellington. Uncharacteristically, he made an error of navigation. Instead of straightening up on a southerly heading for Masterton, he continued to turn to the west and entered a blind valley (a steep valley with no way out). Cries of alarm echoed over the radio. The leader realised his error and scrambled to pull into a tight-G turn to escape the rapidly closing sides of the narrow ravine, overlying cloud preventing a climb out of the trap. Each aircraft behind him needed to pull tighter G than the one ahead. As the number six, I almost blacked out with the effort of avoiding the bush-clad hills sliding by just beneath my nose. Rattled, we continued on our way and landed at Wellington in rough conditions. In the gale northerly, I was grateful to have arrived. The navigation error was a bad omen.

Confusion reigned in Wellington. Aircraft had failed to arrive due to the weather, and people who had kindly offered to host the visiting airmen were milling about at several functions where they were supposed to meet their guests. No one had made arrangements for us, so it was every man for himself. I went to a function and met a kind dentist and his wife who couldn't locate their American guests so they invited me instead. I spent a pleasant evening with them.

Conditions on the Sunday were little improved: they were marginal at best. This was difficult given the time constraints of many of our visitors. After much discussion, it was decided the display would go ahead.

As the amazing Wellington Air Display began the northerly conditions continued, with scudding cloud base at about 2000 feet and strong turbulence in the circuit area. The show began before a massive crowd on and around the airfield and surrounding high ground.

Alarming scrape after alarming scrape ensued. Showcasing its arts, a top-dressing aircraft made what is best described as a St Vitus Dance down the runway, but flew off without mishap. A Handley Page Herald and a Fokker Friendship, two aircraft competing for National Airways Corporation business, flew one after the other. They were anxious to demonstrate their short landing techniques, many New Zealand airports being rather short. Each was flown at the absolute minimum speed to touch down, swerving and pitching about in the turbulence and landing on the very end of the runway with the tyres pouring smoke from maximum braking. They pulled up in incredibly tight distances We military pilots awaiting our turn were full of admiration for their skill. We weren't so sure about their wisdom.

A large formation of Harvards and Devons from the RNZAF training school absolutely waltzed across the sky, somehow managing to keep roughly to their formation positions in the churning winds. Some of the pilots in the middle of the circus later confided that they had barely sufficient control to avoid hitting each other, despite the full application of ailerons and rudder. This was risky flying and probably shouldn't have been attempted with such a large number of aircraft.

A Sunderland flying boat of Number Five Squadron swung about at an extremely low level above the runway. It lurched in the turbulence, and the hull touched the runway, grinding along for several yards with smoke pouring from the planing bottom.

Fortunately, the captain managed to recover and climb away to return to base in Auckland. The chief flight engineer on board claims to be the only man to have flown from Wellington to Auckland upside down as he stuffed rags in the hole to keep out the water when alighting in Auckland Harbour. The aircraft was recovered onto the slipway at Hobsonville without further damage.

More stories emerged. A forward-thinking wing commander had acquired 300 stretchers and discreetly placed them in storage ready for instant use. Those in the know ribbed him about this at first but as the display progressed many people began to congratulate him on his foresight instead.

The smartest pilot of the day, in my view, was my friend who flew the Centuries Series American fighter aircraft. On arrival, he took one look at the weather, cut in the afterburner and departed with a thunderous roar. He made it plain that he would not be coming back. Nice guy. Smart guy.

The near disaster of the Vulcan

It was almost the turn of Red Formation (us). We strapped ourselves into our Vampires – very tightly, given the weather, I might add – and taxied to the takeoff point for the northerly runway. Ours was to be the last demonstration of the opening display but we were held at the takeoff point to await the arrival, two touch-and-goes and final landing of the RAF Vulcan. This magnificent great white bomber looked superb as it made its first approach to the runway from the south. At the sight of it, the crowds all over and around the airport stirred with excitement.

On the first touch-down, the Vulcan's heavy multi-wheel undercarriage contacted the tarmac in front of our nose, a mere 10 feet from the start of the runway concrete. With a tremendous roar an overshoot, or go-around, was executed as planned, and the big white bird flew an impeccable circuit to make the second touch-and-go. This time, the undercarriage touched down right on the end of the runway. I considered radioing the pilot a warning to watch it but decided it wouldn't do to interrupt the busy display control frequency. The Vulcan completed the second practice circuit and made its final approach, with the intention of landing.

Shock and horror! The aircraft touched down in the soft grass area short of the runway.

The left undercarriage bogie slammed into the ground. A big spurt of earth erupted. The rear undercarriage strut broke, and the heavy gear rotated around the fulcrum of the main undercarriage attachment to smash into the underside of the wing. Immediately, a flood of fuel spurted out, straight into the exhausts of numbers 1 and 2 engines. The aircraft lurched to the left (away from us), towards a densely packed crowd about 300 feet from the runway. The wing-tip dropped towards the runway. I braced myself, certain I was about to witness a huge tragedy.

I found it difficult to believe what then took place before my very eyes. The sudden roaring flow of the exhausts showed that all four engines had come instantly up to full power: the aircraft wasn't flown, but rather blasted off the ground, like a rocket!

Normal jet engines of the time took several seconds to accelerate to maximum power. Too rapid application of the throttle, or thrust lever, would cause pressure fluctuations through the engine and lack of acceleration. Typically, it would take about 30 seconds to get full power. But this aircraft had Olympus Spey engines fitted. They had a free spool, which ironed out the pressure fluctuations and permitted instant acceleration – the device was secret then. This was the explanation for the near-instantaneous achievement of full power that enabled the Vulcan to stagger away, avoiding a calamitous crash into the dense crowds so close to the runway.

With the gush of fuel into the now high temperature exhausts of numbers 1 and 2 engines, it was a marvel it didn't blow up. The left wing-tip came very close to impacting the ground. Had it done so, the aircraft would probably have cartwheeled into the crowd. The immediate recovery of control was a superb piece of flying.

And so, my jaw dropping, I watched the giant lurch into the air and accelerate. The difference between that outcome and what could have been the tragic loss of several hundred lives had come about in a few crucial seconds. What a lucky day for Wellington!

As the Vulcan climbed away from its fateful encounter, an English voice, cracking with strain, came over the radio. 'Can you tell me what I have done?'

Immediately came a reply from someone: 'Shut down one and two.' Instantly the exhausts of these two engines, blasting into the fuel leak, disappeared. The aircraft nose yawed wildly from side to side as the pilots fought for control. Then the colossal white aircraft turned north and set course for Ohakea. It had just enough fuel remaining to get there: 18 minutes fuel for the 16-minute flight. The Vulcan was still in serious trouble.

Word of a looming disaster spread with incredible rapidity, and at Ohakea cars piled up at the airfield boundary fences. A flood of people jumped the fences and surged forward. All available airmen were given wooden staves and rushed to beat back the foolhardy crowd. The Ohakea Flight Safety Committee hurriedly convened but before it managed to decide anything, the aircraft arrived.

There were ejection seats for only the two pilots. The other three crew members were unable to bail out. The undercarriage couldn't be raised with the smashed-up left gear. The extended nose landing gear, which sat immediately behind the parachute exit hatch, prevented a successful egress.

Practically out of fuel, the captain elected to carry out a forced landing with the gear remaining. The nose gear and the starboard undercarriage held up, and with his tanks nearly dry, the captain executed a superb emergency landing. The big aircraft slewed to port off the runway. All five crew members escaped without injury.

Later, the Vulcan was recovered from its crash position. The aircraft was jacked up, and the port undercarriage was repaired. Dragged by several army tanks with a complex array of steel cables — a detail admired by ex-teamster me —

the behemoth was returned to the runway by being dragged over railway sleepers placed one by one in front of the wheels. New Zealand Railways insisted on a hire charge of five shillings per sleeper per day. The technique, reminiscent of the ancient Egyptians building the pyramids, earned high praise for Wing Commander Salmon, our technical officer, as the only man who had ever retrieved a crashed V-bomber without substantial further damage. The aircraft was eventually flown back to England.

The near disaster of the aerobatic team

Meantime, back at Wellington, we of Red Formation received our takeoff clearance. After all the things that had happened at the display that day, we were ready for anything. We got plenty.

The takeoff clearance call brought me back immediately to the close attention required in high-speed formation aerobatic display. With safety harness tightened as much as possible for the rough conditions, we rolled down the runway.

Low cloud covered the airfield. 'It's clear over the Strait; we'll do our display there,' came our leader's measured voice over the radio.

We completed the display sequence up to the entry into the downwards bomb burst. Then the leader's voice interrupted the routine. 'It has cleared over the airfield. We will run in and do the bomb burst over the runway.' Diving to attain the speed necessary to the manoeuvre, we followed our leader as he pulled up to the top of a loop and entered the vertical dive before the expected 'Breaking, breaking, *go!*' call.

From seemingly nowhere, cloud suddenly formed, and in an instant we were fully enveloped by it. I will never, ever, forget the feeling of dismay this caused. Interminable seconds ticked by as we awaited our leader's call to break. But he couldn't give it while we were in cloud – if the four aircraft lost sight of one another, they would have collided in the zero visibility. Nor could he continue the loop with all four aircraft from that level – we were too low. The adrenaline came flooding as we realised we were in mortal danger diving vertically at the ground we could not see.

As we approached the bottom of the cloud and the visibility started to clear, there came a frantic call from our leader, shockingly different from his usual calm, measured commands. 'Break *go!*' he screamed.

Instantly transferring my eyes from the leader to the ground, I was aghast. We were terribly low, far lower than the minimum safe altitude for a break. It was going to be a very close thing. I immediately turned 90 degrees then yanked back on the control column to pull as much G as I dared. Pulling heavy G stops the blood flow progressing into the brain; this can lead to a blackout or temporary shrinking of the visual field or even complete loss of sight. I was pulling so much G that my sight narrowed down into a cone in the middle of the visual field, straight ahead. But I dared not relax the G forces when the ground was in such close proximity. Even pilots may find this difficult to believe but I genuinely think I was subject to perhaps 12 G.

A witness on the ground later described what he saw. 'There was a Vampire, nose high in the air, streaming condensation trails from every rivet, desperately trying to pull out of its dive. It came within 10 feet [3 metres] of the ground.'

That was me.

The other three aircraft were in similar straits, or worse. Number four, who had to rotate through 180 degrees, twice my 90 degrees, told me he actually high-speed stalled his aircraft and commenced a flick roll. That was a specially perilous situation, particularly in a Vampire. He managed to recover. He was fortunate to live to tell the tale.

And so, I managed – with the most narrow of margins – to pull out of the death dive. I was unbelievably lucky my aircraft didn't enter a flick roll with the very heavy wing loading. But I wasn't yet done! The quadrant in which I was recovering from the bomb burst was the one pointing into the city. I realised I was at risk of impacting the rising ground near the Hataitai tunnel. Holding the high G, I had to cautiously feed in aileron to turn in order to slide through a gap in this skyline. This was highly dangerous in any aircraft but particularly a Vampire, and my heart was in my mouth as I turned to the right. With almost nothing to spare, I managed to avoid ground contact.

People who were on the ground there later describing the scene to me spoke of a crowd running, screaming and leaping into ditches in their suits to avoid what seemed to them to be a certain ground impact.

After some confusion, we rejoined our leader in formation. Everyone was badly shaken. The smoke from our exhausts was lying on the runway. The intention was originally to depart to Ohakea but because of the Vulcan emergency there, we landed again at Wellington.

It was hours before our leader could bring himself to speak to us. He thought he'd killed us all. Our normal minimum break height for the downward bomb burst was 3000 feet, but at Wellington it was upped to 3500, especially for the aircraft required to break east over the hills near the Hataitai tunnel – this turned out to be me. Suicide height was reckoned to be 3200 feet after some theoretical aircraft performance calculations. The pilots of the aircraft following the leader had, of course, to keep their constant attention on the lead aircraft and had no time to look at the altimeter as the break was called, although we all sensed in our bones that we were dangerously low. Finally, our leader admitted he had called (screamed!) the break at 2800 feet.

After some confusion as to the availability of Ohakea, where clean-up after the Vulcan emergency landing was continuing, a chastened team flew back to our home.

All in all, there were several close-run things there at the opening of Wellington airport. It is a place where pilots must always take special care.

Wellington airport carries on

Perhaps because of the obvious need for pilots to take extra care in the topography surrounding the airport and the regular boisterous wind conditions, Wellington airport has performed without major mishap since its opening. It has been lucky in some instances though.

Probably the most serious incident happened to an Air New Zealand DC8 making an approach from the north in cloud. The instrument approach procedure in use called for a descent after passing over an NDB – non-directional beacon, a somewhat antiquated aid where in the cockpit passage over the station is shown by the needle in the tracking instrument in the cockpit reversing from ahead to astern. Observing the expected reversal, the captain closed the throttles and began his descent Luckily, he broke out of cloud in mid-descent. Shockingly, straight ahead was the sight of the houses of a Wellington suburb: he was about to crash straight into them. A violent application of power and a rapid rotation saw him clear the houses, but by the slimmest of margins. Suburbanites spoke later of the terrifying sight of the sudden appearance of an airliner from the cloud and the roar of its engines as it climbed away. A close-run thing there.

Subsequently, the co-pilot, an ex-pupil of mine, told me that the captain was so shocked that he maintained a steep climb to the point where airspeed dropped to the vicinity of the stall. The co-pilot had a real battle to wrestle the controls from him to correct the situation. The aircraft then carried out a safe landing at Wellington.

There was some scepticism of the captain's explanation of his descent being correctly commenced on the reversal of his NDB instrument … until another pilot reported a reversal in exactly the same place. An investigation followed. It was discovered that the radio propagation pattern centred over the beacon had been somehow picked up by power lines running up the Hutt Valley and was being re-radiated from a position about 10 miles (16 kilometres) from the actual beacon. The captain was vindicated. Nevertheless, the near-miss so shocked him that he gave up flying altogether.

Yet again, aviation had produced a shocking surprise for everyone. The lesson seems to be: always be alert for the unexpected.

* * *

Wellington boasts not only the airfield but also alighting areas in the harbour. On a regular basis, 5 Squadron RNZAF used these lanes for flights to the Chatham Islands. Some years after my Vampire days, I flew to the Chathams regularly in Number 5 Squadron's Sunderland flying boats. On arrival after securing to the buoy in Wellington Harbour, the aircraft would be refuelled from a barge. On one occasion, I noticed that the barge was moored in such a position that it was directly under the trailing edge of the wing. I knew the captain of the barge was a pretty crusty old salt so I was especially tactful in suggesting I would be more comfortable if he shut down his engine, in case there was a fuel spill. This sally elicited a scornful look from the ancient mariner. About ten seconds later, there was a fuel spill, and a solid sheet of Avgas (aviation petrol) flowed off the trailing edge of the wing and straight down the exhaust pipe of the barge's idling engine. Rarely have I seen such a rapid movement as that man shutting off his engine. I managed to refrain from saying, 'I told you so.'

Despite the controversy surrounding its siting, Wellington airport has justified the expectations of its proponents. Long may it continue its wonderful service to travellers to our capital city, minutes from downtown Wellington.

But the day of the opening display of its airport luck just managed to hold for the inhabitants of the city.

9

DISPLAYS, BIRDSTRIKES AND BONE DOMES

Aerobatics

Following the dramatic opening of Wellington airport, our aerobatic team toured the South Island. Displays were performed at Nelson, Hokitika, Christchurch, Dunedin and finally Invercargill.

Hokitika airport doesn't have a sealed runway. I performed a full-instrument takeoff in the dust cloud kicked up by the preceding aircraft getting airborne for our show. The dust ceased at the point that aircraft had become airborne. At near takeoff speed I burst out into clear air and there, standing right in front of me, was a man with a camera. Realising his danger, he cast the camera aside and threw himself down. I just managed to pull up over him. My exhaust must have singed his hair. Lucky guy!

Our departure from Hokitika to Christchurch was delayed by weather. On arrival at Christchurch, there was little time to spare so we all slept on the tables in the operations room, and were roused in time to be briefed and fly the display.

Dunedin was a happy visit. The press made much of me as the local boy. Our performance within the fairly tight confines of the hills surrounding Taieri airport was immaculate.

And so, on to the final display at Invercargill airport.

Birdstrike

The team was on top of its game for this last display and we were looking forward to entertaining a large crowd. During the display, in close proximity, we carried out a series of manoeuvres and entered into gooseneck formation, with number two and three tucked tightly in behind number four. Our wings overlapped by half their length – this is a demanding formation. Pulling through in a loop, we were diving vertically at low level when suddenly there was a puff of white on four's windscreen. A large bird had collided with him, and the debris from the smashed windscreen pulverised his safety visor, blinding him as the debris entered his eyes. He had enough sense to pull back on the control column and radioed a frantic call for help.

Number three broke away from the formation to go to the aid of our stricken comrade and was able to guide him out of the dive. 'Pull up, Rus. Pull up, pull up!' came the dramatic calls. Three did a magnificent job guiding the blinded pilot around a wide circuit, getting him aligned with the runway and talking him down the approach path. We remaining two kept well out of the way and listened to the reassuring voice: 'Left wing up a bit, Rus. Ease off the throttle. Lower your nose. You are lined up with the runway. Passing 100 feet. Chop the power. 50 feet. Good, you're on. Bit of right rudder. Hit the brakes. Well done, Rus, you've stopped on the runway!'

Sighs of relief.

This bird-strike story has a happy ending with a bonus. In hospital, the flight gear was cut away and the patient was rushed into theatre to have his eyes washed out and treated. As sight returned, he was able to see that the theatre nurse was most attractive. Today, he remains happily married to the beautiful lady.

Some years later, a Kiwi pilot flying in a jet-fighter Skyhawk aircraft in the United States – during an exchange posting with the USN – was instructing an American pupil when a bird struck and penetrated the windscreen. Our pilot was completely blinded, and his helmet – containing his radio – was carried away in the air blast now entering the shattered cockpit. He reached for the ejection seat handle above his head and ejected from the cockpit. This was the only course open to him. His pupil, in the rear seat of the Skyhawk, was able to retain control and actually landed the aircraft successfully at a nearby airfield.

Meantime, the ejection seat worked as advertised, and the automatic features soon had the pilot swinging on the end of his parachute, safely separated from the seat. Sightless, he was unable to do anything until he was deposited with a jolt on the ground, luckily without further injury. With blood streaming down his face he searched for something to stem the flow. He took off his flying boot and used the sock to wipe his eyes. This not being effective, he suddenly remembered he was in rattlesnake country so put sock and boot back on and awaited rescue.

The highway patrol weren't long in finding him, and in short order he was in a naval hospital. By a stroke of luck, the chief ophthalmic surgeon of the US Navy was in the vicinity on leave and came in to operate. Hour after hour he worked, and with outstanding skill was able to save partial sight in one eye. Sight in the other eye was lost. Finally, the patient was released from the theatre and taken to intensive care, where his remaining flight gear was stripped from him. Consternation! A bloodied foot! Back to theatre he went for X-rays and examination. Nothing found! It was only when consciousness returned that the explanation for the bloodied foot was forthcoming.

This pilot made a good recovery with partial sight remaining in his good eye and was allowed to continue flying under the supervision of an instructor pilot. The Navy provided him with an artificial eye fashioned to look like his remaining one, and this moved in sequence with his good eye, so that persons in conversation with him had no reason to detect any abnormality. The Navy amused itself by also providing him with an additional artificial eye which had the stars and stripes of a miniature US flag in place of the iris. He could interchange these two artificial eyeballs quickly, and this enabled him to put on a great party act. Talking to girls, appearing like a normally sighted person, he would momentarily turn aside, and when he looked back there were the stars and stripes following the girls' every move! They used to freak out, to the vast amusement of partygoers in the know.

* * *

There is another amusing tale connected with birdstrikes. Aircraft windscreens, which are of complex, multi-layered structure built to resist the shock of birdstrikes, are required to be designed to withstand a certain number of simultaneous hits. This ability is tested in a wind tunnel where a special cannon fires chicken carcasses onto the windscreen. The cannons are manufactured by, I think, the famous English firm Rolls-Royce.

An American rail company, concerned about the safety glass panel in front of the drivers of their fast trains, heard about these cannons and ordered one from Rolls-Royce. They were thunderstruck when on their first test, the chicken went right through the glass and dented the driver's (empty) seat as well. Assembling all the details and data of their test procedures, they sent the lot to Rolls-Royce and asked for advice.

Back came the reply: 'Thaw the chickens first.'

The advent of 'bone domes'

At Cranwell, I admired the college medical officer. A squadron leader, he was one of the original doctors at the Royal Air Force Aviation Medicine Unit at Farnborough. The doctors there were fine people. It was their tradition that if they invented something in the way of personal safety equipment, they tried it on themselves first. One doctor designed a new life jacket. To test it, he went to the end of a pier – obviously with safety people in attendance – injected himself with a knockout drug and fell unconscious into the water. He thus proved his design would safely support an unconscious person.

The Aviation Medicine Unit rather discouraged pilots from visiting their establishment. The visitors might catch sight of equipment that had been tested to destruction and lose confidence in those items.

After one college dinner, the medical officer told me of the difficulty the RAF had in persuading the British Government to stump up with the considerable cost of providing protective helmets, 'bone domes', to fighter pilots. All appeals failed; the bureaucrats wouldn't come up with the money. That is, until an accident report reached the desks of the decision makers. A twin-jet Meteor aircraft was making an emergency asymmetric approach to land, with one engine shut down due to failure. For some reason, the pilot commenced a go-around from a low level – a tricky and unforgiving procedure with only one engine remaining. He mishandled the aircraft, climbing at too steep an angle and approached the stall. The asymmetric thrust overcame the power of the rudder to prevent the nose yawing towards the dead engine. Still at very low altitude, the Meteor stalled and flicked upside down, descending sharply to the concrete runway. Now this aircraft had one of the early Martin Baker ejection seats and the pilot made a good decision – to use it. Unfortunately, his timing was the worst – he ejected just as the inverted descending aircraft was about to impact the runway. The combined forces of the descent and the ejection seat rocket engine drove seat and man through the runway concrete block, with obviously fatal results.

When the autopsy report was filed, it stated that had the pilot been wearing a protective helmet, his head injuries would have been less severe. On the strength of that, the Treasury relented and authorised the issue of bone domes.

10

IT'S YOUR BEST PUPIL WHO'LL KILL YOU

My years of captivating flying on the Vampire Squadron, which incidentally changed from number 14 to the famed 75 during my service, were wonderful but eventually came to an end. I was posted to RNZAF Wigram, for an instructor's course and eventually became the chief flying instructor – A Flight Commander – of the Air Force's flying training school.

The flying training school at Wigram, near Christchurch, operated Harvards and Devons for the training of pilots and other branches of Air Force air crew. It also possessed three Austers for teaching army officers to fly so that they could become artillery spotters.

The North American Harvard T6 entered service with the RNZAF during World War II and was an excellent training aircraft. It was somewhat unstable on the ground run of a landing and, unless watched carefully, would ground-loop and often dent a wing-tip. This was easily repaired, and the experience would send a young pilot on his way chagrined but much wiser. This was far preferable to the pilot having an accident later in his career on an expensive operational aircraft.

The ground loop would occur when the tail-wheel assembly would unhook and allow the wheel to freely pivot, upsetting the on-ground longitudinal stability of the landing craft.

In the 1960s, when the Harvard had been in service for about 30 years, a young airframe mechanic corporal thought the tail-wheel mounting simply didn't look right. His opinion was greeted with hoots of derision – 'Do you think we've had it wrong for 30 years?' – but the astute young man stuck to his guns and managed to obtain the manufacturer's original drawings. Sure enough, we were pumping the tail-wheel shock absorber far too high, leading to early disconnect and ground-looping accidents. The procedure was corrected. We never had another Harvard ground-loop, so far as I am aware. To their credit, senior officers apologised to the corporal and wrote good reports about him.

The Devon, manufactured by de Havilland, was another interesting story. Originally, it was designed with a revolutionary glued wing structure and was to be a medium-range high-speed turboprop. Ha! When the prototype wing was tested, it was so weak that the two halves of the wing would have clapped hands in front of the pilot's nose if engines of the design power had been attached. And the turboprop engine design, utilising the previously unknown feature of an S-bend in the compressor/turbine airflow, was an equal failure; on the first run-up, the engine went to design rpm, and cigars were handed around among the engineers; however, as load was fed in, the revs died away. The engine was producing just enough power to run itself and no more.

What to do with an airframe and an engine that plainly doesn't work? De Havilland had the answer. Produce the airframe and call it a Devon. Junk the engine design and replace it with a development of the ancient Tiger Moth Gypsy engine – blown up to plus 6 pounds (2.7 kilograms) boost, inverted, inline and air-cooled. Then sell it to the New Zealand Government.

Problems arose from the fitting of heavy gear for the training of navigators and signallers. The aircraft was used also for flying training of ab initio pilots. The dual-engine aircraft was suitable for training pilots in the art of flying multi-engined aeroplanes with an engine shut down.

In those days, we were quite mad. Instead of throttling back the 'failed' engine, so it could be brought back to full power if required, we used to actually shut it down. In the Devon, vastly underpowered in its overly laden state, the instructor would reach around behind the pupil's seat and pull up a cock that failed that engine. The pupil would immediately apply full power on the remaining engine and climb away. We would do this at 200 feet at Wigram, where we were climbing out over housing estates, just 200 feet above the chimney pots! At its best, the Devon could manage only 100 to 150 feet per minute climb in this configuration. By the grace of God, we never had a failure of the live engine in circumstances that involved the housing estates. Yet, if anyone said, 'This is insane, let's just throttle back the engine', in those days they would have risked being thought of as LMF, cowardly.

Eventually, the inevitable happened. A flight commander making an approach at Wigram in a Devon with one engine actually shut down suffered a failure of the other engine. A rapid forced landing ensued. The aircraft ended up in the base rubbish dump – thankfully without injury to crew. Staff officers in Wellington came to their senses, and thereafter engine failures in training were to be simulated only.

Before it was discontinued, that crazy practice also caused an accident at the Air Force base at Whenuapai, Auckland. One night, a woman rang to say she could hear loud swearing coming from the mudflats of the Waitemata Harbour adjacent to Whenuapai. It turned out to be the crew of a DC3 that had been practising asymmetric circuits and had dutifully shut down the right-hand engine. After a one-engine go-around had been commenced, the captain ordered his co-pilot, who was inexperienced, to restart the right engine. The hapless young fellow managed to shut down the left engine. With no engines running, the venerable old DC3 was soon settled on the mud over which it had been flying. The language that upset the lady caller was the grizzled old captain telling the younger man exactly what he thought of his abilities.

Instructing ab initio pupils at Wigram, I worked extremely hard but found the passing on of knowledge of correct flying practice very satisfying. Sometimes I would fly eight one-hour details in the circuit with new pupils, six by day and two by night, and totter off to bed at night completely exhausted.

Instrument flying

I was pleased to be selected and qualified as an Instrument Rating Examiner, a coveted qualification. Instrument flying is the hardest skill to master on a flying course.

People have always interpreted their relationship to the world about them through sensory inputs in the body. The three semi-circular canals of the inner ear provide major inputs. But the dynamic motions of aircraft act upon the senses and provide illusions. In flying solely by reference to instruments, the trainee pilot must learn to ignore certain sensations and trust in his instruments to maintain the aircraft attitude to achieve the desired flight patterns. There are many traps leading to spatial disorientation which can – and often have – caused accidents. A common example of these is 'the leans': on recovery from a turn, the pilot may have the sensation of turning in the opposite direction and apply ailerons to re-enter the original turn. If he attempts to recover by pulling back on the control column, he will enter a tightening downward spiral and, if sufficient height is lost, will impact the ground. Other examples of illusions that often cause trouble are viewing an isolated light surrounded by darkened terrain, approaching a runway of different width and length to what the pilot is accustomed to or flying in the mountains, where the usual flat horizon is concealed by the terrain.

It is essential that the physiology of the body in spin recovery is fully understood by pilots. In a spin, the aircraft is usually in a steep nose-down attitude and is turning and yawing (nose moving left or right relative to the airflow). The initial entry causes the fluid within the semi-circular canals to move, bending the sensory hairs and giving a sensation of turning. The eyes now lock on to a prominent object – usually the sun – for a brief period then flick to the next object. The eyeballs oscillate rapidly from side to side. After about 20 seconds, the fluid stabilises, the hairs are no longer deflected and the eyeball oscillation stops. The pilot has the impression the spin has sped up. When recovery from the spin is effected by full opposite rudder, the sensory hairs are deflected in the opposite direction, and nature causes the eyeballs to oscillate in the reverse direction. There is a strong sensation of disorientation. It is vitally important that the pilot looks at and believes his flight instruments or he may misapply the controls, re-enter the spin and continue to the ground.

The involuntary rapid oscillation of the eyeballs (nystagmus) can be replicated in a special training device called a Barany chair, in which the subject can be rotated. The person is securely strapped in and rotated quickly. Upon the rotation being stopped suddenly, the eyeballs can be seen to be flicking wildly from side to side. If the subject's head is now tilted sideways (simulating looping) the eyeballs flick up and down extremely fast. If the head is placed so as to look up to the ceiling, the eyeballs will swiftly rotate first one way then the other – this is an astonishing thing to see. It is most important that the subject be strapped in as the sudden stops may cause sufficient disorientation for the person to throw themselves violently out of the chair.

Pilots intent on obtaining an instrument rating (their licence to fly in cloud or other limited-visibility environments) are well advised to plan their activities so that the whole phase of this training continues without gaps and interruptions. There are difficult lessons to be mastered.

A case of pilot disorientation which resulted in a fatal accident is a sobering lesson. In July 1999, John Kennedy, son of the assassinated US President, was making a night approach over the bay off Martha's Vineyard, Massachusetts. The airfield of intended landing was a single bright spot in a large black expanse of water. In this situation, a properly trained pilot would use instruments to ensure he was turning at a rate that would intersect the correct inbound course to the runway, and losing height at the correct rate (generally, the rule of three – at 3 miles from the threshold, you should be at 3 x three = 900 feet; at 2 miles, at 600 feet, et cetera). But in this situation – where there is a brightly lit destination surrounded by a black, featureless expanse – an untrained pilot would likely experience the leans. He would fail to constantly monitor his instruments and become disorientated. The turn towards the runway would then tighten up as the pilot attempted to recover by pulling back on the control column. This situation could be expected to culminate in a crash into the dark water, short of the runway and inside the turn. Since this is precisely the pattern of John Kennedy's doomed flight, we can be reasonably sure of what happened.

This accident, in which not only Kennedy but also his wife and sister-in-law died, tragically illustrates the predominant lesson of flight in instrument conditions – never persist into worsening conditions beyond your abilities. If caught out by the weather, climb on a safe heading (something you should be constantly aware of) to a safe altitude where you can sort things out with the help of air traffic control.

Accidents involving low-level flight in adverse weather conditions often are caused by two errors. Firstly, there is an error of judgment in penetrating weather below safe levels for the pilot's competence. Secondly, there is an error of navigation: failure to turn on to a safe heading. The second factor is particularly important in mountainous terrain, where the choice of safe escape headings is likely to be limited.

Businesses chartering aircraft to take executives, often the CEO, to conferences in smaller towns should be aware of the dangers of disorientation if the weather deteriorates. There is typically pressure on the pilot to return the VIP on time. If the pilot is young and inexperienced, there may be a tendency to try to oblige and get through when the weather conditions are marginal – tempting fate. My advice to businesspeople chartering aircraft is that, unless there is a high-pressure system giving glorious weather over the whole country and it is summer so there is no risk of fog, it's better to pay the extra for an instrument-rated pilot and an aircraft fully equipped for Instrument Flight Rules (IFR) operations.

My second experience of jammed controls

As an instrument rating examiner, I spent a lot of time teaching pupils instrument flying and in carrying out regular checks on other instructors. On one instrument training detail in a Devon, I was instructing a pupil in recovery from unusual positions, where the instructor puts the aircraft into a steep climb or dive and hands back control to the pupil to recover.

This skill enables resumption of level flight after a disturbance, perhaps caused by severe weather or pilot inattention. I gave control to the pupil after placing the aircraft in a steep diving turn. His recovery to straight and level flight was satisfactory so we went on to the next exercise, a steep climbing turn. He made another satisfactory recovery. I hadn't intended to give him one more steep diving turn but changed my mind and told him to fly the aircraft into a stall and recover.

The pupil was progressively moving the control column backwards to maintain level flight as the speed decreased towards the stall, a normal expected movement. The seating in the Devon cockpit is side by side. Unexpectedly, I saw the pupil jerking on the control column. His face lost its colour in an instant. 'Sir, the elevator is jammed.'

'I have control,' I said, taking over. Indeed, the elevator was solidly jammed, able to be moved neither back nor forwards. Quite probably, my face went ashen, too. The elevator controls nose up or down movement and is necessary to control speed and the flight path of an aircraft. To have it jam is a frightening and serious emergency. It might not be possible to keep the aircraft airborne, let alone land it successfully.

On the plus side, the control jam was experienced in straight and level flight. Had it happened in the steep diving turn we nearly entered, we couldn't have recovered from the dive and almost certainly would have struck the ground at a steep angle. That was lucky!

I checked the mechanism for loose articles that may have blocked movement – nothing. I experimented with engine power and was able to get a very small and slow response, the nose rising with increase of power and falling with decrease. We didn't have parachutes on board – if they had been there, I would have ordered the pupil to bail out and would then have followed him. But we didn't have that option so I had to fly back to the airfield and land somehow. I declared an emergency, returned to Wigram after ATC confirmed that the longest landing run was available there, rather than at the nearby Christchurch International Airport. Back we went very carefully, laboriously correcting every turbulence-induced deviation with the so-slow response to engine power changes. I didn't dare to run out flaps, which reduce landing speed, because they produce a marked change of 'trim' (tendency to nose movement), and I judged this would be beyond my ability to control with engine power. A no-flap landing is at much higher speed than normal. This was going to be tricky, with a good chance of running off the far end of the runway at high speed. The airfield had, of course, been closed to other traffic and a full complement of emergency services was in position.

Carefully, I flew a wide circuit and settled on final approach as low as I dared, almost among the tree tops at about 2 miles out. My aim was to set up a stable attitude and speed, with just enough rate of descent to intersect the runway as close to the start as I could manage – without hitting the obstacles on the approach path, of course. By 200 feet, I judged I was in control, with stable airspeed, nose attitude and rate of descent. At 100 feet, a bit more power, going too low, too close to the fence. At 50 feet I was in a good position, without too much runway behind me, conscious of the high speed. When I judged myself at round-out height, I gave the engines a mighty burst at full power to raise the nose and arrest the rate of descent, then pulled off the power roughly to descend to the ground. I got it just right; we touched down quite lightly and, immediately, I applied full braking to hold the nose down and keep us on the ground. Elated, I knew we'd made it, despite the end of the runway approaching fast. We pulled up about 50 yards short of a prized flower bed, two pilots thankful to be down.

I'd survived my second case of jammed controls. A bearing in the auto-pilot mechanism, which could not be isolated from the main flying controls, had picked up metal and solidly jammed. The Air Force awarded me a Green Entry for my logbook, a commendation that praised me for skill and cool judgment in handling this situation.

Later in the bar that evening, a fellow instructor taunted me that when I'd declared the emergency, I'd sounded bloody scared. 'I *was* bloody scared,' I retorted. That shut him up.

Training flying, including a fright in a Harvard

Training flights at Christchurch were often affected by the weather. The prevailing winds over the South Island are westerly, and a depression approaching from the south-west would cause the famous Canterbury nor'wester to blow. The air arriving over Christchurch, having deposited its load of moisture in passing over the Southern Alps, would be dry and hot on the lee side of the ranges where we were. This phenomenon is known as the Fohn effect. As the weather system advanced to the east, the wind over Canterbury would turn southerly. The cold wet air, no longer passing over the mountains to be stripped of its moisture, would then pass around the southern end of the Alps and advance up the Canterbury Plains. This cold and wet air mass would then meet the hot dry air. Where the two air masses met, there would be a spectacular drop in temperature, and a violent front would move up the Canterbury Plains. The roiling front, accompanied by dark scudding clouds at the surface, strong wind gusts and heavy rain, was not a good place to be flying in. As it approached, warning cries would issue from airborne trainers, and all would come flocking back to Mother Earth ahead of the deluge.

Other situations might produce widespread low cloud that could last for several days. On one occasion, the low overcast over Wigram had persisted for three days. I was in a Harvard with my best pupil — let's call him P. He was good, intelligent and quick to learn. It was usually a relaxing experience to watch P perform well in the exercises I'd just taught him. He was at the stage in his course of intensive circuit training so, unable to get on with upper-air work because of the low cloud, round and round we went. We'd actually spent the previous two flights practising takeoffs, circuits and landings, and were both getting bored with going round and round. To create a break, I told P to head for nearby Lake Ellesmere, where we would practise steep turns. The lingering low cloud ruled out other training manoeuvres.

It was foggy below the main base, and over the lake the grey water blended with the misty horizon, making visual flight marginal. That should have alerted me to exercise special care, but it didn't. My pupil put the aircraft into a steep turn just below the main cloud base at 2000 feet, increased the bank to about 75 degrees and pulled about three G in a tight turn.

'Okay, now roll out to level flight,' I said. High-G situations are common in the training world, and I was still quite relaxed. Startlingly, though, the pupil kicked in a boot full of rudder and pulled back hard on the control column. The force caused a high-speed stall. Classically, yaw at the point of stall produces a spin. The coarse handling flicked us into a spin — an inverted spin, very flat. All this was below 2000 feet. Standard orders were to bail out of a Harvard if still in a spin below 3000 feet, but there was no time. There was not enough altitude to use our parachutes.

I still don't know exactly what P did. Inexperience was a factor but I think the low visibility conditions obscuring the horizon disoriented him. Also, he was new to instrument flying. The fault was mine; I asked too much of him in the misty conditions, which were worse over Lake Ellesmere, where the featureless surface provides no visual clues. However we'd got there, we were in a violent inverted spin. And we were low! I had to fix this mighty quick.

Classic spin recovery is full opposite rudder, control (the 'stick') slowly and centrally forward, when the spin stops, centralise, recover the nose to the horizon and apply full power to climb away. Normal spins feature a steep nose-down attitude with rolling and yawing. Power isn't used initially, as it would accelerate the loss of height when the nose is steeply down. In an inverted spin, there are important differences in recovery technique, and if altitude is critical, these must be applied correctly without delay. A flat spin is unusual: it takes quite a bit of unusual handling – or mishandling – to get into one. But there we were in an inverted flat spin, too low by far to bail out.

Adrenaline spiked. Thank God I'd been thoroughly trained in spinning recovery techniques and was able to distinguish that we were inverted, not right side up. I knew to immediately check the turn indicator to apply the rudder opposite to the direction of turn – the mistake of applying rudder the wrong way would have cost us our lives. I instantly appreciated that, contrary to usual practice, immediate application of power was needed to drag us out of the stall. The big engine roared as I slammed the throttle fully forward. I was right; the thrust pulled us out of our stalled condition without using up our precious remaining height. I could also see it was necessary to delicately apply full aileron at once – despite the risk of doing this in a near stalled condition – if we were to have any chance of rolling upright and pulling out of our developing dive before ground contact. It all worked, but we were scarily close to ground impact before we recovered.

It was a close-run thing. Two very shaken pilots headed home.

It's Your Best Pupil Who'll Kill You

This incident illustrates a lesson for pilots. If you train yourself properly (and regularly practise emergency drills) even when an emergency bursts on you without warning, your training will take over and you will rapidly perform the correct actions, often scarcely aware of what your hands are doing flashing around the cockpit. But if you haven't properly trained, very likely you will make a mistake right when you can't afford to.

And there is another lesson – for instructors. This incident caught me napping; I was relaxed because I was with my best pupil. I didn't expect him to make the mistake of gross mishandling and I was not ready for it. So, instructors, be aware of the old saying – it's your best pupil who will kill you. Watch everybody, all the time.

At debrief, I carefully went over what had happened so that the pupil could learn the valuable lessons available from this experience. First, I admitted the fault was mine in that I'd placed him in conditions (poor visibility, no clear horizon) beyond his ability and experience to carry out steep turns. He'd then become confused and instead of calmly taking recovery action from the turn, he'd used rough application of controls, something you simply cannot do in an aeroplane. I said he could learn from my deep knowledge of aerodynamics, particularly of an inverted spin, which allowed me to instantly assess the situation and apply appropriate recovery action, even though it was non standard. He thanked me for this wisdom and said it had taught him that every pilot must have a thorough understanding of aerodynamics.

Occasionally it was necessary to terminate a pilot's training, and when later I became the Flight Commander at the pilot training school at Wigram, often I was the arbiter when these tough decisions had to be made. This was always shattering for the individuals who failed, but many trainees went on to civil flying careers. The military course is conducted to a high-pressure syllabus, and some people couldn't keep up the pace. Some merely required more time to absorb the lessons, as shown by the individuals who built on the training we'd given them to complete a civil course successfully.

Several times, I took parties of students to my skiing club at Mt Cheesman in the Southern Alps. There, I kept an old Model-A Ford converted to a canopy-covered truck. Filled with cadets to hold it firmly on the ground, this old champion, with its narrow tyres, would snort its way to the very top of the high access road, leaving in its wake all the shiny Land Rovers stuck in the snow. We trained several pilots for the Malaysian and Singapore governments. It was amusing to see them experiencing snow for the first time. 'Look, white rain, white rain,' they called out.

We sent one Malaysian student home with his wings. A year later, I was embarrassed to hear he'd killed himself in an air accident. Such doleful news about a past pupil is always distressing, and I felt badly until I learned the circumstances. Supplying army units in the field, he'd taken off on the fatal flight, climbed into cloud to cross a mountain range and, after a timed run, descended out of the cloud into the next valley. He did this twice but on the third attempt collided with a mountain peak. I no longer felt any responsibility.

11

TROUBLE IN THE MOUNTAINS

In February 1962, an old, twin-engine Dragonfly aircraft, registration ZK-AFB, carrying international tourists, disappeared on a flight from Christchurch to Milford Sound in Fiordland. A major search by mainly Harvard and Devon aircraft based at RNZAF Wigram was conducted over about seven days, believed to be the largest air search ever carried out in New Zealand. The high, wild alpine terrain between Christchurch and Milford presented many difficulties, especially in the cloudy conditions.

There were several incidents in this extensive search, and it was pure luck no further accidents occurred. Cloud covered the higher parts of the mountains and made search conditions demanding; the terrain was precipitous and rescuers were doing sweeps high and low of wild valleys. Frequently, pilots had to pass from one valley to another beneath low ceilings; in some cases only 50 feet of clearance lay between the cloud base and the rocky terrain. The flying required good judgment and steely nerves but even more so for our rather underpowered Devons. It would be difficult to maintain safety in the event of an engine failure.

One Devon captain, whose name was Dyer, made the mistake of penetrating too far into a narrowing steep-sided valley and found he no longer had enough room to turn back. Thank heavens the visibility was okay. The pilot and his navigator standing beside him in the cockpit observed that the valley floor was rising sharply and the ability of the aircraft to climb fast enough to clear the summit was doubtful. With the throttles firewalled (as far forward as possible) and the engines roaring, the pilot traded airspeed for altitude. He was near stalling speed when, to the crew's relief, the summit passed just beneath them.

Quick as a flash, the navigator said, 'We'll call that Dyer's pass, shall we?' Dyer's Pass is at the summit of a prominent highway over the Port Hills, to the east of Christchurch.

At first, my part in this search was flying a Devon based in Hokitika for three days, searching the mountains, valleys and glaciers between Hokitika and Milford Sound. It was certainly adventurous flying. I prided myself that I never went where I couldn't get out if there was an engine failure. This meant having constantly to be aware of the safest course to turn onto in the event of an emergency. This is a good habit in the mountains. The mountains, steep valleys and narrow coastal plateau on the scarcely populated West Coast of the South Island were difficult searching territory, but knowing that a moment's inattention might result in missing a sighting of desperate survivors was a sufficient spur to keep trying day after day.

I was then assigned to a group of eight pilots with four Harvard aircraft operating from Queenstown. Our task was to search between the Queenstown and Wanaka areas and the West Coast. The area was divided into blocks, each to be thoroughly searched by one Harvard with two pilots. The area included the forbidding Mount Aspiring and its approaches.

The technique employed was to fly around the mountain in altitude bands and then fly down all major waterways. Frequent cloudy areas made it necessary to pass under cloud over high alpine passes, often with a mere 50 to 100 feet of airspace above the rocky or snowbound terrain. This made for difficult and sometimes dangerous searching.

Additionally, one of the Harvard aircraft had a history of rough engine running and excess fuel consumption. Several times, in routine flying at Wigram, I'd written up a requirement to check this engine in its Form 700 (the technical record of each aircraft). In each case, the engine was signed out as serviceable by an engine sergeant. At Queenstown, a fellow pilot and I, jointly commanding the detachment, decided this aircraft should be treated with caution. We assigned it to ourselves and reduced the planned normal endurance time from three to two hours.

Now, fuel drill on the Harvard called for the right fuel tank to be used until the gauge registered 10 gallons (45 litres), when supply was switched to the left tank. Unknown to us, the right tank gauge had developed a fault – it stopped reducing the indication of fuel remaining at 12 gallons (54.5 litres). Even though more fuel was burnt, the gauge continued to indicate 12 gallons. Between that flaw and the high fuel consumption, it was a recipe for disaster.

On a sortie searching high up on the alpine slopes, above Queenstown, we had to fly through a pass with less than 100 feet clearance below cloud, to pass from one valley to another. The terrain was rough, mostly huge boulders. I was flying, and as we approached this tricky situation on our search plan, I checked the right fuel gauge. It indicated that there were 12 gallons remaining – no problem. I was alert to the need to change tanks in the next while. The col, or pass, was quite a flat surface and long enough for us to have to fly for about two minutes through the gap between the cloud base and the boulders strewn about. This was pretty daring stuff and we were certainly paying strict attention to what we were doing.

In the middle of the gap, without warning, the engine cut. With large rock outcrops just below us, we had to move fast – there was no chance of a successful forced landing among those boulders. It was a case of get that engine going again at once or die. In the restricted airspace, there was no alternative but to steadily bleed off the airspeed to gain a little time, although we only had a few seconds before reaching stalling speed.

Suspecting a fuel problem in the right tank, I turned the selector cock to the left tank as my associate furiously worked the 'wobble pump' (a hand-operated fuel pump) to build up pressure in the fuel lines with fuel now coming from the left tank. I closed the throttle while trading off airspeed and managed to squeeze in a brief Mayday call to our base. Even at our low airspeed, the slipstream was sufficient to keep the engine turning over. Then it coughed, coughed again and then caught with a roar as fuel from the new source reached the carburettor. Powered again, after what seemed interminable seconds, we flew out into the new valley. Close-run thing that.

We realised that we now had a critical fuel situation and turned for the Queenstown airport at once. We were able to throttle back to save fuel as we were descending the steep mountain slopes, virtually gliding down. We landed at Queenstown, both of us mightily relieved. We had the fuel tanks checked with a dipstick: right tank, empty; left tank, half a gallon only. Our instinct to conserve our remaining fuel had just saved the day.

A technical party was flown in and changed the engine, and that aircraft was flown back to Wigram while the search for the Dragonfly continued.

Eventually, the search was abandoned. No trace was found of the aircraft. It may have been flown out to sea to the west of the rugged coastline and crashed into the ocean. Or it may have come to grief in the mountains or valleys and disappeared beneath the canopy of the thick bush, or forests, typical of the region. The brutal truth was that the performance of this ancient aircraft following an engine failure was limited, so it wasn't well suited for passenger flights over alpine mountains.

Remarkably, hopes of finding some trace of the missing Dragonfly persist and enthusiasts continue to search. In 2017, some clothing appropriate to the period – ladies' boots – was found in a remote location, and this has sparked renewed hope that the mystery of the disappearance may one day be solved. Those mountains are mostly heavily vegetated, and it is likely any wreckage is concealed beneath the bush canopy in some lonely spot – if, in fact, the aircraft didn't crash into the seas off the West Coast. Perhaps some day it will be discovered by a deerstalker or adventurous tramper.

Back at Wigram, I took the faulty aircraft's F700 (maintenance record) to the office of the engine fitter sergeant. Naturally he'd heard of the incident and visibly paled when I appeared. I pointed out the entries where on several occasions I'd reported the engine for rough running, and the corresponding entries where he'd signed out the aircraft as serviceable. He was, I think, convinced I was going to have him court martialled.

'Let that be a lesson to you,' I said, and walked out.

Christchurch was a marvellous place to live, with outstanding skiing and shooting opportunities, and I relished my time as a flight instructor there. Instructing can be very satisfying, and it is true of flying, as of everything else, the best way to learn a subject is to teach it. All of my past pupils have remained lifelong friends, including some who were airline captains when I served as their co-pilot.

I spent my last months at Wigram on immediate call to go to Vietnam as a 'Bird Dog' pilot, an airborne forward air controller. When for some reason the requirement was suspended, I was posted instead to fly the Air Force's venerable old flying boat, the Short Sunderland.

I guess I was lucky to miss the sad warfare in Vietnam, enjoying instead many interesting experiences in New Zealand and the Pacific in the maritime role.

12

THE SUNDERLAND

The Northern Ireland firm Short Brothers and Harland designed and built the four-engine flying boat, the Sunderland, in the early 1930s.

The Sunderland featured some innovative design, being the first aircraft to incorporate semi-monocoque construction (the outer skin forming part of the load-bearing structure of the airframe). Sections, such as four T-shaped wing bars of constant cross-sectional area running from wingtip to wingtip, reflected a lack of knowledge of metallurgical science in those days. Heavy metal components provided strength through bulk. On conversion courses, some time had to be devoted to teaching newly arrived pilots obscure terms of nautical components so they could radio back for the necessary items for repairs if damage occurred in remote locations. A 'garboard strake' is an example. The aeroplane was sturdily built, except for the planing bottom, which was light enough to be susceptible to damage from the aircraft butting through heavy seas at speed.

The large amount of flare built into the planing bottom was perhaps the worst feature of the design. If the flying boat was flown into the face of a large swell with a high nose attitude, the planing bottom was too wide to slice through the water cleanly and would throw the craft up into the air in a sufficiently high nose attitude to cause a stall. If one wing dropped first before the other and caught the water, then the aircraft would cartwheel, with fatal results. Essentially, if forced to accept a landing into the face of a large swell, one had to grit one's teeth, hold a low-nose attitude and deal with a series of crashes through the swells accompanied by clouds of spray until the speed fell off.

I did my conversion course at the lovely old base Hobsonville, on the Waitemata Harbour, Auckland, adjacent to the landplane base at Whenuapai. The big, heavy machine took some getting used to and I now experienced flying regularly with the same crew members. A Sunderland crew normally included two pilots, two navigators, two flight engineers, a radio operator, two or more radar operators and a cameraman/weapons specialist. The crew members obviously had a great interest in the man piloting this wayward beast, in the air and also on the water. Mooring up to buoys in bad weather could be tricky, and careless operation by the pilot could result in injuries to the crew members struggling with heavy mooring lines. I started lifelong friendships in this environment. Crew members often had to clamber out of the astro hatch onto the top of the wing to service engines or assist in manoeuvring in restricted waters. The top surface was often wet with spray and slippery, so moving about had to be done with care. Sometimes it was necessary to turn the engines over by hand. The engineer did this from a special little platform which could be lowered beside the engine. The seawater often flung through the propellers abraded their leading edges, which could become razor sharp. Refuelling was carried out from a special barge; the heavy fuel lines were hauled up with ropes. This barge had a powerful engine, and if lightly loaded after refuelling an aircraft, was quite fast.

On one glorious occasion, the barge happened to be overtaking the admiral's launch from the navy yard at Devonport, a large, very shiny launch filled with the admiral's guests. Each helmsman inched throttles forward bit by bit until both craft were racing at full speed. Magnificently, our barge steadily drew ahead and left the admiral and company in its wake. We never let the Navy forget their defeat.

We shared the waters of the Waitemata Harbour with Air New Zealand's Solent flying boats and a twin-engined charter craft flown by the redoubtable Captain Fred Ladd. Fred was famous for his pre-takeoff cry, 'A shower of spray and we're away.'

My conversion course completed, and newly married to my lovely June, I was soon posted to the relaxed atmosphere of tropical Fiji. Social life was lively. We made lifelong friends. In the next two years I had many interesting experiences living in Fiji and in flying the Sunderland to a huge variety of tiny communities all over the southern Pacific. Very often our task was to bring back to Fiji persons who had suffered accidents or become ill. Frequently, the patients would be suffering from tetanus, a painful malady often caught from horses, which were plentiful throughout the islands. Several unfortunates died from this awful thing while on my aircraft – it isn't a nice way to go.

I learned a lot about the peoples of the Pacific by visiting them in their homes in Fiji, Samoa, the Tokelaus, the Cook Islands, the French territories of Tahiti and New Hebrides and the (then) Gilbert and Ellice Islands. It was interesting to observe the customs of these mainly Polynesian peoples. Invariably, we were treated to a warm welcome in these communities scattered about the vast Pacific Ocean. They knew well we were their lifeline in times of trouble and illness.

The people of Fiji are an example to all the world in containing what could quickly become a violent racial confrontation between the two predominant races, Fijians and

Indians. The first Indians were brought to Fiji as labour for the sugar plantations; they were from southern India and were mild-mannered people. Later arrivals were from Gujarati stock – people who carry the genes of the warlike Germanic Huns (who invaded north-western India) and are demanding and clever. Fijians may beat up on Fijians but rarely on Indians. Indians shoot each other but never, never a Fijian, knowing that that would precipitate a bloodbath. So, the two races exist, not in perfect harmony but peacefully, and therein lies their example.

One mysterious activity the two peoples share is fire-walking. The amazing ability to walk through beds of red hot coals of fire has never been explained by medical science. This is no dash from one end of the firepit to the other; it is a slow ceremonial pacing, with the feet constantly in touch with red hot coals. Yet no harm befalls the firewalkers.

The Fijians seem to have fun during the activity. The Indians have a more religious attitude; for example, a man may walk through the fires in gratitude to a deity for the recovery of a child from an illness. The Indians commonly have metal skewers through their noses and pectoral muscles bouncing about, yet there is no blood and the skin is whole, without any sign of perforation or bleeding when the skewers are withdrawn. No explanation for these amazing phenomena has ever been given.

I went to one Indian ceremony where it was necessary to walk through sticky red mud on the access path. I soon gave up on my sandals and went barefoot, carrying the mud-encrusted footwear in my hand. Rather tired of the smelly things, when I spotted a 40-gallon drum full of clean water, I went over to it and started washing my sandals clean. Immediately, I realised I was in trouble: there was a sharp outcry and Indians started running towards me gesticulating and shouting. Fortune smiled on me in the form of a sturdy Fijian policeman who dashed over and was able to shepherd me away from the mob's hostility. It turned out that the drum was full of cows' urine, holy water to the largely Hindu crowd, who venerate the cow as sacred. Riots have been precipitated by actions such as mine, innocent though they may have been. Lucky me to have got away with that one. That taught me to be more attuned to the customs of local people for the rest of my time in the Pacific.

The RNZAF had a remarkably safe run during its years of flying the Sunderland, considering the wide range of remote areas in which it operated and the difficult nature of some tasks. Only one airframe was lost in the Chatham Islands, which lie to the east of New Zealand and to which we made regular calls. Our flights usually originated from Wellington.

The alighting area at the Chathams is a large lagoon. During a storm, a wall of this lagoon was breached and the water level lowered by several feet. No one thought to tell 5 Squadron, and on the next aircraft landing, the planing bottom was opened up by a rock in the now shallow water. The aircraft began to sink but it was beached without injury to anyone. The Air Force removed valuable components and turned the derelict airframe over to the islanders, who, not being short of time, laboriously drilled out rivets, recovered the sheet metal of the wings and body and built a woolshed.

There has always been great crew spirit in 5 Squadron, people are friendly and help one another. In the Sunderland crew spirit was particularly strong. Pilots who could handle the rough water conditions often experienced during takeoff and landings were practically worshipped by crews. They could do no wrong. It wasn't hard to see why. If the approaches to mooring buoys were mishandled, for example, crew members could easily be injured. That also explains why, as a newly arrived pilot with 5 Squadron, I knew my performance was being closely observed.

During the route-experience part of my conversion training, I flew the aircraft into Funafuti Lagoon. It is the largest of the Ellice Islands (now Tuvalu), which are situated some hours north of Fiji. Funafuti is an enormous lagoon, one of only two which proved capable of holding the entire American Pacific fleet in World War II (the other is Florida Island in the Solomons).

Arriving at Funafuti, I was under the supervision of an instructor. Unaccustomed to the ways of the sea, I made a very rough landing that thoroughly scared the crew – and me too! Essentially, I was sucked in by a feature of wave (swell) behaviour which isn't obvious at first sight. When an established swell pattern (commonly from the south-east in the Pacific, being formed by the steadily blowing south-easterly trade winds) passes through a large gap in a reef, it doesn't die away. It spreads out in a hemispherical pattern. At the big lagoon at Funafuti, there are several sizeable gaps in the reef. The prevailing south-easterly swell pounds on the outside of the reef. But inside the lagoon, the orientation changes, and the swell may in some areas be coming from the south-west, at right angles to the swell outside the reef. This is exactly what fooled me. The alighting direction chosen, into wind, was to the south-west. The swell, not easily distinguishable from the air, was head on to an aircraft landing in that direction. And it was large, even though its presence wasn't obvious to someone flying overhead.

On arrival at the lagoon, I noted the wind direction and, in the absence of any clues to the contrary, assumed the swell in the alighting area to be from the same direction as that outside the reef, from south-east. Following standard practice, I made a low pass to check for floating debris or other hazards and then commenced a circuit to land. I can still picture that circuit distinctly. I was getting used to the Sunderland and anxious to fly accurately in front of the instructor and the critical crew. My performance was immaculate – height, airspeed, rate of turn and descent on final approach spot on, with the nose high just before touchdown, correctly set up for a no-swell landing. I was full of pride and satisfaction just before touching down on the water, telling myself, 'Tom, you've flown beautifully and set this up exactly right for this landing.'

Smash!

Abruptly, the nose was way up in the air; I could see only blue sky. We'd struck the face of a large swell and been bodily flung into the air. Out of the corner of my eye I could see the crew members on the flight deck diving for their bone domes (safety helmets) – which of course they should have been wearing but weren't. The instructor and I pushed fully forward on the heavy control column and brought all four throttles up to the firewall for maximum power. We were lucky; we forced the nose below the horizon and the wings didn't stall so we avoided the danger of catching a wingtip and cartwheeling across the lagoon. The instructor pilot should now have relaxed the forward position of the control column and taken off power to round out for a second touch-down. But he didn't, and with a high rate of descent we came down until we smacked straight into the face of the next swell for a repeat performance of being flung into the air. This time we corrected with more skill, and the big white bird settled onto the water after a few more teeth-grinding bashes by the oncoming swells.

That night, I apologised to every crew member. They were all pretty nice about it. Damage to the aircraft was limited to a few rivets in the hull, soon replaced.

Thereafter, throughout my flying career, whenever I felt smug and on top of things, I would remind myself of that landing at Funafuti and tell myself to always be ready for the unexpected.

Sometime later, a crew member said to me over a relaxed beer that everyone liked flying with me after that. When I looked astonished, he said they figured I'd learned my lesson. He was right.

13

AROUND THE PACIFIC

The Pacific is a vast area. We of 5 Squadron RNZAF constantly travelled hither and yon, evacuating sick people, finding persons lost at sea, conveying government VIPs to remote territories, surveying damages after hurricanes and carrying out military tasks. We periodically surveyed many islands, alighting areas and abandoned military installations.

Our rather creaky old flying boats were a far cry from the smooth, fast high flight of 75 Squadron, but they were immense fun to fly and sail. Crews very much depended upon one another to stay safe and great friendliness developed. The base at Lauthala Bay, adjacent to Suva, was a happy place, and June and I soon had many friends in the expatriate community. Our role as guardians over the wide area for which we were responsible brought us much respect. I formed many friendships and had most interesting experiences in this unconventional life.

27,610 feet

The Sunderland Flying Boats of 5 Squadron RNZAF, like most anti-submarine aircraft, had more and more equipment added as new anti-submarine devices were invented. They became overloaded for certain conditions, such as high temperatures, glassy seas and no wind, not having enough power to take off. At slow speed, when making way through the water or in the early stages of a takeoff run, the trim of the aircraft is such that the nose is higher than in flight and the tail is down. Thus, the four propellers are inclined backwards. As a result, the down-going blades, going forward into the slipstream, are at a higher speed relative to the air than the upgoing blades. This produces an asymmetric torque, or turning force; the force generated by four engines is large and causes the aircraft to turn to the left away from the required takeoff path. This tendency to turn has to be countered. Initially, the aircraft is kept on a straight path by coarse use of the rudder and ailerons, but when this control is insufficient, it is necessary to reduce the power on number four engine. In hot and windless conditions, when the sea surface tends to be glassy, and it is difficult to break the suction on the planing bottom, it may be necessary to take off so much power to stay straight that the aircraft cannot accelerate to takeoff speed and simply wallows along at perhaps 30 to 60 knots (takeoff requires 90 to 110 knots, depending on weight).

Flying the Sunderland requires strength to handle the heavy controls. We had a saying that the Sunderland pilot had to have arms like coconut trees and fingers like bananas. If the wind changed, say from left to right, the pilot while holding the large control wheel back with considerable force had to rotate it a long way from left to right, at the same time reversing from full right to full left rudder with the feet and concurrently stretching right across the console to advance the number four throttle to full power then retard the number one throttle. If the wind changed again, all these actions had to be reversed! Flying the Sunderland is a physically taxing activity.

On one duty, I was out on the water at Lauthala Bay, Fiji, at the crack of dawn. The Queen was flying from California to Sydney in one of the new Boeing 707s. The Royal route transited the extensive area of the Pacific for which New Zealand had Search and Rescue (SAR) responsibility. I had come up from New Zealand to fly the royal SAR escort flight. The plan was to take off so that the 707 would pass near overhead us at the mid-point in our area of responsibility. We carried specialist rescue gear. Thus, we were prepared to render the best possible assistance if the Royal aircraft had an emergency.

Lauthala Bay is a vast expanse of water. The limit of our alighting area to the east was the Rewa River and to the west a narrow shipping channel that ran for about half a mile down to Suva Harbour

It wasn't a good morning for me. The previous evening, I'd received word of my mother's death in a motor accident. But I had to put my emotions to the side as there were only two crews in Fiji that day. The base was being run down and was lightly staffed. One crew had to remain available for any SAR emergencies which might arise. It would be unthinkable to fail to provide Her Majesty with support, so I was forced to command the royal escort flight.

Naturally, for this task, maximum fuel was loaded. Conditions weren't good for the heavy takeoff. Temperature was truly tropical at 37 degrees Celsius; there was no wind; and not a ripple disturbed the glassy surface of the bay. Off we went for an attempted takeoff but as expected, a turn to the left developed, necessitating reduction of power on number four engine. The best speed we could achieve after wallowing across half the bay was 45 knots, so that attempt was abandoned. It took 30 minutes for the engines to cool down enough for another attempt, so I took the opportunity to position to the extreme edge of the bay, which was in fact up the Rewa River about a quarter of a mile. This gave the maximum distance available for the second attempt at takeoff, sure to be a protracted affair.

I briefed the crew that I was going to try a technique I'd discussed with experienced flying boat captains. The technique was to put the aircraft into a sharp right-hand turn at the start of the run, so that the turning force to the left would take some time to overcome the right turn. Thus, the retardation of power on number four engine would be delayed, and full power would be available for longer, giving a good chance of being able to rock the control column back and forth sufficiently to break the suction on the planing bottom and get the craft to rise up 'on the step'. Once on the step, takeoff was assured, provided there was about a mile of clear water ahead.

The crew looked slightly doubtful but had sufficient confidence in me to refrain from comment.

Modern pilots will note that 'seaman's eye' judgment was necessary to take off in this environment, unlike the fine calculations used in land-based jets. In this case, I realised that I might end up close to the shipping channel to Suva Harbour. This channel twists and turns and is quite narrow. As a precaution, I had my navigator, a yachtie experienced in this area, stand beside me in the cockpit in case I needed guidance in the channel.

With cylinder-head temperatures below limits at last, we were ready for another go.

I advanced the four throttles, the mighty Pratt and Whitney engines bellowed, and we surged forward. I applied coarse right rudder to enter a right turn and held it until we were turning as tightly as I dared. Then, with the torque effect of full power progressively slackening off the turn, I rocked the control column backwards and forwards. I'd learned to speed up the rocking motion as speed increased, so that with each pitch cycle the nose came down a bit nearer to the takeoff position. It all worked! We got up on the step, very tentatively at first, but getting steadier, firmly established on the step and accelerating. But with all the cavorting about, we'd used up a lot of the bay. I took a good hard seaman's eye stare and estimated I had about a mile to go before the entrance to the shipping channel. Once firmly on the step, the Sunderland could be depended upon to get airborne in a further run of a mile. So – decision – go for it! I was now committed.

But things began to go pear-shaped. I was getting some increase in airspeed but not enough. About 10 knots below the minimum needed for lift-off, speed stabilised. I was thunderstruck. With engines roaring and the flight engineer shouting about his cylinder head temperatures, this aircraft wasn't responding as expected. We gobbled up that precious mile, but still couldn't achieve our planned takeoff speed. The edge of the bay and the entrance to the shipping channel were approaching at alarming speed.

The personnel of the station were just coming to work, and life stopped as all watched in astonishment at what was happening on the bay, the great white flying boat with spray flying closing fast on the shipping channel. Only once before in the long history of Lauthala Bay had a penetration of the shipping channel happened. (The captain of that flight was a legendary flying boat pilot.)

My guide needed no urging; he recognised we were indeed going to be in the channel. If we misjudged and strayed across the coral reef, we would tear the bottom out of our craft and undoubtedly kill everybody aboard. The eyes of the rest of the crew were, by this stage, out on stalks. Down the channel we pounded, and thank goodness no shipping was coming the other way. (Flying boats on the water, being fast, have to give way to surface vessels but I was in no position to manoeuvre around any ship.) Calmly, the navigator steered me through the labyrinth. 'See the red pole? Keep it to port – good, now the green pole coming up, go to the port side of that', and so on.

Why couldn't I get those extra 10 knots? I had to do something. I decided that if I came to the end of the channel, I would execute a steep right turn into Suva Harbour. This would probably mean I'd knock off the starboard float and so would have to get crew members up on the top of the wing through the astro hatch to run out onto the port wing to prevent the old boat rolling over – we could sit on the port float without difficulty. But, first, I had to try the only thing I hadn't attempted – to push forward on the control column and lower the nose. This technique was normally a strict no-no. I duly pushed. Hoorah, the speed started to creep up. As we passed the end of the shipping channel, I was able to pull that heavy old machine out of the water at last, and we were on our way to our date with Her Majesty.

The poor aircraft performance was probably due to barnacles on the hull. The aircraft were customarily left afloat for long periods in the water.

Later in the flight, after completing our task of supporting the 707, we were about to set course, as planned, for New Zealand. But the engineer noticed a broken engine air intake flapping. Our response was to shut down that engine for fear metal would be ingested and wreck the engine. The proper course of action was to head for the nearest suitable alighting area where the aircraft could be serviced. So, we returned to Fiji.

The small aviation community of Fiji heard about all this and my mother's funeral. Every airline operating through Fiji rang and offered me a ride to Auckland on the jump seat of their cockpit. What heart-warming courtesy.

An RNZAF De Havilland DH82 Tiger Moth. This robust and reliable machine was the RNZAF *ab initio* trainer from 1939 to 1956. I made my first flight and first solo on this aircraft. *(P A Images)*

The Blue Lake at Saint Bathans, near my childhood home. Gold-bearing material was evacuated with high pressure water jets. Abandoned, the site flooded to form the Blue Lake, nowadays an aquatic playground. *(Tom Enright)*

The Royal Air Force College Cranwell, Lincolnshire, England. *(RNZAF Official)*

The First Sea Lord, The Earl Mountbatten of Burma, and party arrive at Cranwell for the graduation of 70 Entry. *(Barratt's Photo Press)*

Graduation Day RAF Halton 1954. *(author collection)*

A Harvard formation goes over the top of a loop. The Harvard T6 served the RNZAF as its main trainer from 1941 until the mid 1970s. *(RNZAF Official)*

A neat line of Harvards awaiting their crews at RNZAF training base at Wigram, Christchurch. *(RNZAF Official)*

The hard working De Havilland Devon, used to train RNZAF pilots, navigators and radio operators. *(CC 3.0 RuthAS)*

Eleven Vampires of 14 Squadron RNZAF in a formation flight. *(RNZAF Official)*

The last flight of NZ 5771 after my wild ride through several fences and into a ditch. *(RNZAF Official)*

Presentation of 75 Squadron Colour by the Queen Mother at Palmerston North. I was selected for the honour of receiving the Colours. *(RNZAF Official)*

Queenstown Airport. Surrounded by alpine terrain, pilots take special care here. *(Otago Daily Times)*

Wellington Airport, landing from the south. *(Rob Suisted/Natures Pic Images)*

A Sunderland accidentally touches the runway during a flypast at the opening of Wellington airport display, 25th October 1959. Smoke from the planing bottom can be seen behind the aircraft. (Frame from National Film Unit's Pictorial Parade [No 94, 1959] sourced from Archives New Zealand. Provided by Gabor Toth at Wellington City Libraries)

A Vulcan bomber struck the ground in the undershoot area on an attempted landing at the opening display of Wellington airport, collapsing the port gear. This photo, taken seconds after the accident, shows how close the aircraft came to a calamitous port wingtip contact with the ground. A close-run thing for the crew and spectators! *(RNZAF Official)*

The crippled giant flies away after its landing accident at Wellington to a crash landing at Ohakea. Note the swinging port undercarriage. Vampires can be discerned positioning at the takeoff point – I occupy the second from the right. *(New Zealand Herald Glass Plate Collection, Auckland Libraries 1370-3-14-3)*

De Havilland Dragonfly ZK-AFB at Milford Sound. In 1962 this aircraft, carrying overseas visitors, went missing on a flight Christchurch to Milford Sound. An extensive air search was made but nothing was ever found. *(Photo by Mike Kerr, provided by Richard Waugh)*

Mount Aspiring, wild, dangerous and a menacing presence throughout our difficult search for the missing Dragonfly. *(Age Fotostock/Alamy)*

Crewmen carry out pre flight inspections of the Sunderland flying boat, at anchor with a tender alongside. *(RNZAF Official)*

Tropical takeoff by a RNZAF Sunderland. *(RNZAF Official)*

A missile launch test at Kwajalein Atoll – America's first defence against nuclear attack. 5 Squadron RNZAF's involvement with this Pacific base is described in chapter 16. *(DOD Photo/Alamy)*

Survivors of the *Tuaikaepau* on the wreck which was their sanctuary. Minerva Reef, 1962. *(RNZAF Official)*

Atafu Atoll among the Tokelaus Islands. Barely submerged coral in the lagoon makes for a demanding alighting area. *(World history Archives/Alamy)*

A southern royal albatross. A noble creature, but not one you want to see through an aircraft windscreen. *(Galaxiid/Alamy)*

The magnificent SS *Canberra*. A Sunderland of 5 Squadron made an emergency drop of eight oxygen cylinders to her in a remote stretch of the Pacific Ocean thus ensuring the survival of a sick child on board. *(Trinity Mirror/Mirrorpix/Alamy)*

The *Kaitawa*, a collier, was lost in a 1966 hurricane off Northland. Twenty-seven souls perished despite the best efforts of my crew and myself to locate the stricken vessel. *(I. J. Farquhar Collection)*

Kiwi aviation legend Sir Tim Wallis with his Mk 16 Spitfire. *(Photo by John Coom, from Wairarapa Archive)*

Goodbye to the free life. Sir Tim Wallis pioneered the use of helicopters to capture wild deer. *(Alpine Helicopters, Wanaka)*

An RNZAF Orion aircraft overflies nuclear-powered cruiser USS *Truxton* during an anti-submarine exercise near Auckland. *(RNZAF Official)*

The Hajj terminal at Jeddah, Saudi Arabia, awaits the Guests of Allah. *(AGE Photostock)*

An Air New Zealand DC10, about to land at Kai Tak airport, Hong Kong, passes the 'chequer board'. This prominent visual aid assisted pilots turning onto the runway from the displaced instrument approach. *(The Air New Zealand Flight Engineers' blogspot provided by Gary Sommerville.)*

A B747 on final approach to Kai Tak airport, Hong Kong. Massive skyscrapers are in close proximity. *(Frances Li/Alamy)*

Afterwards, the navigator and I got out the charts and measured the distance from power application to final lift-off of that takeoff. The run had lasted five and a half minutes, exceeding the engine limits. The distance, in a more or less straight line, not taking account of the cavorting around the bay, was 27,610 feet (8.4 kilometres).

They still talk about that takeoff at Lauthala Bay.

Tarawa

At the time of my visits there, Tarawa was the administrative centre of the Gilbert and Ellice Islands, a British outpost of empire that in 1916 had progressed from protectorate to colony status. Today the islands are incorporated into the independent nations of Kiribati and Tuvalu. Rather than conventional islands, they are coral atolls, the tops of undersea volcanoes. There are 33 atolls, the total of the former Gilbert, Phoenix and Line islands, but most are uninhabited.

About every three months, one of our Fiji-based Sunderlands visited Tarawa, alighting on the enormous lagoon. The British families of the administration liked to take the opportunity to gather to entertain us and practise life in the English way. The first time I visited, I found it onerous having to change into formal evening uniform for this social occasion: Tarawa is only about 20 minutes of latitude north of the Equator and extremely hot.

Refuelling the aircraft – which we did soon after our arrival – was also trying in the heat. About two and a half thousand gallons of Avgas had to be brought alongside in 40-gallon drums in whaleboats and pumped by hand-operated wobble pumps up over the wing and into the fuel tanks.

We had to become comfortable with low-tech problem-solving on that route. Because the hull of a Sunderland is vulnerable to damage, when we operated in isolated areas like Tarawa, our repair kit was stocked with plasticine, a special pencil to block the hole left by a ripped-out rivet and, for the king hit, quick-setting concrete. (Yes. Truly!)

Our accommodation was in an RNZAF-maintained open-sided building with beds. We brought linen with us from Fiji and paid the local women to make up the beds. After refuelling, I finally got to sit down on my bed – smelling of fuel and drenched in perspiration – I would see a stirring in the coconut trees surrounding our little camp. Next thing, there would emerge a tall and magnificently attired Gilbertese, a member of the administrator's staff, who had been watching out for me. Wearing a white *sulu* (a male skirt) and jacket with gleaming buttons, our visitor would present on an enormous Georgian silver tray and an invitation card. Couched in formal language, it requested the pleasure of our company at the Residency that evening. Hastily, I'd write a formal reply to be borne off on the silver tray.

This set the pattern for subsequent trips. When the card-bearer appeared from the coconut trees, however, I knew to be one step ahead. I would have pre-prepared a suitably worded acceptance note in my best penmanship. To my relief, after my first visit, the convention of formal evening uniform was dropped.

Conversation with the locals was always interesting. For example, they related how on one island at a certain time every year, the locals sang on a beach and masses of turtles would come out of the sea, to the benefit of the locals' larders. Marriage between closer than sixth cousins was forbidden, and the island chiefs who policed such edicts had the status of British magistrates. A sentence pronounced by them was a valid conviction in British law.

Two English doctors, a married couple, spent up to two months at a time voyaging around the outlying islands. Some islanders would welcome them as honoured guests but when the pair asked to see the sick, they were told there were none. On these islands the white man's medicines weren't welcomed as they tended to lead to overpopulation and pressure on limited food supplies.

A favoured drink was toddy, which is sap bled from coconut trees and fermented. There is one-day toddy, two-day toddy and three-day toddy; I never dared to sample the last.

In 1943, Tarawa was the site of the first battle between American and Japanese forces in the Pacific, that is, the first time there was serious opposition to an American amphibious landing. The Japanese were entrenched, mainly on the heavily populated island of Betio, in the south-west corner of the lagoon. Local lore has it that on the eve of battle, the on-scene American commander was advised his tide tables were six hours in error. He said he didn't have the authority to change the orders of battle. The following morning, hapless marines were trapped on the coral reef at low tide, too far out to storm ashore but well within the range of murderous clusters of machine guns manned by Japanese soldiers. These had unexpectedly survived the massive barrage of the accompanying American ships.

Three thousand marines died over the ensuing three days of the battle. It is recorded that only 17 of the 4700 Japanese soldiers survived. When the marines had finally subdued the garrison, they found they had been under fire from British guns which the Japanese had relocated from Singapore.

The Japanese left behind massive dumps of artillery shells, munitions and bombs. Unexploded weapons fired by the attacking American ships and warplanes added to the tremendous load of live munitions on Betio. Having defeated the enemy, the Americans then established further dumps of explosives. The theatre of war moved on, and an Australian garrison was installed. At the end of the war, the Australians went home leaving Betio as the dumping ground of an unbelievable quantity of munitions. They were lying about all over the place, especially on the beaches. Over time the big shells buried in dumps sweated a sticky green coating of explosive powders. These substances were highly sensitive, and a small knock was sufficient to set off an explosion. In the 1950s, when I visited regularly, the local population had developed a blasé attitude to these common hazards and if they found a bomb or shell would load it onto a tractor-drawn trailer, transfer it to a launch and jettison it beyond the reef. Occasionally, some unlucky individuals would pay the penalty when an explosion occurred.

One time, a 345 pound (156 kilogram) US depth bomb was uncovered, and for something of this magnitude, the locals had the good sense to ask the RNZAF for assistance. Following that request, the next time I flew to Tarawa, I had an armament officer aboard. He examined the bomb where it lay and felt there was a good chance something buried beneath the visible bomb would also go up. The local police chief, an Irishman, provided prisoner labour to dig a blast channel seawards for in situ demolition. The appropriate manual specified a danger area of 10,000 yards and the policeman asked me to reduce this to 5000 yards to avoid moving several thousand people living nearby. I would have none of this and thank goodness – when the bomb was detonated, there was a second explosion from beneath the bomb crater, probably another bomb. The two created an almighty blast, and there were broken windows and damage to houses up to 15,000 yards away.

While the channel was being dug, the policeman pointed to one of the prisoners and told me the fellow was serving his third sentence for incest. He had married his fifth cousin. He'd received a six-month sentence on marriage and a further 12 months had been added for each of his two children. To me, the prisoners on Betio seemed a happy lot. They were supplied with boots, shorts and two meals a day – munificence not necessarily available on their home islands. They wandered about fairly freely doing jobs such as emptying the rubbish bins. Most had mistresses, things being free and easy in the island community. So, dear reader, if you have to serve some time and get a chance to choose where you will be incarcerated, you could do a lot worse than selecting Betio.

Quite a few of the children of the colony suffered from night blindness, and so a dietitian from Fiji was aboard one of my flights. She promptly analysed the cause as lack of vitamin A in the children's diet. With the assistance of the locals, she found a widespread plant rich in vitamin A and had the mothers make soup from it. The children's sight improved immediately, to the immense joy of the people. They venerated the dietitian as a saint and gave a swinging departure celebration to thank her. Having brought the lady to them, I basked in some of the glory.

Returning to the subject of the World War II-era live munitions lying about all over Betio, the extent and diversity of the issue was staggering. For instance, among them were tens of thousands of rifle and machine gun rounds, mortar bombs and the like. It was difficult to set foot on some beaches without stepping on something live. Local lore has it that the Duke of Edinburgh visited and kicked a small bomb lying on the beach (fortunately it remained inert). This was proudly exhibited to visitors as 'The Duke of Edinburgh's Shell'.

I was incredulous that such a situation persisted so long after the war and questioned the Resident Commissioner about it. He showed me a letter accurately describing the dangers from unexploded bombs and smaller munitions which he'd sent to the War Office in London, requesting a clean-up. The reply suggested such a mess could not possibly have continued to exist and that the administration had obviously 'gone tropo'.

The villagers moved about and did their fishing in dugout canoes. A large woven sail supported by two poles provided motive power, capturing the trade winds that blew steadily over the vast expanse of Tarawa lagoon. To tack, one takes down the two poles and sail then remounts them in the opposite direction. These canoes are reputed to sail at three times the speed of the wind. I can vouch only for the fact that they moved fast: Sunderland crew members had enormous fun scooting about on these little craft.

* * *

Tarawa was the base for some prolonged search and rescue flights and medical evacuations in the North Pacific. One flight is worthy of special mention. A stricken lady had to be picked up from an isolated island several hours' flight away. The mission went almost to the limit of the Sunderland's endurance. No fuel was available at the remote island and sufficient had to be carried for the return journey to Tarawa. The young navigator was newly checked out in the maritime role and, knowing that his records would be rigorously checked on his return to Fiji, anxious to perform creditably. The technique used to find an isolated island without radio aids in the wastes of the Pacific was a 'sun line homing'. A calculation was made of the elevation of the sun (measured by a sextant) over the island at a particular time. The aircraft was then flown on a course maintaining that elevation. (Normally the course was set by DR – deduced reckoning – deliberately to one side of the island, so that on arrival at the sunline one knew which way to turn.) On reaching the calculated point, the navigator turned to fly the path where the sun elevation is constantly kept at the required value. The aircraft must pass over the island. Once established on the course, the navigator can sit back and wait for the lookouts to call their sighting of his target.

On the flight in question, having established on the sun line, the young man took the opportunity to check the accuracy of his calculations to that point. Ohhhh! He discovered he'd made a mistake – he'd miscalculated and had flown a whole hour too far. He was aghast; fuel reserves were now endangered and he would have to answer for his stupidity back in Fiji. He made a frenzied re-check but to no avail – the mistake was clear. Ashamed, he picked up his microphone to confess his error to the captain and crew. At that exact moment, the bow lookout sang out over the intercom, 'There it is. Right on the nose. Good old Nav.' This was pure luck – a huge piece of luck.

This navigator went on to become quite a legend for his expertise in squadron operations. One evening, years after that flight, he told me the story and remarked on the fact that great reputations are sometimes built on shaky foundations.

In the annals of 5 Squadron's meanderings over the expanse of the Pacific, Tarawa occupies a special place.

The Tokelaus

The three islands, coral atolls to be precise, of the Tokelaus lie to the north of Samoa. The islanders speak three languages: English, Samoan and their own dialect. Politically, the people are citizens of New Zealand by their own choice and so were regularly visited by the Sunderlands based in Fiji. Invariably the first item on the itinerary was an overnight at Aggie Grey's hotel in Samoa, always a convivial affair. Aggie was reputed to be the person on whom the character Bloody Mary of the musical *South Pacific* is based. She made a fortune during the war entertaining the American troops who'd been sent to Samoa for acclimatisation to the tropics before advancing to the battles against the forces of the Japanese Emperor. Young feisty American soldiers and uninhibited Samoan girls made for an explosive mixture.

After Samoa, we would visit first the island of Fakaofo, then Nukunono for an overnight, with the aircraft anchored in the lagoon. The next day's routine was to visit the third island, Atafu, on our way back to Samoa.

Facilities in the three islands were limited. Everything coming ashore from visiting shipping had to take on the hazardous crossing of the reef in whaleboats. The New Zealand Army had blasted channels in the reef to reduce this hazard but not very successfully.

The people in those places were religious, adherents either of the Catholic Church or the London Missionary Society (LMS). Sad to relate, the local representatives of the Catholics and LMS allowed the competition for converts to become excessive. Perhaps 80 per cent of the capital development of the islands comprised the shells of two side-by-side churches, each of which had no hope of being completed.

During our overnight stays, apart from the fact that all the girls on Nukunono would be locked up, we were welcomed enthusiastically. Our engineers and radio operators were always busy repairing electrical and radio equipment for the locals. Able to roam, I observed daily life with fascination. The children were superb swimmers. They'd dive to the bottom of the lagoons for squid, surfacing with the tentacles wound around their arms. They then killed the squid by biting them in the head. The people learned their genealogy by singing and miming; they were natural mimics. The New Zealand Army had donated World War I rifles. To welcome us – and occasionally New Zealand Government VIPs – squads would perform military drills they'd devised. They seemed unable to resist adding a few dance steps, which made a parody of the drills and it was hard to keep a straight face during their performances.

The welcome for one VIP, a gentleman fresh from United Nations duty in New York, was especially colourful. After we'd anchored, the VIP canoe came alongside. In the islands, your status is recognised by the height of your seating, so the canoe had an enormous leather armchair strapped on top of a very rickety framework of poles. As the VIP was a heavy man, anxious moments ensued as my crew members and the locals shepherded him from the aircraft door to his throne atop the creaking structure. All went well and soon he was being paddled ashore. The orator took exactly 27 minutes to give his speech of welcome in the local dialect (I timed him). He resumed his seat and another stood and repeated the speech in English without a single note in his hands for reference. He, too, finished in exactly 27 minutes. This seemed to me to be a remarkable feat of memory even though much of the oratory was probably flowery traditional phrases.

Once, a Sunderland alighting at Nukunono holed itself on a coral reef. The captain headed the sinking vessel straight for the nearest beach, coming to rest with the nose section in a grove of coconut trees. No one was hurt. At considerable expense and difficulty, repair parties were flown to the scene. They restored the hull to flyable condition.

Now there was a serviceable Sunderland sitting on an isolated beach pointed away from the sea with its nose in the jungle. Kiwi ingenuity was called for. With the islanders' help, it was supplied. First, blocking coconut trees were felled and removed. Then 100 sturdy island men placed their backs against the hull. Inspired by the chants of the island cheerleader and admiring women gathered to observe this enthralling scene, the men lifted mightily and moved the old girl around about five degrees. Repeatedly, the men heaved, and after a long time the Sunderland was facing its natural environment, the water. It remained only for the tiring workforce to inch it forward bit by bit. Finally, gloriously, it was floating and could be turned over to the waiting air crew for return to Fiji. This aircraft continued flying for many years. The story must surely be unique in the recovery of crashed aircraft.

Atafu

Military authorities maintain surveillance over a surprisingly large number of old airfields and alighting areas in the Pacific. The source of information about these is a classified (ie not available to the public) publication, the *Joint Intelligence Bureau Journal* (the JIB). Atafu was the third call on our Tokelaus circuit. It is a restricted lagoon requiring special care. Before my first visit I consulted the JIB. It said, 'Atafu should be used only in the most extreme of emergencies, and even then only by pilots with recent local knowledge'. Cor! This seemed to be a place to approach with a good deal of caution. Let me assure you it is!

The alighting area consists of two sections of a lagoon separated by a coral wall, the top of which is only about 6 feet below the surface of the water even at the best of tides. Since the Sunderland draught (the amount of clear water required beneath the lowest point of the hull) is approximately 5½ feet, it was necessary on both takeoff and landing to traverse the wall at a minimum speed through the water so that the planing bottom was raised well above its taxiing level. This was an unusual requirement and required careful piloting. After crossing the coral wall, when the landing run had been completed, it was necessary to locate a coral outcrop about ten fathoms (60 feet, or 18 metres) deep, as this was the only anchoring ground available. It all made for a stressful arrival.

Ashore, we were like Doctor Livingstone in Africa as we traded our old khaki uniforms for beautiful, fine woven baskets made from 'millionaire's salad' (the heart of the coconut tree, the removal of which caused the tree to die, hence only millionaires supposedly could afford the precious fibres). The children would await us with excitement and go wild over a lolly scramble.

Handling the anchor at Atafu needed special care. The anchor was an essential piece of equipment in this isolated roosting place. We carried a large and heavy one, about 10 feet long, and it came equipped with a crown line, a rope attached to the crown by which the anchor could sometimes be pulled free of the coral in which it was embedded. We carried two spares. At Atafu, where there was little space to restart the engines and recover the situation if the anchor pulled out, the wise captain ensured on arrival his anchor was well and truly driven into the coral way down below. As a consequence, when it came time to depart dragging the anchor free of the coral could be difficult and frustrating. If, after hauling manfully on the crown line the anchor remained stuck, the crew would stand clear. The pilot would call for all to vacate the bow compartment and progressively pour on more and more power. The engines would roar and the aircraft, while still tethered, would jerk and jump about, to the alarm of our passengers. Finally, either the anchor would be dragged free or the chain would break and the aircraft, held nose down by the reluctant mooring, would surge forwards as the restraint was removed. We were accustomed to these rough antics but they worried our passengers.

On one departure a flight engineer was irritated as he dragged on the crown line to find a pair of hands reaching over his shoulder to help. '**** off' he shouted, then turned to find his would be assistant was our VIP for the trip, a very senior government official.

On my first departure from Atafu, the chain broke and off we went, having written off that anchor. But on my next visit, as we completed our mooring, I was aware of two grinning figures approaching in a canoe. In their hands was the missing anchor! Apparently, with infinite patience, they had free-dived repeatedly to the coral outcrop using heavy stones to take them down. Bit by bit they had freed the abandoned anchor. We were astonished and thanked them profusely. On the next trip to Atafu, we presented each of them with a bag of flour. The men's wives were ecstatic.

Like most alighting areas in remote lagoons, the boundaries of safe water at Atafu were marked by old 40-gallon fuel drums painted a bright colour and mounted on posts. The restricted space at Atafu meant these markers were tightly bunched. One carefully counted the markers before advancing the throttles for takeoff and set off to pass between numbers 11 and 12, counting from the right to left.

Squadron lore has it that once a storm knocked down one of the markers but no one told the crew. On the next takeoff, what seemed to be markers 11 and 12 were in fact markers 12 and 13. The takeoff course was displaced to the left of the safe route. A coconut tree protruded into the takeoff sector and shortly after liftoff the aircraft struck the tree quite heavily, scattering branches and coconuts. But the magnificent old seaplane sailed on and completed the flight with only a few dents to show for the experience. The Sunderland is a tough old bird. Manufacturers Short Brothers and Harland of Belfast would have been proud of their creation, although I doubt their design calculations took into account airborne collisions with coconut trees.

A visit to the Northern Cooks

At irregular intervals, 5 Squadron visited Manihiki Island in the isolated Northern Cook Group. The Northern Cooks are actually the tops of sunken volcanoes forming atolls. The coral reef that is Manihiki is renowned as a breeding ground for the fearsome great white sharks. Coral heads cover the lagoon thickly, restricting aircraft passage. The alighting area includes two quite sharp turns necessary to avoid obstacles.

Our flights to Manihiki were always made from our regular Southern Cooks base at Aitutaki. Because it was the lagoon used by Air New Zealand in its Solent flying boats on their famous service to Tahiti, the people of Aitutaki were used to flying boat operations. 5 Squadron crews were especially welcome guests as the islanders knew we were their lifeline when emergencies occurred. The RNZAF maintained a building there, where we were always entertained by the Number One or Number Two Aitutaki Drum Dancing Teams. These two groups were skilled performers who wouldn't have been out of place on the stage in London or New York. They were invariably the winners and runners up in annual competitions between a multitude of South Pacific Islands hosted in Tahiti.

No fuel was available at Manihiki so we had to take off from Aitutaki with enough for the return journey plus prudent reserves. The takeoffs were thus at heavy weights and in the warm tropical temperatures required a prolonged run before lifting off from the water (engine power is reduced by higher air temperatures). Fortunately, Aitutaki lagoon had long, clear takeoff paths available. Once airborne, we had to fly at low levels, usually 1000 feet, being too heavy to scramble much higher.

There were no radio aids at Manihiki so navigation, including sextant shots on the sun, and moon if visible, called for a high standard of proficiency in basic principles from the navigator. Even with maximum fuel loaded, we had just enough for the journey out and back so there was little latitude for error in this task. There are no surface features, such as reefs, between Aitutaki and Manihiki to provide a check on our progress, so all eyes were upon the navigator performing a difficult task. Standard navigation drills crossing featureless ocean legs called for a smoke float to be dropped into the water once every hour. The aircraft then flew a three-minute pattern to cross over this marker and an instrument called a 'wind finder attachment' was used to establish the wind at the aircraft's flight level.

On my first flight to Manihiki, I had a skilled and highly respected navigator, Rex. He and I agreed that losing three minutes in every hour on the smoke float drill, virtually adding five per cent to the length of the journey, wasn't the most prudent course for this fuel-critical flight. The alternative agreed on was to have the pilot judge the surface wind by eye and use that, with small standard corrections, for navigation at our 1000 feet cruising level. Sunderland pilots develop a good eye for water conditions and generally could read the surface wind over the ocean within five degrees direction and five knots speed. For the first few hours as we droned on over the sparkling blue sea, I called out the surface wind to Rex every thirty minutes and all seemed well.

As local midday approached, I observed Rex preparing for his 'noon-day fix'. This would be his sole opportunity to obtain a fix to check on his course so far. Local midday is more correctly referred to as 'mer pass', or meridional passage, when the sun passes across the observer's meridian of longitude. At a small interval, say 10 minutes, before mer pass the sun will be to the east. At mer pass, the sun will be directly north. At the same interval after mer pass, the sun will be to the west.

Thus, three position lines can be obtained, and where they intersect is the observer's position. Notorious for errors, as the angle between the three position lines is obviously small, noon-day fixes are usually not given too much credence but on this flight, it was all we had. I awaited Rex's completion of the procedure, expecting there would be some course correction. When it came, I was flabbergasted: 'Turn 90 degrees right.'

I immediately turned 90 degrees right and sat there silent, knowing Rex would come up to my seat to talk about this extraordinarily large, almost unheard of, change of course. Being far out over the empty ocean when fuel was critical and being told to head off at a right angle to our previous course was worrisome. Sure enough, Rex was soon there. He was playing it cool, but I could sense his anxiety.

'Noon-day fix, Rex?'

'Yes.'

'Good one?'

'Yes.'

Then Rex unburdened himself. He'd taken considerable care with the sextant sights and had confidence in his fix. He thought an extraordinary wind shear had developed between the surface and our cruise altitude. This unforecast wind had taken us well to the west of our intended course and our new course should take us over the lagoon. Rex was looking for the greenish tinge in the sky that on a bright day can be seen from afar over an isolated large lagoon. He calculated the distance at which we would see this and expected to sight the shimmering light 16 minutes later.

Exactly 16 minutes later, we saw the greenish tinge and soon were approaching the huge lagoon. But our troubles were far from over.

Traversing the large lagoon with its thick population of coral heads, some invisible under the water, and myriad great white sharks needed care. One could not afford to strike a coral head and sink in those waters. After landing on the three-way dogleg alighting area, the crew picked up a local waiting in his canoe and he was soon aboard and guiding us between the coral heads. This local had to be trusted completely and so we had the unusual situation that the safety of the aircraft was in his hands. No maritime captain would be happy with this, but at Manihiki there was no alternative, only a local could navigate across this water.

The easterly trade winds were blowing at about 15 knots, tending to turn the aircraft into the wind. This had to be corrected by positioning the rudder and ailerons but mainly by use of power on the outer engines, and as some of the corners were sharp, a lot of engine power was necessary. In turn, this increased the speed beyond comfortable levels. The RNZAF maintained mooring buoys on all lagoons where we anchored overnight. The one at Manihiki was on the extreme east side of the lagoon, about 3 miles from the settlement where we would spend the night. On arrival at the buoy area we searched for some time but were unable to find it. We realised it had sunk or broken loose, a common event in isolated areas subject to storms. This was very problematic at Manihiki because the only mooring option was anchorage to a specified coral head. This was across the lagoon, adjacent to the main village. A long taxi, guided by our local pilot, ensued. By now it was late in the afternoon. One cannot afford to be traversing coral lagoons with setting-sun glare on the water blinding the lookouts. It was a relief to finally identify our coral head opposite the settlement and anchor to it. I was pleased to get out of the cockpit at last and relax.

The relaxation didn't last long. Our documents mentioned a coral head adjacent to the one to which we were anchored, within the anchor-chain swing distance. That is, if a thunderstorm came through in the night and the aircraft was swinging about on its chain with gusty winds, the hull would pass over this coral head. According to the books, this coral head was two fathoms (3.6 metres) deep at the lowest tide so the hull would swing over it easily. But when I looked, the coral head was at shallow depth. This needed investigation. I commandeered one of the boats disembarking our passengers and crew and went over with the leadline. Sure enough, the obstruction was barely 3 feet below the surface.

Here was a pretty pickle. It was too late in the day to go hunting for another anchorage. If I did nothing, there was every chance a thunderstorm with strong wind gusts would arrive in the middle of the night and blow the aircraft onto the coral head, hole her and sink her. And the anchor watch of four men could end up in the shark-infested seawater. I decided to try to secure the seaplane nose and tail so that it wouldn't swing around. The nose was simple – we put out all three anchors we had on board. Then I went ashore to the harbourmaster's store and managed to borrow a long hawser and a strop. With a bit of scrambling, we passed the strop around the tail and secured it to the hawser. We then dragged the hawser ashore and tied it securely around a coconut tree. Enlisting some manpower, we pulled everything up tight – the aircraft wasn't going to swing anywhere!

It had been a long day and I went thankfully to bed. Next morning, the anchor watch reported that overnight a vicious tropical thunderstorm did pass through and buffeted the old aircraft strongly but our unusual fore and aft mooring held tight and the hull did not swing across the shallow coral head.

Next day I was quite glad to open the throttles and zigzag my way down the three-dogleg takeoff. Adieu, Manahiki. That was the first time I had slept with my aircraft tied to a tree.

Kwajalein

Our merry crews thundered around the Pacific in our venerable machines visiting far-flung places. Among them was the fascinating Kwajalein Atoll, part of the Republic of the Marshall Islands. The southernmost and largest island in the atoll is named Kwajalein Island. During World War II, the Americans' second major battle against an entrenched Japanese garrison took place here. Profiting from the lessons of Tarawa, the Americans operated with a far less costly butcher's bill. The Japanese weren't fully prepared but the garrison fought off the attackers with commendable determination, and only 51 of the 3500-strong garrison survived.

Aviation buffs will be interested to know that at the end of the war in the Pacific, some 150 operational aircraft were jettisoned off Kwajalein Atoll, this course being cheaper than transporting them home. The list included Dauntless dive bombers, F4U Corsairs, Grumman Avengers and F4F Wildcats, Helldivers, B-25s and C46 Commandos.

With a mid-Pacific location, Kwajalein Atoll is ideally placed to fire defensive missiles at intercontinental rockets aimed at America from the west. A four-billion-dollar space tracking and missile defence facility has been built on Kwajalein Island. The island is run by contractors to the United States Army, which controls the administration. It is subject to rigorous security, and few if any visitors have ever been permitted – except Sunderlands of the RNZAF.

The privilege was granted to us so we could attend the regular anti-submarine exercises run by the United States Navy from its base at Manila in the Philippines. It was necessary for us to refuel at Kwajalein, on both the outward and return trips. Because there were no seaplane handling facilities, we had to make do with the shipping gear. This meant mooring to large, hard-skinned ship buoys, a procedure requiring care to avoid damaging our soft-skinned aircraft.

There are always new lessons to be learned in flying. One crew, tired after the long transit from Fiji, took what they thought was the fuel hose from the taciturn crewman on a Navy refuelling barge. The nozzle was placed in the fuel tank and they pumped away – until the crewman shouted up, 'You guys sure take a lot of oil.' They had connected the oil hose, something used often for ships but rarely for seaplanes. The poor fellows were a lot tireder that day by the time they'd drained the oil and refilled with aviation gasoline.

On one transit, we received instructions to delay refuelling until the morning of departure. We were waiting at the crack of dawn but no barge had appeared by 5.30. We were cutting it fine if we were to join our associates in the Philippines in time for the exercise briefing. I rang one person after another without obtaining any answer. In desperation, I rang the admiral himself. The phone was promptly answered by his manservant, who was reluctant to wake the admiral. But I insisted. The gentleman listened politely to my problem and said he would fix it. Not five minutes later, a refuelling barge with a real bone in its teeth came speeding towards us. The admiral had been as good as his word.

We arrived safely for the briefing and, as usual, held our own in the exercise. Despite our ancient craft competing with the modern equipment of the latest anti-submarine aircraft, we got our fair share of kills thanks to the skills and savvy of our experienced operators, especially the radar operators. They astonished our hosts with the information they gleaned from their flickering screens.

Kwajalein was, and probably remains, a key component of the American missile defence system and no expense was spared in maintaining its effectiveness. Some of the finest – and best paid – engineers in America were there. To compensate for the isolated island life, they paid reduced tax on their considerable incomes for the first few months and no tax thereafter. The upshot was that they had full pockets and little to empty them on.

We were the only outsiders permitted to visit Kwajalein, so visitors to this close-knit community were rare. The presence of new faces drew crowds to the lavish entertainment centre and each man could hardly wait to buy us all a drink. The island favourite was a Mai Tai, duty free of course. No one could possibly consume these rum cocktails at the rate they were being bought and so soon our tables were surrounded by seas of Mai Tais. Heaven! We wished it happened more often.

Florida Island, the Solomons

At irregular intervals the squadron sent an aircraft to the Solomon Islands. There is no anchorage in the vicinity of the capital, Honiara, as the seabed drops away sharply to considerable depths just off the reef. We therefore landed at Florida Island, north of Honiara. This is one of the largest lagoons in the Pacific and in World War II accommodated all the ships of the United States Navy fleets operating in that part of the Pacific. A base grew up dedicated to transferring supplies to the fighting ships, and large quantities of goods were stored wherever space could be found. At the end of the war the sailors departed as soon as they could, leaving behind all manner of stores.

Burns Philp, the Australian shipping line and merchant company, which subsequently became a major trading firm in the Pacific, received a huge boost by filling up three liberty ships with Lucky Strike cigarettes from Florida Island and selling them at enormous profit in Hong Kong. Possibly this is the reason why that company never received compensation for war damages to their island properties.

Our stopovers on Florida Island always included a day getting organised, adapting to the sparse facilities. Refuelling was a protracted affair, fuel being pumped by hand from drums in a flotilla of small boats. Servicing the engines from platforms bolted to the wings was hard on the engineers in the tropical heat. After the work was over, the locals delighted in showing us around. The piece de résistance was a concrete wall within which the bodies of several murdered Japanese soldiers were said to be buried.

There were no hotels or facilities on Florida Island, so crew members were hosted in the homes of government staff. Several European families lived there and attended to the maritime affairs of the Solomons government. As captain of the visiting crew, I was the guest of the harbourmaster and his wife. These good people always invited all the crew and, it seemed, just about every other person in the community for a social hour and dinner during our visit. On one occasion, when all were assembled and my fellow crew members were looking forward to their tipple, I was asked my preference. There being no flying scheduled for the following day, I asked for a whisky and soda. Consternation! There was whisky but no soda. A search of the house failed to discover a single drop.

In vain I pleaded that water would be quite sufficient: I had asked for soda and the honour of the community required that it was soda I got! Meantime the crew, who were well aware that they wouldn't be served until their captain had his soda, were looking absolute daggers at me.

One of the local ladies saved the situation by driving her ancient Jeep to her plantation nearby. Triumphantly, she came back with a large box of rather rusty soda bombs and in short order Captain Enright and his crew were happily sipping away. When I commented to my saviour that I hoped I hadn't depleted her supplies, she laughingly said she had several hundred thousand soda bombs! Fossicking about on her estate, she'd found a cave, and in it the huge supply of soda. Obviously, some US supply sergeant had stored the treasures in the cave and was no doubt happy to forget about them when the great day came to go home from the war.

A hair-raising visit to Satapuala

Late one afternoon, when I was captain of the duty crew at Fiji, we received a call for help from American Samoa. Two school teachers, citizens of the United States, had been canoeing along the southern coast and had gone missing. A Coast Guard cutter from Pago Pago was on its way to the search area. It was the hurricane season and no less than three tropical revolving storms were live in the South Pacific. The combined swell systems spawned by these storms had generated sizeable rough seas.

We were airborne with all haste and arrived in the search area with one hour of daylight to search before departing for the night to our nearest overnight alighting area, Satapuala, a coastal village on the north-western side of Upolu Island in Western Samoa. There are no night facilities at Satapuala so we continued searching for the lost teachers till the last moment and timed our landing for last light. Thus it was dark by the time we were secured to our mooring buoy, awaiting the arrival of the refuelling barge. This was a pig of a little craft carrying two thousand gallons of aviation fuel and towed by a launch manned by Samoans. One would suppose that these people, living beside the sea, would be expert small boatmen. Unfortunately, they are not. The crew of the launch and four persons aboard the barge were further stressed by operating in the dark, which was unusual for them.

On their first attempt to bring the barge alongside so that we could pick up the hoses to pump fuel into our tanks, the Samoan coxswain managed to get into a classic dangerous position where the launch was upwind on one side of our soft-skinned craft and the barge was on the other. He then froze. The wind, blowing at about 15 knots, rapidly pushed the two craft past our bow, so that one was on our left and one was on the right. Inevitably the tow rope between launch and barge would be tautened by the aircraft bow. Should the two craft be blown alongside us and trapped there, grinding up and down, we might have been sunk.

We screamed and shouted at the coxswain to power up, pull the barge away and make another approach but the man seemed mesmerised and did nothing. By chance, the launch presently drifted under our port wingtip. Crew members were then treated to the spectacle of me dancing up and down with rage on the wingtip screaming curses in several languages – at least, that's how they enjoyed telling the story. In desperation, I leaped down into the launch and (I'm a tad sorry to say) kicked the coxswain in his cockpit in the head. Coming to his senses, he applied full power and, with my crew members fending off the barge as it passed, he managed to get clear of the aircraft with just the loss of a bit of paint.

By this time, it was fully dark and I decided it was just too dangerous to let this man have another go. I knew we had enough fuel remaining aboard for about six hours' search the following morning so decided to discontinue our refuelling efforts. I motioned to the coxswain to go to the long jetty a few hundred yards away to moor the barge. Being now in the launch, I had to go with him and anticipated returning to the aircraft to pick up the crew.

About 50 yards out from the jetty, the coxswain charged ahead at full speed, the ungainly barge bucketing along behind him. Then he turned 180 degrees without slackening speed, and when the towline became taut, the barge was jerked and overturned. Now there were four crewmen in the water with a flood of gasoline. Once again, the coxswain froze, and the launch started drifting over nearby rocks. I could hear the propeller clanging as it bounced up and down on the rocks. Any second now, I expected it to break off and the launch to drift out to sea. Enough! I leaped out onto the rocks and scrambled onto the jetty. There I watched as the men in the water were blown down to the jetty. I leaned down and helped to pull out the first soul, slippery with fuel. The air was thick with gasoline fumes. As I reached for the second man, I noticed the first one reach down to a bundle lying on the jetty and pull out his cigarettes. Enough again already! I sprinted the length of the jetty and took shelter behind a coconut tree.

Miraculously, there was no explosion. Eventually, we got the launch back out to the aircraft and soon the crew were in taxis on their way to Aggie Grey's hotel. After a few hours of sleep we returned to the aircraft. There being no replacement for the sunken barge, we abandoned hope of refuelling and set off at first light to resume the search for the missing teachers in cooperation with the Coast Guard cutter. It wasn't to be a straightforward flight!

Shortly after leaving Satapuala for the search area – to the south-east of American Samoa – buffeted by severe turbulence in the lee of the land mass caused by the still blowing hurricane winds, number three exactor failed. In the Sunderland, engine revolution speed is set by hydraulic controls, known as exactors. If the system develops a leak and the hydraulic fluid is lost, the engine rpm goes to minimum. The idling engine is at virtually zero power. This presented me with a tricky situation. Normally, the condition would be cause for a turnback for repairs. But the lives of the two school teachers were at risk, and when life is at risk the rescue pilot must go to the limit. Since there was no chance of a refuel, even if we repaired the exactor leak, and since we were able to maintain satisfactory flight on the remaining three engines, I judged that we should continue the flight. I told the crew of my decision and invited comment. There was none, and we pressed on.

An aircraft cooperating with a surface vessel passes over that vessel on each leg of a creeping line-ahead search and can thus correct any navigation error that might have occurred on previous legs. We had just commenced our third leg when – bang – there came an explosion on number one engine, which immediately started vibrating and shaking the aircraft.

'Recommend you shut it down,' called the flight engineer, and I promptly did so. At that moment, the second flight engineer saw, he was convinced, a canoe with two people in it. But with virtually two engines lost, we ourselves were in a state of emergency. There was no choice but to set course for Satapuala immediately as our ability to remain airborne was doubtful. With deep regret, we turned away from the search after having given details of the possible sighting to the cutter. The vessel searched that area carefully but nothing was found.

After declaring an emergency, we analysed our performance and options. The hurricane-induced seas were high, and the prospect of a ditching was unwelcome. By applying as much power to the remaining two engines as could be controlled by the rudder, and applying five degrees of bank towards the outer live engine, we were able to maintain height but only within a 5-knot airspeed range. Faster or slower than that and we lost altitude. We were at the search height of 1500 feet.

We set course for Satapuala, about an hour and a half away, but I had to make some more decisions. First, I was reluctant to go to the leeward, or northern, side of the land after experiencing the turbulence there on our outwards flight. I felt the Sunderland wouldn't maintain height, and there was the distinct possibility of encountering downdrafts (sinking air as the wind flowed down the mountainsides). I therefore elected to go via the southern coast, even though this increased the distance to be flown significantly. This turned out to be a good decision as I was able to ride the updrafts on that side to gain some much-needed height. The thought of flying a Sunderland as a glider was enough to bring a smile to my face.

Next, I had to consider whether to divert into Pago Pago Harbour. This was risky strategy as Pago Pago Harbour is landlocked by high hills. Once I entered the harbour mouth, there'd be no chance of turning around or of being able to execute a go-around.

As a precaution, I sent a message to the harbourmaster warning of a possible diversion into his bailiwick. This created quite a stir at home base Lauthala Bay and at Pago Pago. Meanwhile, we limped along handling our heavy old aeroplane carefully to keep our exact speed. After what seemed a long time we turned for the headland south-west of Satapuala and set up for a two-engine landing in rough conditions. It had been a grim day.

The media around the Pacific had lots of fun with 'Troubleshooters In Trouble' type headlines. It turned out the trouble with number two engine was that a cylinder head had blown off. After the cylinder was changed on the water, we returned to Fiji and awaited further adventures. The school teachers were never found.

Discomfiture of an aide

Squadron lore tells of a flight (rather before my time in Fiji) to take the Governor General of Fiji on a State visit to the Kingdom of Tonga. Governors General in tropical regalia were an impressive sight, their uniform including a helmet trimmed with white ostrich feathers cascading down to the vice-regal waist. This magnificent headpiece was not of course worn journeying to and fro; it was transported in a big box while the Governor General wore his military hat. It was a principal duty of the Governor General's aide-de-camp to ensure the box was brought along and safely held until required. On the flight in question, the vice-regal party, including aide and helmet box, was loaded at Lauthala Bay in an aircraft commanded by a senior pilot and was soon winging its way towards Tonga. In the wardroom, sherry was being drunk as delicacies were passed up from the galley. 5 Squadron was performing at its best. However, at the rear of the flying boat in the bomb room a different scenario was being enacted by a master signaller, a man who was invariably found at the centre of any trouble. He had undone the locks on the helmet box, taken out the helmet with its feathers and was parading up and down with the helmet on his head and the feathers flowing down his back. Suddenly the aircraft lurched as it passed through a stray cumulus cloud and our joker stumbled and lost his footing. Alas, the helmet and plumes managed to find their way through a gap between the flooring and the fuselage and rolled down into the bilges.

Now, in most vessels, bilges are not nice places to be, and the Sunderland was no exception. When the helmet was fished out, it was covered in old oil and sludge. The once white feathers were a bedraggled mess. The laughter that had accompanied the posturing quickly died away and the messy remains of the Governors General's fine headpiece were hurried to the galley. Water was quickly boiled and scrubbing started. A large door in the rear fuselage that could be opened in flight was quickly prepared to accept the feathers for drying in the slipstream. All to no avail – the feathers were never going to be white again!

Crewmen listened with dismay as the order to prepare for descent and landing in the Tongan roadstead was given. What to do? This was going to be the worst diplomatic incident in the squadron's history. The Governor General of Fiji would insult the Kingdom of Tonga by appearing in finery that was no longer fine. But the miscreant who was responsible, eyeing the open fuselage door, was equal to the occasion. He put the tarnished helmet and the filthy feathers back in their box, closed the lid and heaved the whole ensemble overboard.

On arrival, when the aide-de-camp called for his helmet box, he was asked, 'What box? We haven't seen any box.' The distressed official was forced to confess to the Governor General that the box containing the helmet and feathers was nowhere to be found; the Governor General would have to face the guard of honour and subsequent formalities wearing his plain old military cap.

The loss was never explained officially, despite extensive inquiries. 5 Squadron members knew when to keep their mouths shut. The aide's career was not enhanced.

Survivors of the Minerva Reef

Tongans are interesting people. They and the Thais, or Siamese as they used to be known, were the sole peoples of the South and West Pacific who were never colonised by European races. Consequently, they bear no burden of resentment and are natural, relaxed and happy people to know.

Tongan men and women are large and powerful figures. In the last few centuries, when many of the peoples of the Pacific were fierce cannibals, the Tongans were the mercenaries of the region. Several would go to fight for a particular Fijian chief, whose enemies would promptly surrender rather than face the powerful Tongan men on the battlefield. The Tongans would often take payment from the Fijians in the form of the large ocean-going canoes, capable of carrying 100 people, which were unique in the South Pacific.

In the villages adjoining the sea, the navigator was of higher mana than the chief. Navigational skills were handed down in the family from grandfather to grandson or, occasionally, granddaughter. Lacking a latitude and longitude grid, the Tongans navigated by Polynesian methods from star to star. A voyage from A to B might involve changing from one to another of several stars; the sequence was committed to memory by chanted verses. Clever use of natural phenomena enabled these sailors to zero in on their target islands. For example, the outwards direction of long-range seabirds in the early morning, or inwards in the evening, were a pointer to the nearest land. The sailors could also recognise a trail of humps, or upwellings, spreading out from an island caused by the bouncing of the trade wind south-easterly swell from the target island. This reflected wave intersected the swell itself, causing an upwelling. A succession of these little disturbances provided a trail at 45 degrees to that swell, leading back to the island. In general navigation, direction was maintained by reference to the predominant swell system, caused by the south-easterly trade winds. It was important to read this correctly and it could be difficult as this dominant swell was often overridden by several other swell systems of more local origin.

As mentioned above, some navigators were female. At the risk of bringing down on my head the wrath of those who claim girls can do anything, I have to demur. Female navigators struggled to read the underlying swell accurately. It was generally agreed there is only one truly accurate indicator – the freely swinging testicles.

To the Tongans, being at sea was a natural and relaxed state of being. A French sailor of considerable experience, including a raft voyage eastwards to South America, recounts going from one island to another with some Tongans (they were in search of cigarettes). When the single engine failed the Polynesians broke up floorboards and began to paddle. They were unconcerned – they'd been travelling to their island under power; now they were travelling by paddling. The Frenchman was ashamed to find himself panicking as the target island dropped below the horizon when a head wind blew them backwards, but his companions carried on calmly – even a nursing mother, who picked up her paddle when her infant was satisfied.

The navigation skills of these people were excellent. An Australian doctor whose hobby was learning and documenting their techniques made a long ocean voyage with some Tongan boatmen and said he surreptitiously used modern gear he carried to check their performance. They were rarely more than two degrees off course.

**

Something which exemplifies the seafaring talent of the Tongans is the amazing tale of the survivors of the Minerva Reef. That reef is situated on the direct track from Nuku'alofa, the capital of Tonga, to Auckland. It's an extensive lagoon, most of which is underwater at high tide. At one stage, an American company was planning to build above-water structures on it and declare it to be an independent republic. Apparently the United States didn't feel threatened by the emergence of a new nation there, but the plans came to nothing after hostility to the idea was voiced by Tongan, New Zealand and Australian governments

In 1962, a Tongan-registered vessel set off for Auckland from Nuku'alofa. But after several days routine radio reports were not received. When the ship failed to arrive in Auckland on schedule it was declared overdue. It had, in fact, run onto the Minerva Reef one dark night and sunk. Near the point of impact, there happened to be the wreck of a Japanese fishing boat – the Pacific is littered with them. This wreck, lying on its side, wasn't badly damaged and proved to be a shelter for the shipwrecked crew. They set themselves up in reasonable comfort after retrieving good quantities of supplies which were floating around the lagoon. The Tongan captain, Tevita Fifita, settled back to await the arrival of a searching Sunderland from Fiji or New Zealand, confident that he and his men would soon be spotted and rescued. But day after day then week after week passed and, inexplicably, no aircraft arrived. Admirably, the captain kept his men in disciplined order. Food was augmented by the plentiful fish from the lagoon and a solar still supplied sufficient water for the survival of all persons. Finally accepting that no rescue was forthcoming, the captain set his crew to gathering wood and materials from the flotsam and jetsam of the lagoon with the intention of building a small sailing boat.

The reason for the non-arrival of a searching flying boat reflects no credit on the two group captains in charge of Sunderland operations at Lauthala Bay in Fiji and Hobsonville in New Zealand. They couldn't agree on the border of their respective areas of responsibility for SAR actions. The Hobsonville commander insisted the northern boundary of his area of responsibility lay to the south of Minerva Reef. The Lauthala Bay commander was equally adamant that the southern boundary of his area lay to the north of Minerva Reef. This left Minerva Reef outside the areas admitted by both commanders and no aircraft from either base was allowed to go to the area. Navigation leaders of both bases tore their hair out with frustration, knowing that Minerva Reef was the obvious place to look for survivors of a lost Tonga–New Zealand vessel. Still, the two commanders squared off like a couple of old walruses and forbade their crews to search the disputed territory.

Meanwhile, the Tongan captain and crew, which included his son, were living on their wits in the Japanese wreck refuge. Sadly, several perished. After a total period of about three months, sufficient materials had been gathered to build a little sailing boat, constructed without tools. This was stocked with supplies and a few volunteers set off in the small craft for Fiji, propelled by a makeshift sail filled by the reliable trade winds.

Interest in the fate of the survivors had faded after three months and the world at large forgot the missing men. Until ... electrifying news flashed around the world. Survivors had arrived on one of the southern islands of the Fiji group. The little sailboat, in the expert hands of its Tongan crew, had proved equal to the task; although it had taken them a week to make landfall.

Tragically, Captain Fifita's son had been lost, in heart-wrenching circumstances. The tiny craft had foundered in rough waters about a mile off the coast of the island and its crew had to swim for it. The captain's son, weakened by his long ordeal, couldn't keep himself afloat. Bravely, he insisted the others go on to raise the alarm for those left behind at Minerva Reef. The captain and remaining crew left him and swam on. But within minutes the reason for the rough water became clear – they were standing on a submerged reef. They turned back for the son, but he was gone.

On notification of the survivors' arrival, a Lauthala Bay Sunderland was despatched to the reef. The crew managed to find an alighting area free of obstructions, landed and taxied to the Japanese wreck to safely recover all the remaining survivors. Soon, they were recuperating in a hospital in Fiji. Remarkably, these men were in quite good condition. Queen Salote of Tonga (who'd endeared herself to the London crowds by riding in an open carriage in torrential rain at Queen Elizabeth's 1953 coronation parade) asked that the crew who'd rescued her subjects fly them back to Tonga after their recuperation. Naturally this request was granted, and the lucky fellows flew off to a state party in Tonga which was talked about for many days.

Interviewed by the world's media, Captain Fifita was asked what he would have done if they hadn't found the wreck of the Japanese fishing vessel. His reply: 'We would have built a raft from the wreckage and been back in Tonga in a week.'

My great respect for the Tongan people makes me believe he would have done so.

Deepsea rendezvous

One afternoon, a call for assistance was received at Lauthala Bay from the steamship *Canberra*. One of the largest luxury cruise ships of her time, *Canberra* was regarded as unlucky. She was launched at Harland and Wolff's shipyard, Belfast, Northern Ireland, on 6 March 1960. Designed by a young naval architect, she floated well down by the stern. Plainly, the centre-of-gravity calculations were in error. Reportedly, 2000 tons of pig iron ballast were required in the bow to restore an even keel. As a consequence, there were massive bending stresses in the hull and this prompted her insurers to strictly limit the seas and places *Canberra* was permitted to operate. Several times, she had created headline news with unfortunate happenings, including a serious fire while moored at Gibraltar when a switch was thrown the wrong way dealing with a wayward generator. Bad news travels fast and the sensation-hungry world media were always alert for some more news about her.

Canberra made the call from the vicinity of the Tokelau Islands, a little north of Samoa. A child on board was ill and desperately required oxygen. *Canberra* advised that all her medical oxygen supplies had been used up and half the engine room supply as well. She was still a long way from a rendezvous with the American Coast Guard cutter from Pago Pago, Samoa, which had medical facilities and plenty of oxygen. Could we help by dropping cylinders of oxygen to her?

Well, this was an unusual task; oxygen cylinders are dangerous cargo and no one had ever heard of their being delivered by dropping them into the sea. They were liable to explode on impact with the water, causing lethal metal pieces to fly out in all directions. We kicked ideas around until a bright spark thought of encasing them in sheets of kapok, the material which gives life jackets their buoyancy, to cushion the shock of entry to the water and provide flotation until they could be retrieved. We obtained kapok from the firm of Morris Hedstroms, merchants in Suva, strapped it around an oxygen cylinder and threw the package into the base swimming pool. It floated, so we advised *Canberra* that we would drop eight cylinders to her and arranged a rendezvous for first light the following morning. *Canberra* was to be hove to at that location.

To reduce the danger of the cylinders exploding on impact, I determined to drop them from absolutely minimum altitude. This was 50 feet, as low as I dared go. (To any pilot reading this, a word of warning, don't dream of going so low unless you're in a specially equipped aircraft – as maritime surveillance aircraft are – and have been properly trained. There are optical illusions low over the water which can easily trap you.)

En route to our rendezvous, we made radio contact with *Canberra* and described the procedures we would follow to avoid endangering the crews of her pick-up boats. I wanted the boats to remain in the vicinity of the ship before each cylinder was launched so that there was no risk if the cylinder exploded on impact. I also suggested to the commodore that he consider sending his boats to a nearby Tokelau Island lagoon, where we would land and pass the oxygen to his crew without the risk of explosion. He declined this offer because his sailors were unfamiliar with reef crossings and tropical lagoons.

On schedule, *Canberra*, hove to on the empty ocean, loomed up in the dawn light. What a magnificent sight this majestic vessel was. Her massive, gleaming white structure towered above us. Even at that hour her decks were lined with passengers and crew, cameras at the ready. She really looked quite stately and beautiful. As arranged, her boats were well clear of the explosion danger range. So, I lined up on our drop zone and called for the first cylinder to be launched by hand from the bomb bay hatch, carefully maintaining 50-feet altitude, fully expecting an explosion. But no, a big splash and the cylinder was floating and soon retrieved by *Canberra*'s best crew. All eight cylinders were safely received and the sick child was soon breathing our pure oxygen.

Photographers on *Canberra*'s decks, far above our low altitude, gained some spectacular shots, which were soon on their way around the world. With her history of unlucky happenings, *Canberra* was highly newsworthy. I was surprised to find that our drop made six-column headlines in America and Europe as well as Australia and New Zealand.

It was publicity gold: the child survived with our oxygen supplies which were sufficient to stabilise his condition until *Canberra* met the Pago Pago Coast Guard cutter. The father was a Canadian, the mother Australian; *Canberra*, of course, was a British ship; and our New Zealand aircraft was based in Fiji. The oncoming American Coast Guard cutter from American Samoa completed the quite lengthy list of nations involved in this international rendezvous on the high seas.

Farewell to Singapore

The Sunderland was well known to Singapore. In wartime, one managed to take on board a huge number of persons escaping from the advancing Japanese. There were so many that there was no possibility of taking off and the seaplane was taxied many miles to a safe evacuation port. In the Malaysian emergency, Sunderlands patrolled hour after hour, dropping anti-personnel bombs onto rebel-held jungle areas.

Following an exercise in the Philippines, a ceremonial call to Singapore was made so that RAF personnel could say goodbye to the old flying boat. Mine was the first aircraft to arrive and we were met by several air commodores and group captains who'd been flight lieutenants in charge of the British Sunderlands in their day. The mooring at the arrival wharf was tricky as, if one failed to secure the mooring line on the first approach, there was no room to abort the approach and try again. So, we knew there were many critical eyes upon us as we lined up. Nods of approval accompanied our successful hook-up.

During the next two days, the British hosts entertained us royally. Shopping trips, games, entertainment – nothing was too much trouble. We felt quite honoured by the genuine friendship and interest in our activities. An all-ranks evening function, common in large maritime squadrons, was a merry affair at which the grizzled veterans of earlier days relived their experiences. One old warrant officer sought me out and said he was pleased to see the strong crew spirit exhibited by our squadron members. He was able to point out, one by one, the members of my crew, observing our attitudes to one another. He was right, too; our old craft fostered excellent crew spirit as we went about our multitudinous tasks.

14

A NIGHT TO REMEMBER

In Auckland, I was captain of the duty crew called out in response to a distress call from a collier, the *Kaitawa*, off the west coast of the North Island. She had 27 persons on board and had been making her way via the northernmost cape of New Zealand to her destination, Auckland. The position given in her distress message was off 90 Mile Beach, in the vicinity of the underwater Pandora's Reef. There was immense concern as the radio operator had interrupted a routine position report to send a mayday call, reporting extreme difficulties in mountainous seas. After this call, there was silence from the vessel despite repeated attempts at contact by the maritime radio services. Immediately, RNZAF Whenuapai was alerted and the duty crew called out.

An additional concern was that the position given in the distress call was in proximity to the submerged reef. An underwater reef reflects energy back to oncoming swells and makes them higher. In the prevailing hurricane conditions, even the open ocean swells were known to be of the order of 60 feet (18 metres). Experienced skippers would normally stand out into deep water in heavy swell conditions. The situation of the distressed vessel was most alarming.

Three days earlier, a tropical depression in the Tasman Sea (between Australia and New Zealand), had atypically been travelling south, hugging the eastern coast of Australia. It collided with an active cold front moving north. What meteorologists call an intense thermal gradient existed between the warm, moist northerly and the cold southerly air masses. A severe storm was generated, and hurricane winds and 60-foot-high seas spread across the Tasman Sea.

I'll never forget receiving that call. My wife and I had been out. As we walked in the door, we heard the telephone shrilling above the noise of the shrieking wind and heavy rain of this stormy night. We both knew what that signified and exchanged dismayed looks. June looked frightened as I answered the phone and received details of the emergency. Five minutes later, I was driving to the air base.

On the way, I had a good think about what I faced here. Twenty-seven lives were in dire peril. We of the duty crew were about to put our own lives on the line in order to find them and hopefully rescue them. With lives at risk the rescue must go to the limit of our aircraft's capability. I was acutely conscious that conditions on Auckland Harbour, from which we would make our takeoff, might well be at, or even beyond, the limit of safe operation. Extreme care was called for.

One by one, the crew appeared in the operations briefing room. My co-pilot, two navigators, two engineers and four radio and radar operators were joined by three volunteer lookouts. All were grim-faced. The briefing officer, an older man of much experience, looked worried as he recounted the conditions on the Auckland Harbour – wind gusting to 85 knots (157 kilometres per hour), six-foot (1.8-metre) waves, heavy rain reducing visibility to near zero and rough conditions. Everyone looked at me – it was my decision as to attempting a takeoff. My comment – 'We must go and try. I won't make a final decision as to takeoff until we're in position. Be very careful moving about on the aircraft during pre-flight inspections' – met with nods of approval from each crew member.

By 1.30 am, we had gathered our gear and were out in the hurricane wind and rain on board the launch taking us out to the aircraft. She was pitching and tossing about on her mooring buoy in the Hobsonville channel. With some difficulty we boarded, completed our checks, started the engines and taxied to a takeoff position appropriate to the hurricane winds. We carried two sets of Lindholme Gear, several rafts roped together for dropping to survivors in the water. They might well prove to be the last chance for the 27 persons in distress. At the takeoff point, we had to wait for the report from the safety maritime patrol launch that the takeoff path was clear of debris. The sweep was something I'd insisted upon: there was a high probability of storm debris floating on or just under the surface. Imagine the havoc that could cause. More than an hour passed which I well knew would be the subject of critical comment in the media. The operations officer unable to contact the captain of the launch, he'd asked the police to go to the man's house to rouse him. Finally, the man was found and he assured us the takeoff area had been searched and cleared. The crew completed their checks on the wildly pitching aircraft and we taxied into position for takeoff. It was decision time.

I stared through the windscreen at the towering swells, driven fast by the 85-knot hurricane. We were pitching violently, and spume and spray were flying. Auckland Harbour was being lashed by a dangerous storm, pitch black with heavy rain. The grim faces in the darkened cockpit wore sombre expressions. I reminded myself that rescue crews must go to the limit but with these winds and seas we were at the absolute limit of safe operation for takeoff. Were we beyond the limit? That was the question. It would be of no use to those in distress if the aircraft crashed and the crew were killed attempting a takeoff.

Another wave swept by and I decided. We go. I gave the order for takeoff and resolved to abort if things were too rough at 50 knots. 'All clear above and astern, standing by booster pumps,' came the standard cry from the astro-hatch lookout and, adrenaline pumping through our veins, we started our takeoff. Four throttles forward brought the mighty Pratt and Whitney R180D engines screaming up to full power and we butted into the first wave. Smash! Hull rivets screamed and broke (89 of them, we discovered later). A solid sheet of water came green right over the cockpit. I was having trouble controlling the heavy machine, trying to keep an even keel. Now the second wave! The smash was slightly less violent and then each successive wave was a little easier than the last. Gradually, we climbed onto the planing bottom step and I knew we would make it. Relief! No one hurt!

Flying conditions airborne were barely better than seaborne. The aircraft shook violently amid turbulence, wind gusts and lightning. But once the radio altimeter showed we had climbed to 300 feet, I breathed easier and pulled the throttles back to reduce to climb power.

Suddenly, sickeningly, the bottom seemed to drop out of the atmosphere. We commenced a fast descent as we crossed the boundary of Whenuapai airfield, adjacent to our takeoff path. I was flung straight into the most demanding test of instrument flying skill of my entire 23,000-odd flying hour career.

The human mind can make about five decisions per second. My mind raced:

0.0 seconds	Dangerous downdraft.
0.2 seconds	Max power.
0.4 seconds	Why is this happening? Dunno, but dangerous.
0.6 seconds	Scream over the intercom, 'Firewall, firewall everything!' This prompted the flight engineer and co-pilot to push the engine controls as far forward as possible – to the firewall – to gain every last skerrick of power.
0.8 seconds	Dismaying – terrifying rate of descent at this low altitude.
1.0 seconds	Can only counter by bleeding off airspeed; have emergency power already.
1.2 seconds	Little margin, stall speed about 90 knots at our weight.
1.4 seconds	Instant recall of long-ago aerodynamics tutor saying, 'In a propeller-driven aircraft, in a power-on stall, the forced draught over the wing will reduce the stalling speed.' Thank God for my training.
1.6 seconds	Okay, assume 75 knots stall speed.
1.8 seconds	Losing speed fast, scary. Crew's lives at great risk now; suppress fear.
2.0 seconds	Conditions terrible, buffeting, turbulence, heavy rain! *Dear God, I must be super careful!* I was approaching a stall in frightful conditions and in danger of hull impact due to low height.

At about 200 feet with a descent rate of 800 feet per minute – 15 seconds to impact – hammered by the heavy buffeting, I managed to trade airspeed for height. But it was down to 110 knots – only 35 knots above the power-on stall speed.

In a manoeuvrable training aircraft in blue skies, approaching the stall, one has to be careful with the controls as coarse movement of aileron or rudder causes yaw, which leads to a spin. But here I was with heavy controls in this old aircraft desperately trying to keep an even keel in solid darkness, turbulence and slashing rain.

No sooner did I have balanced flight on an even keel than I was slammed by turbulence and jerked away from straight and level flight and had to fight for control again, always aware a rough move would precipitate a spin with immediately fatal results. I found myself sobbing with the strain but I was utterly determined to get every last ounce of flyability out of this old machine.

In the '60s, the phenomenon of down bursts was unknown to aviation. It occurs when a cold air mass, heavier than the surrounding air in a cumulus storm cloud, forms and commences moving downwards. Sometimes the downward movement will gain high vertical speed. The descending column of air then strikes the ground and flows outwards. The unwary pilot encountering this phenomenon mightn't realise he's got, perhaps, a 60-knot head wind component coming from the downdraft until he crosses the boundary between the outflow and the descending column of air. Without warning, loss of airspeed (say 60 knots) hits as he experiences entry to an awful rate of descent in the descending air. Even in simulators, this phenomenon – generally called wind shear – is dismaying as the runway threshold rises before your very eyes and you sink below the planned approach path. Some real-life wind shear conditions cannot be escaped by the most skilled pilots and the most powerful aircraft. (Sorry, travellers, but that's the way it is.) The wise pilot avoids such conditions that have destroyed many aircraft. But search-and-rescue flights often have to press on until reaching the limit of their abilities.

I was now approaching the stall despite the engines screaming at absolutely maximum power and my crew was in grave danger. This was becoming a very close-run thing; we were in extremis. My airspeed above the stall had all been traded for the maintenance of height, the engines were roaring at absolute maximum power and I had nothing left but utter concentration on maintaining level flight. A burst of turbulence or rough movement of the controls would be enough to cause loss of control and a fatal spin. Worse still, I couldn't be sure of my height in the blackness and lashing rain and the radio altimeter appeared to be reading zero, so I was obviously in danger of ground impact.

Then suddenly, magically, the ASI (air speed indicator) kicked up 5 knots. I must have passed out of the column of the descending air. Little by little, the airspeed went up and after what seemed an eternity I had 90 knots. Flick flick, 100 knots. I was going to fly out of this! In retrospect, I felt that I'd kept that old flying boat airborne by sheer willpower. We were going to survive. I was slowly gaining height; we were going to fly out of this death trap. Thankfully, we were accelerating away. I knew that this storm had far from finished with us, but deep within myself was a warm feeling: I hadn't failed my crew at the closest call.

Sobered by this experience, we set out for the search area. Bucketing and banging about in the severe turbulence, we made our way north and soon were lined up for our first approach to datum, the position given in the vessel's distress call. The turbulence had now increased to extreme and flying conditions were most uncomfortable.

We descended to 300 feet and I handed over control to my co-pilot, who was very reliable. I trusted him with our lives, which is indeed what I was doing right there. He didn't need to be reminded to remain locked onto the instrument panel and to not take his attention from it for a single second. The navigator advised wind speed 145 knots (270 kilometres per hour).

With the aircraft in my co-pilot's safe hands in this hurricane, I looked up and called for flares. 'Flares, flares, flares – go.'

The ghostly fluorescent light of multi-million candle-power flares lit up a dread, shocking sight. Mountains of water, heights amplified by the underwater reef, with their tops blown off by the shrieking wind, charged by underneath us. Spray, spume and solid sheets of water lashed this wild scene of malevolent violence. We saw nature's unstoppable power. Once seen, never forgotten. No one would ever go voluntarily into such conditions. By observing the radio altimeter readings as the huge rollers passed beneath us and subtracting the minimum from the maximum indication of this reliable instrument, we were able to calculate the height of these enormous swells. I believe they were 90 feet (27 metres) high – yes, I did say 90 feet. Incredible though that may seem, it must be remembered that the open ocean swell was reported at 60 feet (18 metres) and the underwater-reef reflecting energy increased swell height in this vicinity.

Pity poor humans in this hell! And they were out there somewhere! At a subsequent inquiry, it was proven that some survival equipment from the vessel had been taken and operated. Some persons must have escaped their sinking vessel. I hope our presence was a comfort to the doomed. We started a standard square search, being careful to make all turns away from the nearby land in the 145-knot wind. We peered as best we could into the maelstrom but nothing was sighted. Hour after hour we searched and searched, looking for survivors or rafts, our Lindholme Gear ready to drop to any survivors sighted in the wild waters. Alas, nothing but the wild, wild storm-driven ocean.

A British vessel lay hove to about 20 miles offshore. After some difficulty, we made radio contact and I asked for help in the search, promising the vessel assistance in its navigation. We waited a full ten minutes for a reply. A polite British voice said, 'Not tonight, sir.' Fair enough. There's a limit beyond which SAR efforts shouldn't go, when further action will likely lead to further loss of life. We thanked the British captain for his consideration.

Reaching PLE (prudent limit of endurance) after about 15 hours, we were relieved by a second Sunderland and set course for Hobsonville through the continuing storm. We battered our way to a landing in rough conditions. After refuelling at the mooring buoy, we tumbled into the disembarkation launch utterly exhausted.

Experts calculated that life rafts from the stricken vessel could have been blown around the North Cape of New Zealand and so the search continued. Nothing was sighted. The decision to suspend the search was made after three days, to the sorrow of the families of the missing sailors. Such, all too often, is the world of search and rescue.

When the weather had subsided some days later and Royal New Zealand Navy divers were able to investigate the wreck, it became apparent that the whole superstructure of the vessel had been detached, more or less in one piece. It seems likely that she touched bottom at the trough of the swells and oncoming walls of water had destroyed her. It was amazing that anyone had managed to escape from the vessel, as the deployment of emergency equipment had indicated. The fact that the distress message interrupted a routine radio call highlights the unexpectedness of the disaster. This is certainly a lesson to sailors to stand out into deep water when the going gets rough.

In my mind's eye today, I can still see those roiling mountainous waves rocketing by.

15

SIR TIM WALLIS – A GREAT KIWI

Someone I admire is Sir Tim Wallis, legendary pilot, successful businessman and rancher, collector of antique aircraft. He is best known as the creator of the biennial Wanaka Air Show, War Birds Over Wanaka, which in 2018 had been running for 30 years.

When, early in his career, he looked at the deer industry in New Zealand, it was a feeble affair. Deer which had been introduced to the country ran wild. Exports of venison had started in the 1960s, which helped to control the burgeoning deer population in the mountains, but was too small in scale to be significant. Overgrazing of alpine meadows had led to erosion, blocked rivers and flooding of the lowland farming areas. Government shooters and private hunters found they could profit from the sale of venison meat, skins, antler velvet, tails and sinews. (The latter three products are wrongly believed by Westerners to be aphrodisiacs. They are not. A doctor explained to me that the products are almost pure protein; Asian men often had little protein in their diet so a concentrated burst of it in the form of medicines made from deer velvet, tails and sinews gave them energy.)

The shooters, scrambling through the rugged alpine terrain frequented by deer, made little impression on deer numbers until Tim rationalised the industry. The enterprising Tim introduced helicopters into the battle. Tough and agile sharpshooters started killing the deer and leaping out to retrieve the carcasses. These daredevil marksmen became expert shots from the unsteady helicopters and cases of well over a hundred kills without a miss are known.

Subsequent innovations included the retrieval of deer live, incapacitating darts being fired instead of bullets, and the use of nets spread by small rockets. Farming of the animals became practical with the increased supply of animals. Large-scale deer farming was pioneered in New Zealand, which remains home to the world's largest and most advanced deer-farming industry.

Tim developed his property, Criffel, in Central Otago as the first deer farm. It became the centre for the development of high-quality genetics and the model for other farmers. As the father of the country's modern-day deer industry, he has received a knighthood.

Tim was a large and forceful man, full of energy and go. A member of his family described life with him as like 'living in the centre of a hurricane'. He had a tendency to push his margins, and accidents early in his flying career threatened the viability of the operations. However, he had enough sense to bring in ex-military pilots to train his pilots to cope with the demanding role. Business prospered.

The demands on the pilot and crewman in the wild, steep alpine terrain were enormous and one really has to admire them. The deer, accustomed to the serenity and peace of their primeval surroundings, must have been stunned to find themselves suddenly grabbed, bound and whisked through the air dangling from a chopper. Once recovered from their tranquilliser shot or netting, the animals were placed in dark sheds and the local radio stations were played to them. After some time, they adapted to life with humans with surprising equanimity. Though still afraid of their captors they managed to live and breed on the many deer farms that soon appeared. (I'm not sure if this is a commentary on deer psyches or the radio stations.)

Early in his flying career and shortly after meeting the mini-skirted woman who was to become his wife, lifelong companion and mother of four strapping sons (two of whom perished in helicopter accidents, to the great sorrow of their community), Tim agreed to help a friend by helicoptering feed to snowbound sheep on the steep hills bordering Queenstown. Perhaps distracted by thoughts of the mini-skirted lass, he failed to check the location of power lines in the area – an error that pilots are taught to guard against scrupulously – and crashed into live lines. He paid the penalty for this carelessness by breaking his back. Ever since, he has had to drag his paralysed left leg behind him, sometimes in considerable pain. Illustrating Tim's character, in a magazine article his wife revealed that although Tim's pain was sometimes so serious as to warrant pethidine injections, he had never once complained about his injury to her.

Tim's chosen industry included some tough players. Originally, deer were classified in law as noxious animals. This meant, for example, that if your neighbour was driving a herd of deer along the road, you could lawfully cut out some and make off with them. In the helicopter deer-recovery business, there were some spirited individuals who weren't afraid to take advantage of the law. A large machine might wait for a smaller helicopter, laden to its limits with deer hanging from the skids, to appear staggering out of the alpine valleys, The pirate helicopter would swoop in and hover over the smaller one forcing it downwards in the downdraft from the larger machine. The smaller machine would have no option but to jettison its load, whereupon the predatory crew would swoop in and grab the animals. Such tactics led to defensive measures, and soon bullet holes started to appear in helicopter fuselages. The New Zealand Police Force were not long in becoming cognisant of such activities, and after some stern warnings things quietened down. There were, after all, plenty of deer for all.

Another of Tim's attributes was a knack for developing international business connections. For instance, he facilitated Altai velvet imports into the principal market, Korea. The Altai Mountains, which cross parts of Russia, China, Mongolia and Kazakhstan, are the home of the Siberian red deer. At a celebratory party in Altai, to which he was flown in a Russian military helicopter, he realised the chilled vodka came in cups. Alas, when Tim tried to discreetly pour his first cupful into the local equivalent of an aspidistra, a burly chief noticed. 'Nyet, nyet,' he said and insisted on refilling the cup. Resigning himself to a day's heavy drinking, Tim entered into the spirit of the gathering. For his departure, he had to be lifted into the helicopter by four men, one for each arm and leg. Not everybody was prepared to go to such lengths for business, he later observed.

Going vodka for vodka against the Russians was part and parcel of Tim's expanding his international business. To the Russians, he was larger than life, and they grew to love and trust him.

Nevertheless, not all doors were open to him. Ever on the lookout for means to improve the quality of his deer herds, Tim was well aware that the best deer in the world are in Russia and devoted much time and money attempting to export their genes. He was thwarted at every turn. Eventually, according to some reports, he received a very real threat from the Russian mafia, who told him if he were to export the genes there would be consequences. Tim was wise enough to desist.

An enthusiastic collector of World War II aircraft, affectionately known as 'warbirds', he had a number of Polikarpovs built from original plans found in World War II aircraft factories to join his several aircraft of the Battle of Britain period, including two Spitfires which he maintained in flying status. He also acquired a completely mangled Stuka but restoration was beyond even Tim's skills and it sat in a public hangar at Wanaka for years. For no particular reason, an engineer happened to check the guns – and found they were still loaded with live ammunition. Tim's skills as a pilot were impressive. One day, he helicoptered in two parties each of two scuba divers (his sons and friends) to the remote wilderness of Doubtful Sound, where the crayfish are stacked as on a supermarket shelf. As was his custom, he had an after-lunch sleep. On awakening at the helicopter alighting area, he found the weather had deteriorated and immediately scrambled to check on his charges. Two boys were safe on rocks, but the other pair had been washed out of the sound into large ocean swells in the open sea. Sir Tim flew out and let down above these two boys until each was able to reach up and grasp a skid. But the next ocean swell arrived immediately. To avoid the tail rotor hitting the water, Tim had to raise the helicopter at the rate the swell face approached, pause on the top then descend at the right rate into the trough following. Slowly, slowly, Tim rode up and down just above each swell and finally dragged the boys to safety.

This was magnificent flying. Such precision, presence of mind and determination, with the lives of his family and his own life at stake, was admirable.

Back at camp, the day's events were discussed. The first priority was established: 'Don't tell Mum' as if that smart lady wouldn't worm it out of them. Then Sir Tim made a comment that will ring true to every search and rescue pilot: 'It's amazing what you can do when you have to.'

Sir Tim's flying career came to an abrupt end in his last flying accident at Wanaka airport. Of the two Spitfires he owned and flew, one was a Mark XIV, fitted with an American Griffon engine. The other was a Mark XVI powered by a British Merlin. A propeller-driven aircraft on takeoff experiences a turning force until the tail is raised and a level attitude achieved. Spitfires, with powerful engines and rather small rudder surfaces, require immediate and full application of rudder when the throttle is advanced for takeoff to prevent a sharp swing. If uncorrected, this swing will soon have the aircraft swerving off the runway.

American engines rotate clockwise and the swing is to the left. British engines rotate counter-clockwise and the swing is to the right. An item of takeoff drill is to set the rudder trim fully left or right as appropriate – this quite powerful control exerts a force to counter the swing and if it isn't set properly, the pilot has to exert a large force on the rudder to stay straight on the runway. The problem was that Tim forgot which aircraft he was in and set the rudder trim the wrong way. He was now in trouble because the rudder trim would increase the tendency to swing. Only a significant force on the rudder by the pilot's foot would save the day. But the leg required to stop the swing was Tim's paralysed left leg.

On the throttle being opened, the aircraft accelerated rapidly but swung off the runway. Almost airborne, the Spitfire snagged the tailwheel on a fence alongside the runway and crashed. Sir Tim sustained a serious head injury which left him unconscious for almost three months. By sheer determination and with the constant care of his wife and family, he has recovered sufficiently to be able to lead a fairly normal life. Few men would have achieved this and the renaissance is a tribute to this great New Zealand aviator.

Warbirds Over Wanaka

One of Sir Tim's outstanding achievements was the establishment of the biennial Easter air show Warbirds Over Wanaka. Wanaka is a beautiful resort in Central Otago, north of Queenstown.

Planned by Sir Tim as a showcase for his collection of World War II aircraft, the first display in 1988 attracted 14,000 visitors. In addition to the planes, vintage vehicles and agricultural machinery were featured. The occasion was a financial success and became a biennial event. The 1990 show attracted double the number of paying spectators: 28,000.

In 1992, the star of the event was a Messerschmitt BF-109. Unfortunately, a member of the Roaring Forties team was killed in practice.

Subsequent shows have featured a Mitsubishi Zero replica and 11 types new to Wanaka (1994), the last display of the RNZAF Skyhawks (2000), four of Sir Tim's Polikarpovs in the flying display (2002) and guest of honour Buzz Aldrin (2004). In 2006 a phenomenal 111,000 spectators arrived. The first display of the Royal Australian Air Force F-18 Hornet fighters was in 2010. 2014 saw the last display of the RNZAF's UH-1 helicopters, old favourites which had performed at every show from 1988.

The 2018 show had an extensive list of participating aircraft. The Warbirds' Harvard aerobatic team was followed by NH-90 and Sea Sprite helicopters and the RNZAF Kiwi Blue parachute display team. The RNZAF contribution continued with Hercules and Boeing 757 aircraft, followed by Australian Hawk 127 high-performance jet trainers. French military forces in New Caledonia sent a CASA aeroplane and a YAK-52 team performed formation aerobatics. A spirited dogfight featured the ME109. Other aircraft were an Avro Anson, Spitfires, YAK-3s, a P51, an Avenger and a Catalina flying boat. A formation aerobatics team of Vampires performed for the crowd and L-39s followed. With skydivers, glider and model aircraft displays, a flypast of classic 1930s aircraft, a display of vintage Packard cars and a military re-enactment of a battle, the crowd were given their money's worth.

Sir Tim's brainchild, Warbirds Over Wanaka, is now operated by a charitable community trust whose mission is to preserve and promote New Zealand's World War II flying heritage. According to the WOW website, not only is it the largest warbirds air show in the Southern Hemisphere but it ranks among the world's best. It is an extraordinary achievement.

16

THE MIGHTY HUNTER, THE ORION

It was the end of an era when I came to bid goodbye to wandering the watery wastes in the venerable old Sunderland. The New Zealand Government had decided that the exercise of its Pacific Ocean responsibilities required modern equipment. The aircraft chosen was the Orion, at that time operated only by the United States Navy. Mine was one of five crews despatched to California for training.

The Lockheed Orion, the Mighty Hunter, has an interesting genealogy. It's a development of the civil airliner the Electra. With its four powerful turbine engines and large paddle-bladed propellers, the Electra was a giant step forward in airliner design for its time. However the development did not come without problems. Like any rotating body, a propeller acts as a gyroscope and exhibits rigidity (the maintenance of its plane of spin) unless forced into a change of direction. Because of their size, the four propellers displayed a lot of rigidity. The forces generated by this had to be accommodated by the wing structure as it bent and flexed in flight, as it was designed to do. The resistance of the propellers would send a ripple force back down the wing. By great misfortune, in certain flight conditions this recurring force could reach the harmonic frequency of the wing (that is, each disturbance would arrive just in time to reinforce the next). The wing would then begin to flap – and in extreme cases break off. Several airliners were lost, including an aircraft of the Federal Aviation Authority.

With this background, the designers of the military version of the Electra, the Orion, added plenty of strength to the wing structure. Consequently, the ailerons needed force and the flying characteristics were rather stiff. The aircraft rode hard in turbulence. However, there have been no known cases of wing failure in the Orion.

We arrived in California during the American build-up in the Vietnam War. The United States Navy was under extreme pressure to turn out qualified crews. It was even relaxing medical standards for air crew. Some of our pilots were shocked when they entered the crowded airspaces of California after the open skies of New Zealand and the Pacific. I blessed my experience in the Vampires, which helped me cope with the demanding environment. It wasn't uncommon to hear one instructor radio to another, 'Hey come on over to ____; there's only seven aircraft in the circuit.'

The navy people were hospitable and friendly, for example one of my flight engineers was given the keys to three cars which one of his new friends, off to Vietnam, was leaving behind.

Our initial training was at San Diego, my favourite part of the United States. We took the opportunity to cross the Mexican border and visit Tijuana, supposedly a tough town. But I found the people nice and polite. I rather like the Mexicans. There I saw my first bull fight and regret to say I found it thrilling, although the poor bull doesn't get much of a chance. In contrast, in Portuguese practice, the bull isn't killed and so learns and becomes more cunning with every appearance.

In New Zealand, guns are regarded as tools, kept to do a job. Americans seemed to have an unhealthy fascination with them. One navy officer I met had a gun in practically every drawer and another in his car glovebox. He once looked out the window of his room to see a criminal trying to break in to his vehicle. Reaching into the nearest drawer and extracting the pistol therein, he fired at the miscreant. Later the California Highway Patrolman taking his report made an observation: 'You made only one mistake, buddy – you missed.'

Players of bridge will appreciate this story. I made up a four with three Americans at Navy San Diego. We all played the Goran system, Goran being the reigning guru at that time, and we all got along fine. One player, an attorney doing his reserve navy training, told me he often played in high-pressure tournaments in his home city Chicago. On one occasion, he welcomed a gentleman to his table as players changed by saying he played the Goran system. The man said, 'I am Goran.'

Electronic equipment training completed, we moved from San Diego to Moffett Field at the bottom of San Francisco Bay – I should have said the southern end of San Francisco Bay! This enormous base of about 30,000 inhabitants was the site of some huge hangars built to house dirigibles (airships) of World War I vintage. Again, everyone was most friendly. We attended the Battle of Britain commemorative service at the beautiful Grace Cathedral in San Francisco. The local military services use this occasion to pay homage to the British forces so there were many colourful parties there. A group of Royal Air Force veterans was led by a pilot who'd actually flown in the battle. Now an artist (he looked it too), he carried a tattered ensign he had kept from the war days. The gleaming, chromed helmets and brilliant crimson scarves of the marines looked out of place. Ah well, as my mother-in-law used to say, we all have our little ways.

One of the US Navy commanders told me he'd been flying an Orion north of Cuba during the Cuban crisis. This was when the world came close to atomic war as America disputed Russia's right to position threatening weapons in America's back yard. The commander's orders were to photograph a particular warship in one of the Russian fleets cruising the Caribbean. The Orion is well set up for photography. Equipment includes a battery of powerful flares of sufficient strength to illuminate small targets, such as periscopes, in the night at sea. These flares are deployed by an explosive charge, which makes a loud bang when it goes off. When several flares are fired in quick sequence, the noise is similar to a rapid-fire cannon. The commander spotted his target vessel one night at sea and flew towards it photographing with flares. It was later discovered that the Russians, having never experienced rapid-firing flares before, thought they were being fired upon and raced to return fire to shoot the aircraft down. Fortunately, the American Orion finished its photography before the Russian sailors could bring weapons to bear. After the aircraft turned away, the sailors realised they hadn't been fired upon at all and allowed the aircraft to continue on its way unmolested.

The possible consequences of the shooting down of an American warplane by a Russian warship in the midst of this tense standoff are too awful to contemplate.

* * *

Our flight training on the Orion continued. We were using our own aircraft but of course the instructors were US Navy people. The aircraft flew positively and crisply, and it was a pleasure to get acquainted with this powerful machine. A large crew of electronic specialists, navigators, flight engineers and tactical coordinators crewed the cabin. It was a privilege to be in command of these professional men and we soon all became good friends.

On one training sortie on our magnificent aircraft, we were flying in cloud at 7000 feet over northern California. Our navy instructor, who was a bumptious sort, suddenly announced that we were descending to 500 feet, took control and began a dive. Positive we were over a coastal mountain range considerably higher than that, I took control from him to return to our previous altitude. The navigator, who'd been standing in the cockpit, ran back to his station to check position and returned even faster – we were indeed over the range. Well, this was a pretty situation, mutiny really. I stated that I was the senior officer aboard the New Zealand aircraft and we wouldn't descend until I knew it was safe to do so. Round about then we emerged from cloud and could see the high ground below. It was evident that we would have flown into the mountains concealed in cloud if we hadn't overridden our instructor. The American turned away and said nothing. I made sure we didn't fly with him again.

After completing the course, we flew home via Hawaii. Our overjoyed families were kept busy unwrapping the shopping we'd accumulated in three months' absence.

One morning, the squadron commander called me into his office and said, 'Tom, there's no money for training the next five crews in the States, as planned, so we'll have to train them here. I want you to cease being flight commander and become training officer. Your first course starts on Monday morning. Good luck.'

With no training equipment or facilities, that was a tough one. But I set to with all the section leaders and we coped. Several courses ran under my supervision. Since then, the RNZAF Orions have operated all over the world for more than 50 years. It's a matter of considerable personal satisfaction to me that they've done so without accident. The training foundations we laid were obviously sound. This record is all the more commendable when one considers that the Orion spends much of its time at low level over the ocean. Patrolling at 300 feet with one engine shut down to conserve fuel is commonplace in Orion operations.

During our early days with the Orions, we did have some close calls thanks to autopilot deficiencies. I was conducting a search off Fiordland for a missing vessel and flying at 500 feet when suddenly the aircraft pitched up quite violently – an autopilot fault had caused full up elevator to be applied.

A second incident, which occurred during a night-time exercise with a submarine, was far more serious. We were about 50 miles north-east of Sydney in a 'black nor'easter', a weather system familiar to Australians characterised by dark, low scudding clouds, rain and sometimes severe turbulence at low levels. At our patrol altitude of 300 feet, the turbulence became so bad that I decided to go to 500 feet to increase our safety margin. Just as well! About half an hour later, the autopilot suddenly pitched hard down. Frantically, I hauled back on the control column with all my might as we dived at the dark ocean below. Pulling a lot of G for such a large aircraft, we recovered from the dive in time, but with not much to spare. The navigator in the cabin said his altimeter had descended to 170 feet. That is, we'd plummeted (from 500 feet) 330 feet, even without considering lag in his instrument. Had we remained at 300 feet, we'd have been short 30 feet at least in our recovery.

The culprit proved to be a screw that should have been shellacked in place but wasn't. It had come loose and shorted out two terminals in the autopilot, which caused the application of full down elevator. After this incident, we made it mandatory for any pilot flying at low altitude to keep his finger on the front of the control column, on the autopilot disconnect button. Henceforth, any pitch down would instantly disconnect the autopilot.

Later in that exercise we generated six-column headlines in the *Sydney Morning Herald*. As we approached a submarine, the wily skipper hove to underneath a fishing boat. This vessel shouldn't have been present in the area promulgated for the exercise. Submarine and fishing boat engines share certain characteristics, which can confuse antisubmarine detection equipment, so hiding near fishing boats is a known tactic of submarines. Convinced our target was under the boat, I decided to winkle it out using a technique known as EER (explosive echo ranging). This entails dropping small explosive devices and analysing the echoes from targets. The fishing craft skipper was unlikely to be pleased but I reasoned that if he'd chosen to infringe the exercise area, he could take what was coming. So, at safe range, we dropped the little bombs and indeed secured a fix on the submarine located precisely where we'd anticipated. While this was highly satisfying to us, the fishing skipper was rather upset and contacted his shore base. Next morning 'NAVY BOMBS THE FLEET' screamed the *Sydney Morning Herald* across six columns. I chuckled. The Royal Australian Navy had copped the blame and there was no mention of a visiting aircraft.

Some upset Frenchmen

In Auckland, I was one day assigned the task of checking on certain warships. It was recognised that they might be at anchor in the New Hebrides, albeit they weren't French vessels.

At briefing in Auckland, I didn't ask to see our diplomatic clearance to overfly French territories. It was not then the custom to check on the operations officers. But unfortunately, in this case, operations had slipped up and forgotten to do the paperwork to advise our French neighbours of the intended visit and secure their approval. The flight progressed normally, allowing us the luxury of a low pass by the popular Ile des Pins spotting French beauties on the beach. We duly checked several anchorages suitable for naval use, descending to low level to obtain photographs of all vessels. Our photographer, standing in safety harness in an open door, would have been clearly visible to watchers on shore. What he was doing would have been obvious to them.

The Frenchmen were furious. They thought we were checking on their fleet to gather information on their atomic bomb. This was in the era of French atomic bomb tests in the Pacific and the French were extremely sensitive to any criticism. To appear out of the blue, without diplomatic clearance, and photograph them – what an affront!

Having carried out several other tasks in the area, I landed back at Whenuapai to see my commanding officer waiting for me on the tarmac as I taxied in. I was about to learn how rapidly diplomacy can be conducted. A protest had been sent from New Caledonia to Paris. From Paris, a stinging rebuke had been sent to Wellington. And a 'please explain' had already arrived in Auckland. I was able to assure my CO that nothing untoward had occurred on the flight. An apology for the oversight of not having diplomatic clearance was soon on its way to Paris – and was accepted by the French when they learned the vessels we were looking for weren't theirs. All was well.

This episode astonished me. I'd had no idea that diplomats could move so quickly and resolved to always check personally on diplomatic clearances in future.

During the several years I flew the Orion there were many and varied tasks. One was checking on all shipping in the vicinity of our country. With the range of our radar we could conduct our surveillance no matter what track the aircraft flew, so we often took the opportunity to take in the beautiful sights around our coast. Cruising up Milford Sound dining on a freshly cooked steak from the galley was easy duty. It didn't get much better than that.

Chicken!

Do you want to know what a Royal Albatross looks like through the windscreen of an Orion? Ask me! I've seen it. It looked lethal.

The mission was to photograph a cove on the remote Antipodes Island in the far south of the Pacific: it was a reconnaissance activity for the Navy. The University of Canterbury wished to land an adventurous research party on the island and looked to the Royal New Zealand Navy to transport them there and safely disembark them. The Navy identified the cove in question as their preferred landing spot and asked us to supply detailed information so they could assess the suitability of this cove for a safe landing. To do this, we had to descend to 100 feet so that the photographic detail could do their work. The Orion aircraft is equipped to allow safe descent to particularly low altitudes when required and crews are trained in the techniques.

Ours wasn't the Air Force's first attempt to get these photographs. Various aircraft had made the long journey to the Antipodes on several occasions but each sortie had been thwarted by the area's characteristic low cloud and mist. There was a firm desire to get the troublesome and expensive job done on our flight. The weather forecast was for strong winds, which would tend to disperse the impediments to visibility.

At the briefing we'd been asked to look out for sheep and goats; these animals had been released on the seldom-visited islands some years earlier to provide food should any shipwrecked mariners ever need it. When the island came into view we could see white dots everywhere and concluded that the sheep and goats had adapted magnificently. Closer examination proved the dots to be nesting albatrosses.

We were in luck, with no low cloud or mist. The reason for that was gale-force winds sweeping the area. It meant we were in for a hammering from turbulence created by the gales at the low altitudes required for our photography, the cove being on the leeward side of the island. I ordered the crew to secure everything and strap in tightly. For this task we flew with the main cabin door open to allow the photographer unrestricted views of the target area. Obviously, he'd be secured by safety harness, but as an additional precaution I ordered that he be fitted with a second harness. The photographer in the open doorway in his double harness was supported by two other crewmen, also wearing safety harness of course. Now thoroughly prepared, we lined up to run past the cove and I let down very carefully to 100 feet. We passed the cove (and secured what turned out to be excellent photographs). I was about to ease up in height in preparation for a second run. All of a sudden, dead in front of me, filling the windscreen, was a giant bird, a Royal Albatross.

Birds striking aircraft are an accepted hazard of aviation and aircraft windshields are strengthened to withstand collisions. The windscreens are complex structures, typically of five layers, with the centre layer made of high-impact resistant material heated to an optimum temperature. They're designed to remain intact when impacted by, say, two or three birds of large chicken size. They're not designed to withstand a bird as large as a Royal Albatross (which boasts an average wingspan of over 10 feet or 3 metres). I expected the albatross to smash through the windshield and kill me. At 100 feet, that would most likely cause the aircraft to crash seconds later.

Nearly always, birds about to be hit by an aircraft will dive to escape. But this bird, this clever albatross, managed to climb and pass over the top of us. This was nothing short of a miracle.

Shaken, I pulled up to 500 feet to decide what to do next only to find I had another problem. In the Orion galley, there's seating and safety harnesses for three people sitting side by side. On our pass by the cove, the centre person had vomited violently. Understandably, the person next to him, adjacent to the aisle, undid his harness to escape. Bad timing! A gust hit the aircraft and he flew horizontally across the cabin head first into the fuselage. He appeared to be unconscious with dilated eyes. Suddenly, we had a medical emergency, and it was hot foot for the Air Force medical facility in Christchurch.

The crusty old operations officer who met us there said, 'In all my years, I've never before today had to call an ambulance to an aircraft. Yet you're the second in the last half hour.'

Our injured crew member was kept under observation for a couple of days and recovered with nothing more than an almighty bruise on his skull.

So, what did the albatross in the windshield look like then? In real life, bad news, very bad news!

A few nights later I had a dream. In the dream, the albatross appeared once again, filling my windscreen. But this time, in the dream, as it swept past, the albatross's face cracked into a big grin and it said, 'Chicken!'

Some chicken!

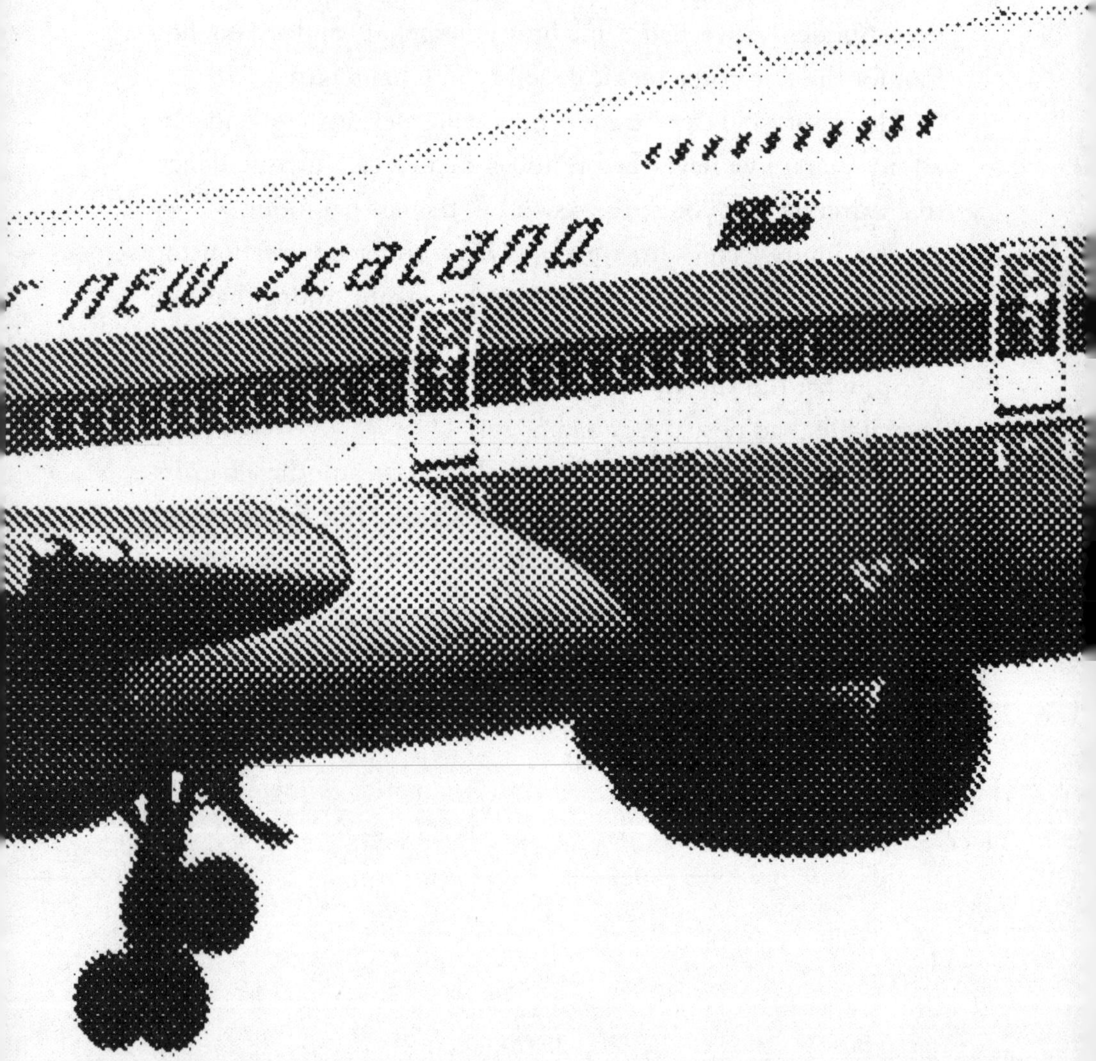
NEW ZEALAND

AIRLINE TALES

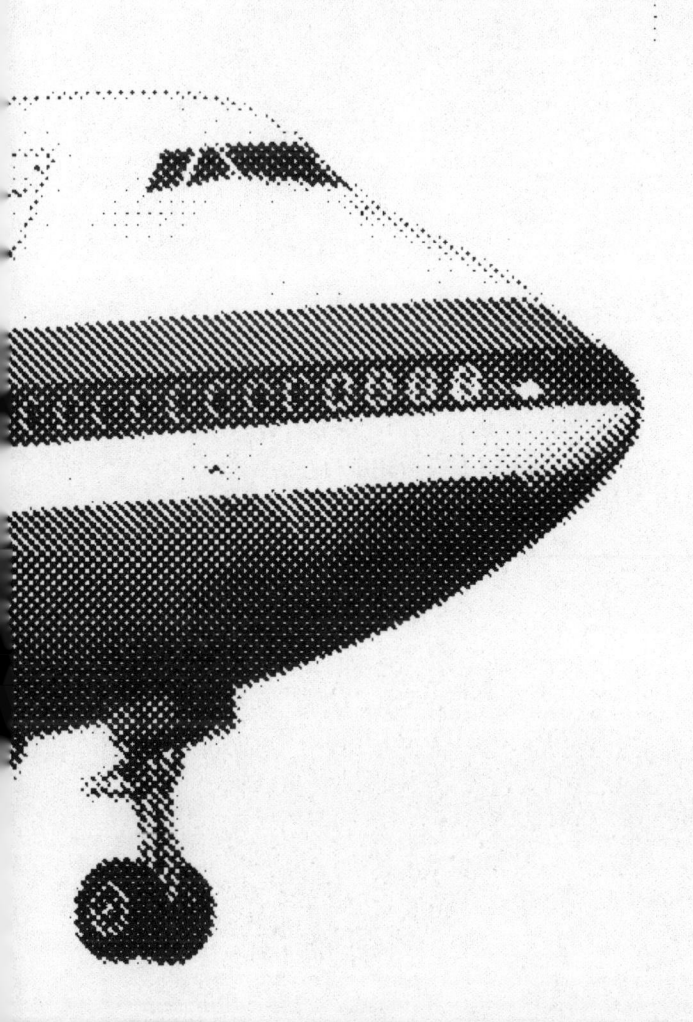

17

OFF TO THE AIRLINE WORLD

Happily, when it was time to hang up my sword and turn from military flying to the commercial sector, there was an opening with Air New Zealand. I joined their Electra fleet, and the conversion from Orion to Electra wasn't too demanding. Life was pretty sweet for airline pilots in those days, with good money and ordered life, so I was content to learn new ways. This included dropping to a co-pilot role, sometimes flying with my old pupils as captain, but I accepted the reduced status. Everyone was most understanding and I never found any difficulty in sitting in the right-hand seat.

Reflecting on my 20-year military flying career, I have to say I'd had rather more than my fair share of close-run things for a peacetime pilot. But perhaps risk is inherent to some degree in military flying. Sometimes it was necessary to persist in hazardous circumstances. By contrast, in civil flying, every effort is devoted to the elimination of any risk and so my subsequent career didn't feature so many headline-grabbing activities. But that isn't to say my experiences were without interest. My civil type ratings repertoire included Electras, DC8s, DC10s and B747s, all sturdy, hardworking craft. The

DC10 of course featured in several disasters but I found it superb, a real pilot's aircraft, well balanced and responsive.

The Lockheed Electra

One Friday in 1971, I completed my duties with the RNZAF. On the next Monday I started my conversion course with Air New Zealand on the Lockheed Electra. On most conversion courses, it's head down and concentrate 24 hours a day, so if family commitments can be minimised they should be. A popular saying among pilots is that if you have a flaw in your marriage, a conversion course will surely find it out. However, as June and I were firmly established, on our way to what turned out to be 50 years together, I was well supported. At that time, June, a dietitian, was engaged in community service where she was much loved by her generally elderly clients. She was a good manager – and needed to be with five sons. We'd bought our first house in Remuera, Auckland, and were now well settled down.

I was impressed with Air New Zealand's strict standards in the classroom and in the air. It's a well-run airline and the people are friendly. Once checked out on the Electra, I was employed mostly operating the Wellington–Sydney service. Wellington is well known for white knuckle arrivals in turbulent conditions in both northerly and southerly winds. Sydney airport can have equally testing conditions, with frequent violent thunderstorms over the field. Consequently, my colleagues and I had plenty of practice in control near the ground in turbulence. We became quite proficient in flying our Electras right onto the ground in these conditions to get safely down, much to the relief of passengers.

There were regular days off in both cities and when not scheduled for flying the next day we enjoyed each other's company at merry parties. On one occasion in Sydney, where the party extended into the small hours, a crew member noticed the local milkman delivering his wares to the hotel in a horse-drawn cart. The milkman was invited in to the party and stayed – and stayed. Two rascals went out, undid his horse from the shafts, led it into the hotel lift and took it all the way up to the roof. When eventually the milkman went out to resume his rounds, he was dismayed to find his steed looking down on him from a balcony high above. The police were summoned but couldn't understand how the animal had got to the roof. No one thought of using the lift to return Dobbin to terra firma and eventually a harness and hoist had to be rigged on the roof to lower him to the ground. Fortunately, no one thought to link the mystery to an earlier party; where the participants had had the sense to close down the festivities.

I've always enjoyed navigation in aviation and constantly pestered our planning staff to get me flights under the supervision of qualified instructors. In those days, before navigation satellites and associated equipment, the sextant was the aid most used in flights over the ocean. To cope, one had to become proficient in spherical trigonometry, star recognition and other arcane subjects, so navigation wasn't to be taken lightly. I'd managed to build up several dozen of the 200 hours experience needed to qualify for a licence while in the air force, on Sunderlands and Orions. The rate of calculations from astral navigation tables and the like needed to be fast, and a navigator who could manage 30-minute fixes was working hard. We were proud to perform at this rate and thought we were really on top of the situation. It's amusing now, with experience of modern satellite-based systems giving continuous position and wind changes, to think how little we knew of what actually went on between our precious 30-minute fixes.

I finally did qualify for a full flight navigator's licence by achieving my 200 hours and passing the flight test. To this day, I'm proud of the achievement. Navigation is an absorbing skill and making an accurate landfall is most satisfying. Before occupying the navigator's chair, I always used to fret a little if not within reach of the aircraft controls. But soon after beginning navigation duties, I found myself totally absorbed in the procedures and was completely relaxed provided I knew the pilots to be competent.

The navigation training process continued after I'd left the Electras and was flying DC8s. The faster speed of the latter called for more intense concentration. I recall one occasion in the middle of the night when I obtained a three-star fix in the vicinity of Tonga en route to Hawaii. A three-star fix plotted on the chart has three lines at about 60 degrees separation; the perfect fix would have all three intersecting at a point, one's actual position. But invariably there's a gap and the lines form a 'cocked hat' (the centre of which is taken as one's position). On this occasion, my three lines did intersect at a point. I laughingly said to the instructor I would like to know which one was wrong. At my debriefing after the flight, he said in fact all my sights were accurate and that I'd established our exact position. He'd checked my position by radar fixes on nearby islands. Thereafter, he referred to a single-point intersection of a three-star fix as an 'Enright fix'.

On the Electra fleet, we had a navigator who'd typically issue perplexing directions: 'Change course ten degrees left', followed five minutes later by 'ten degrees right', then again 'Five degrees left/five degrees right'. His nickname was 'Zig Zag'. On a flight from Brisbane terminating at Wellington at six on a Sunday morning, Zig Zag had a bad day. On top of the usual left, right, left, he miscalculated the westerly wind pushing us along, it was far stronger than he thought; so we flew on, over total cloud cover, for several minutes after we should have started our descent. In a break in the cloud, I spotted an island in Cook Strait, passing abeam. At that position, we should have been descending through about 15,000 feet. I called out a warning to Zig Zag and commenced a descent at fast speed without power. But we were way too high, and there was no way we were going to slow up enough to land at Wellington from that approach. We were doing about 300 knots.

The cloud having disappeared now, it was a perfect, still morning in the dawn light and Wellington, quite spectacular always, looked stunning. As there was no other traffic about at that early hour, we decided to conceal our mistake by asking permission from air traffic control to fly a harbour circuit to show our passengers the view.

Permission was granted and round the harbour we went, pointing out the features to our enthralled passengers. After a turn downwind it was on to finals and we made our landing – all the while with the throttles completely closed. In this way we managed to dispose of the surplus height, but I doubt the controller was fooled.

Douglas DC8

After about 18 months of trans-Tasman and South Pacific flying in the Electra, my number came up to transfer to the four-engine jet, the Douglas DC8. This doughty old warhorse had many successful years' service in Air New Zealand and operated in the Pacific to the west coast of the United States and to Hong Kong. It was a sturdy machine and pleasant to fly.

With a type rating and my newfound navigator's licence, I crewed many interesting and satisfying DC8 flights. These included flights into Aitutaki in the Cook Islands. When the airline commenced flights there with our DC8s no other airlines were operating in competition to this destination. Air New Zealand got away with scheduling flights to land about 2 am Cook Island time without losing passengers.

The Cook Islands way of life was comparatively simple then and in particular didn't include any Kentucky Fried Chicken restaurants, the products of which were much prized by the islanders. Every returning local confidently expected that his whole family, numerous acquaintances and old Uncle Tom Cobley and all would turn out in the small hours to witness the excitement of our weekly arrival. But the welcoming party would expect their KFC treat. So, the returnee absolutely had to have enough Kentucky Fried Chicken boxes to satisfy everyone. Thus, in passing through the aircraft cabin, one saw pile after pile of Kentucky Frieds clutched in passengers' laps.

Once the returned loved one had cleared customs and immigration, the boxes would be distributed and the whole island would sit down by the side of the road munching contentedly. There seemed to be miles of happy islanders gnawing on chicken bones on both roads servicing the airport. The schedule came to be known as 'The Kentucky Fried Special'. It would take days to later get the smell of Kentucky Fried out of the aircraft.

DC8 freighter aircraft of other airlines called frequently at Auckland to uplift loads not normally carried on passenger aircraft. One day, to our surprise, an Irish DC8 freighter arrived in Auckland. It was to convey the first racehorses to be flown across the Tasman to Australia. Racehorses are valuable cargo and the champions are often accompanied by an attendant. They tend to develop dangerous throat infections in the very dry air at jet aircraft cruise levels. Racing stallions can be pretty highly strung. They're carried in the front of aircraft and mares are loaded at the rear (aircraft ventilating air generally flows front to rear). The Irish captain satisfied himself as to the aircraft loading and set off for Sydney.

En route, one of the stallions went berserk and started kicking and lashing out with its hind feet, causing damage to the pressurised fuselage and danger to the attendants. The captain ordered that the animal be destroyed. As there was little experience in New Zealand at this stage in carrying large animals, no one had thought to load a humane killing device. The only thing available to subdue the wildly threshing beast was the aircraft fire axe. It was so horrible that persons present will never be able to forget the dreadful sight. After this incident, regulations were issued requiring all aircraft carrying racehorses to be equipped with humane equipment to deal with an out-of-control animal.

On another occasion, a lion being transported across the Tasman died during a flight. It was reported as having drowned in its own urine in the special cage designed to hold animal discharges. It was never established how the animal had drowned and it seems likely that it had collapsed into the urine due to some unknown cause. Subsequently, the New Zealand SPCA pointed out that the captain of an aircraft is personally liable for the welfare of any animal on board. From then on, captains were required to personally check on the loading arrangements of large animals.

We regularly flew into Kai Tak airfield at Hong Kong. The approach and landing required careful preparation and attention. The official international airport for the colony of Hong Kong from 1925 to 1998, this airfield was designed in the days of DC3s and similar smaller and slower airliners. If the designers had been able to foresee their product being used by giant jet aircraft like the DC8 and Boeing 747, I feel sure they would have been mightily surprised. The airport was in the narrow channel between the mainland and Hong Kong Island

and was hemmed in by sharply rising hills and huge, towering skyscrapers.

The original facilities were expanded many times. During World War II, when the Japanese controlled the territory, two runways were built, using prisoner-of-war labour. For this construction, the wall of the historic Kowloon Walled City was demolished for materials.

For the most commonly used runway, 13, landing to the south-east, there's no room for an Instrument Landing System (ILS), which feeds accurate tracking guidance and vertical approach profile to the landing pilot. The required clear airspace profiles are penetrated by the surrounding high hills. Instead, a modified ILS, an IGS (Instrument Guidance System) is used. The aircraft makes the initial approach to land to the south-east over the sea down a channel bordered by high ground on either side, this track being 40 degrees off the runway heading. At 650 feet, the pilot *must* be in contact with a series of powerful flashing lights leading round the 40-degree turn onto the runway. Incidentally, this approach system is why no flashing lights were permitted in the city – so that pilots wouldn't become confused. In restricted visibility, it wasn't possible to see the runway at this point but what drew the attention were the towering skyscrapers rising up on the left-hand side, on the hills near the approach. They were far above the aircraft, and close. The consequences of an accident here would have been horrendous.

Cabin crew told me that, frequently, when unsuspecting passengers noticed the skyscrapers flashing by with no airport in sight, some panicked and thought their last days had come. The so-called 'Hong Kong heart attack approach' enjoyed notoriety with crew and travellers alike.

In strong crosswind conditions, some tricky aircraft handling was needed. It was always satisfying to put the aircraft smoothly onto the runway at such times.

Kai Tak ceased airport operations in 1998 but before leaving the subject I cannot resist describing a funny cartoon related to the approach. First, bear in mind that laundry is often hung out on long poles to dry on tier after tier of the balconies of skyscrapers in Hong Kong. The cartoon depicts a supercilious instructor captain in the right seat addressing the pilot under check, on whose wing-tip several strings of laundry have been caught up and dragged along. 'A little more clearance on finals please, laundry claims are up this month.'

McDonnell Douglas DC10

As the commercial aviation market developed, so did the need for larger and more efficient airliners. When Air New Zealand bought the Douglas DC10, I transferred. The DC10, like similar aircraft of its generation, introduced the spacious wide-bodied fuselage and changed the concept of passenger flying. But there were accidents early in its history and the DC10 acquired a reputation as an unsafe, or at least unlucky, aircraft. Any bad news about a DC10 was guaranteed newspaper headlines – a case of give a dog a bad name. In reality, over its active passenger-flying career between 1972 (when first delivered to US airlines) and 2014 (when it ceased flying passenger services, although some freighters continued), the DC10 proved to have a reliable record after the initial tragedies.

I enjoyed flying this aircraft, with its unencumbered views from the wide cockpit. The superb quality of the flight instruments enabled very precise flying – setting the pitch attitude to a tolerance of one degree, for example, was easy. The computerised navigation systems were bliss to someone raised on sextants and computation tables. No longer was a professional navigator required in the crew; instead there were two pilots and a flight engineer. The quiet cockpit engendered good communication, enabling each of the three crew members to monitor each other well to achieve a high degree of safety.

It's important in the cockpit of multi-engined aircraft that when an irregularity occurs, a flurry of hands without supervision is avoided. Each of a crew member's actions should be supervised by another member. Otherwise there may be selection and operation of the wrong controls. An example of how this philosophy is applied in practice is the drill for an engine fire. This calls for the flight engineer to close the fuel cock of the burning engine. The flight engineer doesn't reach for the operating lever and close it but simply places his hand on it and says, 'Fuel shutoff number three.' The pilot flying continues to give his whole attention to achieving the right flypath and going in the right direction. The pilot not flying ensures the flight engineer has his hand on the correct control and says, 'Check number three.' Only then does the flight engineer operate the control. In this way, the situation of having one engine failed and a second inadvertently shut down is avoided. For years I flew the DC10 without incident, except for a surprising tussle with turbulence right at touchdown at Sydney airport. I was landing in a black nor'easter and turbulence was to be expected. As always (after my Sunderland arrival at Funafuti) I was ready for the unexpected. Only 50 feet above the runway, we were hit by a sizeable gust from the left side. Reacting swiftly, I applied full aileron to bring back to level the starboard wing, which was rolling rapidly to the right. But it wasn't enough; the right wing continued down and was in danger of touching the runway. Rapidly accelerating with full power for a go-around, I had to use the secondary effect of rudder by booting in full left rudder to control the roll and slowly to raise the wing. The adrenaline was pumping! It was unusual to have to take such coarse action so close to the ground. It's interesting to note that I wasn't caught out unawares, having appreciated the likelihood of turbulence in the conditions. It's the wise pilot who constantly looks ahead and anticipates possible problems; he's the one who'll be prepared for trouble.

A unique minor accident occurred soon after Air New Zealand started flying the DC10. It was the first airline to operate the DC10, with its third engine mounted high in the tail, into Sydney airport. The Australian authorities were concerned that, with the unusual elevation of the engine high above the airport fences and perimeter structures, the exhaust with full power set might cause blast to affect cars on a motorway adjacent to one runway. A test was arranged where all three engines were to be run up to full power with the aircraft positioned stationary at takeoff point. The airport monitoring team were set up with their instruments on the roadway. When the team was satisfied with the readings, the brakes were to be released and the aircraft to continue at full power for 200 yards down the runway before reducing power, abandoning the takeoff run and returning to the terminal building.

The crew assigned to the test boarded the aircraft and found the cabin cleaning crew busily going about their work. Without thinking about it too much, the captain ordered the cleaning crew to leave immediately. They did, but left behind, untethered, three large carts which contained the hundreds of cutlery sets needed for the next flight. All went well with the test: the aircraft was positioned correctly and the three engines ran at full power. With the ground monitors satisfied, the captain released the brakes whilst maintaining full power. As the aircraft hadn't been refuelled, it was very light, and the acceleration was spectacular. In the unoccupied cabin, the three cleaners' carts took off towards the back of the cabin – more correctly, the cabin accelerated round them – and reached quite some speed down the aisles before one of them veered off and collided with seats. As well as the seats being demolished, a great spray of knives, forks and spoons hurtled down to the back of the cabin like a cloud of javelins and embedded themselves in the trim of the rear walls and galley. The damage was considerable – and expensive.

After deliberation, the company blamed the operations manager for not issuing sufficient instructions to all concerned. Air crew chortled with delight – the operations manager was usually the one handing out the sackcloth and ashes to them.

There was at least one other instance of crews chortling at the operations manager. This was in the early days of television in New Zealand, when TV sets were expensive and every overseas traveller who could do so brought back a TV into the country. The operations manager arranged a flight for himself to Fiji and picked up a handsome TV. Carefully, he carried it back to the cabin and strapped it into a safe place, not allowing the baggage handlers or anyone else to touch the precious thing. At Auckland again, only he carried the set through customs and out to his car. He had straps ready and tied the set securely to his roof rack. Unfortunately, driving home he forgot about it and on arrival went straight into his garage. Too late, he heard the awful crash as the low roof demolished the beautiful new addition to the household.

***

An unusual feature of the fuselage design caused tragic consequences. The spacious cargo hold in the DC10 is extended by having the large cargo door outward opening rather than the usual inward-opening plug-type door. This design allows for cargo to occupy the space which a plug-type door would need inside the cargo hold to open. Early on in the DC10's airline flying, a door opened in flight, causing an explosive decompression. Secondary damage was caused by the collapse of flooring, which cut through flight control hydraulic pipes. The American crew recovered the situation with tremendous skill and landed safely, despite having only limited control movement and being deprived of one aileron. The design of the locking system came under intense scrutiny and it was found that the aircraft could be despatched with the locking system indicators showing the locks fully home when they were only partially engaged. Oddly, no Federal Aviation Authority (FAA) order to fix the fault was issued.

A second explosive decompression from the same cause later occurred on a Turkish airliner that hadn't had the lock system modified. The consequences were horrifying: the damage caused the aircraft to crash, with the loss of 365 lives. Bolting the stable door after the horse had gone, the authorities now made sure all crews throughout the world were fully instructed on the cargo door system. Each door was modified so that positive locking of each of the latches could be assured from the external inspection prior to takeoff. Everyone paid strict attention to this check thereafter.

This was a rare case of the American FAA failing to take timely remedial action after a serious design fault had been discovered in an aircraft.

1979 was annus horribilis for the DC10. At Chicago airport, the rear bolt securing a wing engine to its pylon, or engine mount, failed during takeoff. The engine was under full power and it rotated about the fulcrum of the front pylon bolt, causing extensive damage to the wing structure. The crew were unable to control the plane and it crashed about a minute later, with heavy loss of life.

The inquiry revealed an astonishing story. During maintenance, the engine and pylon had to be detached, inspected and remounted. The procedure recommended by the aircraft designers was a lengthy one, and the servicing crew decided to take a shortcut and attach the engine to its pylon whilst the pylon was mounted on the wing. (This procedure infringed FA requirements.) Unwisely they used a forklift truck to lift the engine, and then allowed the fork lift truck to run out of fuel when the rear, but not the front, engine securing bolt was in place. As the forklift engine stopped, the heavy load dropped until restrained by the engine's rear holding bolt. Very heavy shearing force must have been exerted on the bolt. Unforgivably, the maintenance crew didn't report the mishap or arrange to have the bolt inspected. It was this weakened bolt that failed in the takeoff at Chicago. Such carelessness in aircraft servicing, which cost many lives, is extremely rare in aviation. The omission to report the damage was an almost unheard of dereliction of duty.

Then rose up the spectre that will forever haunt Air New Zealand. I arrived home from night flying at about 11 pm to find June crouched over the television. I saw at once something was seriously wrong. An Air New Zealand DC10 overflying the wastes of Antarctica was declared overdue, then missing. June wept when the captain, Jim Collins, was identified as we both knew and liked him. Jim and I had become friends at Ohakea in my Vampire days. He disclosed that his father had been too busy in business to have time to spend with him. Jim was determined this wouldn't happen in his family and spent as much time as possible with his four children when in Auckland. Premonition?

Next morning, the awful news was announced – wreckage had been sighted on the slopes of Mt Erebus. All aboard had obviously perished. An expedition to recover the bodies and search the wreckage for clues as to the cause of the disaster was organised with commendable speed.

The facts, and rumours, began to filter out. The captain of the previous flight to Antarctica, a widely respected pilot, had reported that the co-ordinates of a position, a waypoint, were incorrect. The error was corrected but regrettably Captain Collins and his crew weren't informed. The crew, acting on incorrect navigational information, had descended into what they believed to be a safe valley clear of obstructions. Instead they steered straight into Mt Erebus, a prominent active volcano. Those of us with experience of flying in low visibility in mountainous areas surmised that the crew failed to sight the mountain ahead due to a condition called whiteout. Whiteout occurs when there is white, snow-covered terrain ahead, the atmosphere is misty, the horizon isn't discernible and there is no prominent feature such as a jumble of black rocks. Because of lack of stimulus in the white world ahead, the human eye tends to focus just outside the cockpit and obstructions are not seen.

The initial inquiry accepted the view of the Civil Aviation officer responsible for the investigation of aircraft accidents that the cause of the accident was pilot error.

Airline pilots generally have to accept that with the high pay comes the likelihood that blame for accidents will be laid on them. Years may pass before painstaking inquiry lays the blame elsewhere. But in Captain Collins's case, there was a public outcry against the initial verdict. Prime Minister Muldoon decided to institute a more formal investigation. Mr Justice Mahon was appointed to preside over the new inquiry.

The conclusions of this investigation created much interest throughout the world, especially Justice Mahon's allegation that he'd been forced to listen to an 'orchestrated litany of lies' from Air New Zealand. He cleared the crew of responsibility for the accident.

Not being professionally qualified in flight safety matters, I don't feel justified in expressing opinions on the judgments.

But I am prepared to quote a very experienced old pilot that when there is an accident involving a navigation error, the crew cannot escape some measure of responsibility. In the circumstances of this disaster that measure must be low, particularly because the crew had been despatched into the snowy wastes without training in the effects of whiteout.

Among those lost on this flight was well-known New Zealand mountaineer Peter Mulgrew, who'd been engaged to give commentary on the terrain to the passengers. He was a longtime friend of Sir Edmund Hillary and the two had shared several alpine expeditions.

I met Sir Edmund and he told me Peter was highly regarded by London businessmen. Sir Edmund shared with me an anecdote about one expedition for which the two were seeking financial contributions in London. *The Times* newspaper of London had offered ten thousand pounds. Ed and Peter met a *Times* representative in a Fleet Street restaurant to sign the agreement accepting the gift and, in the usual way that English businessmen conduct their business, the lunch began with a large globule of whisky. After that, Ed was happy to sign anything but Peter kept his head and asserted that it was unfair that *The Times* was to be the sole beneficiary for any news items which could be sold. He asked that the expedition receive half the income generated by the stories after the initial gift had been fully repaid. After some spluttering the English newspaperman agreed. The story spread that Peter could hold his own whisky for whisky and still remain an astute negotiator. In London he was one of the boys.

***

In the years that followed the Erebus accident, I had many superb flights in the DC10. It was a wonderful aeroplane to fly. The controls were beautifully balanced and responsive to a light touch on the control column, so it was easy to fly really accurate flight patterns. There was, however, one disconcerting feature.

The electrical qualities of the pilot's windscreens attracted massive electrical charges from the aircraft's passage through moist air. A blue ball of shimmering energy about 30 centimetres in diameter, probably of several million volts, would form on the outside of the windscreen and remain there for minutes at a time. This is a startling thing to have about a metre in front of your nose. It wasn't of concern, however. All metal parts of an aircraft structure are 'bonded' (electrically connected) so that sparks cannot jump from one metal piece to another if the aircraft has a lightning strike. Most lightning strikes are air to air, and strikes on aircraft occur regularly. The bonding precaution invariably absorbs the massive voltages accompanying them without damage other than a few pinholes in the fuselage. But that ball of fire surely was attention-getting.

After many years of excellent service from its DC10s, Air New Zealand decided to leave Douglas and join the Boeing stable. I bade goodbye to the DC10 sadly; it was such a magnificent aircraft to fly.

Boeing B747

Stepping out of a DC10 into a 747 was like leaving a computerised sports car and getting into a brand new truck. But it was some truck! This was a good, tough, hardy aircraft.

The Boeing 747 was manufactured at Everett Field in Washington State, and that's also where conversion courses were conducted. I was struck by the scale of all things Boeing; the aircraft engineering establishment was massive, as were the aircraft manufacturing facilities. There were many admirable features. Large buildings and super-hangars housed fuselages and wing structures in various stages of construction. People, the engineers supervising the building of these huge machines, were notable for their absence. Many engineering processes were programmed into machinery that worked automatically or were carried out by robots. When I peeped into one huge hangar, where the massive wings were built, machines were clicking away at several of the wings being built simultaneously, with hardly a person in sight. The usual complement of staff, I was told, was five.

Washington State is spectacular, with active volcanoes and alpine regions. In 1980 the most disastrous volcanic eruption in United States history occurred on Mt St Helens. An ash plume rose 25 kilometres high; on the ground, snow, ice and entire glaciers melted, forming several large lahars (volcanic mudslides). Fifty-seven people died.

The fertile soils of the adjacent river valleys running up to the Canadian border are farmed intensively, especially for vegetable crops. The farmers have a fine routine, working hard for six months until all the crops are harvested and despatched to the markets, when they shut up shop. As the winter snows settle, off they go to travel the world for the next few months.

The accommodation provided for the B747 conversion course was pleasantly situated in wooded suburbs adjacent to Possession Sound. Because our families had remained behind in New Zealand, we were spared distractions except for occasional visitors and were able to concentrate on the excellent instruction. Boeing staff were accustomed to dealing with people from all the world's airlines.

By this time, the aviation industry had developed flight simulators to a high standard. The atmosphere inside the simulator cockpit was so true to life that you could forget you were still on the ground. Visual representations of flight situations and airports and their approaches were incredibly realistic. Now, all the training was completed in the simulators before one flew the actual aircraft. This saved huge amounts of time and money as compared to using aircraft. It allowed emergency situations to be experienced and dealt with by students without incurring risks to anyone.

Anywhere in the world, getting sufficient clear airspace for flying training at an airfield is a problem. Boeing maintained several fields in isolated areas in the hinterland of Washington State where circuits and landings could be practised without interruptions from arriving and departing traffic. On one field, a flight engineer was making his way through rather overgrown grass as he carried out his pre-flight inspection. 'Hey!' called out one of the Boeing trainers. 'Don't you know this is rattlesnake country?'

For fun, I told the Boeing representatives that I wanted to lay a claim for fame in aviation: I reckoned I was the last of the Flying Teamsters and the first of them who'd made B747 command. They said they didn't know of any other pilot fitting the description and they'd recognise my claim!

During the time of our conversion course Boeing made its first delivery of a B747 to the famed Pan American airline, the 'world's most experienced airline'. Well, this delivery was an experience I'm sure Pan Am would rather forget. A massive publicity effort accompanied the first commercial flight of their new B747. But on the very morning of the much-heralded flight, another aircraft in Pan Am colours was being delivered to an airport by a Boeing test pilot. He managed to undershoot on his approach and collided with the poles supporting the approach lighting system. The aircraft came to rest in a position that made it look like a praying mantis, with the nose landing gear extended and unharmed but the main gears collapsed. This made wonderful copy and was featured in all the world's newspapers, entirely displacing the glamour reports of a seamless introduction of the glamorous B747 to glamorous Pan Am. Rumours abounded that this caused tremendous bitterness between Pan Am and Boeing.

Air New Zealand had extended services to London and Europe by the time we'd returned from our American training. I welcomed having so many more places of interest to explore during my days off on the new routes. Some people tend to stick around their hotels on layovers but I've always planned ahead and made good use of the travel opportunities available. My sister Beth was living in Haltwhistle, Northumberland, and so during London layovers I was a frequent customer of the long-range bus services to the north, available at very reasonable cost in the United Kingdom.

Haltwhistle is close by Hadrian's Wall, the structure built to keep the wild Scots out of northern England in Roman emperor Hadrian's time. The rather clannish people of this border (between England and Scotland) were suspicious of strangers. Perhaps the locals regarded it as a wonder that my sister had come to marry and settle among them: she became an icon to her community. I also was accepted. A friend, who operated a thriving business marking roads, took me golfing. On one fairway he pointed out the Lepers Tree. In the previous century, the villagers left food at the base of this tree for the lepers, who were required to live in isolation from their people. This was fascinating, but I still managed to win several florins from my genial host.

Tall tales and true were in plentiful supply. The Scots, I learned, were a cheeky bunch to climb the wall and nick the backsides of the English farmers' cows, drawing sufficient blood to make their favourite dish, the haggis.

I was lucky enough to be taken to hostelries known only to Haltwhistle folk. One establishment, which served the most excellent fare, occupied a stable once attached to a castle. The ringbolts (for tethering horses) remained in the walls. A ghost, a French lady in white, was alleged to haunt the premises. The stories goes that she was brought back with a considerable dowry by one Thomas on his return from a crusade against the infidels of the Middle East. After – one hopes – a decent interval, Thomas demanded the lady hand over her dowry or he'd desert her for the fleshpots of London. She didn't; he did.

Apparently Hadrian's Wall was a fortified zone and the many castles were interconnected by tunnels sufficiently wide for livestock to be driven though them. When her castle was besieged by the wild Scots, our white lady could escape with not only her life and treasures but also her livestock. It was widely believed that she secreted her dowry in one such tunnel, though it was never discovered – or at least not by anyone prepared to talk.

One of my favourite haunts in that part of England was Durham Castle and Cathedral, near Newcastle on Tyne. The Cathedral Church of Christ, Blessed Mary the Virgin and St Cuthbert of Durham (Durham Cathedral to you) has been a bishopric since 995. Construction of the present cathedral was started in 1093. Skilled Norman architects incorporated historic improvements in design in this beautiful building. For the first time, flying buttresses were used, enabling taller buildings and wider wall spaces and bigger windows. St Cuthbert had died in the area and his remains were preserved and revered by local folk and pilgrims. But the community was harried by raiding Viking parties, and for safety the relics were carried thither and yon. Once completed, the cathedral provided a permanent resting place for the sacred remains.

I met a priest in London who was conducting a large party of American tourists and recommended that he include

Durham in his future itinerary. He said one of his order's most precious possessions was a relic, thought to be a knuckle of St Cuthbert. It seems that as the holy one's remains were carted hither and thither in those ancient times a profitable trade arose pilfering and selling pieces such as that knuckle. Would it be cynical to suppose that some animal substitutes might have found their way into the market? I wouldn't have dared suggest this to the priest.

I thoroughly enjoyed all my peregrinations, courtesy of Air New Zealand opening up its destinations.

Back in Auckland, my number finally came to the top of the seniority list and my long stint in the co-pilot's seat was over. After numerous simulator checks, route checks and examinations, I was sent off on my first flight as pilot in command of a 747. The duty was to fly to Tahiti and return the next day to Auckland. It resulted in a photograph of me splashed across the front page of the *Auckland Herald*.

Tahiti has always been, and always will be, a glamour stop on the airline circuit. As a people, the Tahitians are graceful with some astonishing traits. The men are strong and big, and the locals claim the *gendarmerie* (police) are issued with two bullets: one for the Tahitian and one for themselves if they miss. Tourists are mesmerised by the women's performance of the hula hula dance, when their hips are swivelled with astonishing speed. The people seem to be psychic. On several occasions, I've seen a crowd of men and women suddenly and simultaneously begin frenzied dancing with no apparent signal given to begin. Once when I was with a group dining in a hotel, we saw three men set upon a fourth at their table. After a short time, again with no apparent signal, all the men in the room started fighting one another. With the utmost speed, we tiptoed off and out of harm's way Those big guys could hit hard and fast – I resolved never to get into an argument with a Tahitian.

In ancient times, there was a practice of burying pairs of very old stone figurines. These relics may be unearthed. Finders are well advised to seek the advice of the local medicine man as to whether they are 'wet' or 'dry'. If dry, no problems. But if wet, failure to pay for an exorcism ceremony may have bad consequences. Locals like to tell a tale of many years ago to illustrate the risks of not acknowledging the power of these figurines. Apparently, a pair was discovered in the fabled island of Bora Bora. They were wet, but no one bothered to ask for a cleansing ceremony. A small French naval vessel was used to transport the pair to Papeete, where a pedestal had been prepared so they could be exhibited in the city gardens. After the work party had mounted the figurines it drove out of the gardens. At the gate there was an accident, with fatalities. Some weeks later, the transportation vessel was lost at sea. This strange and interesting tale was repeated to me several times by different people, so there seemed to be some substance to it. According to the locals the wet figurines carry a curse from the old people which will fall on anyone disturbing them unless there is a cleansing ceremony. When one considers the widespread belief in the power of objects such as holy relics to tap into good forces, perhaps it is also possible that objects can be vested with power to tap into malign forces.

On behalf of the New Zealand Airline Pilots' sports club, I used to supervise two Laser Light sailing boats which were kept in Tahiti with a small catamaran. Basically, flight deck and cabin crew members would book the use of the pleasure craft through me, and I also took them out frequently. Sailing in the clear blue waters inside the reef in the pleasant temperatures of the tropics was a delight

Our sojourns in Tahiti were very enjoyable. Generous expense allowances facilitated travel to the beautiful volcanic island of Moorea, a few minutes' flight from the airport at

Papeete, the capital. The Tahitians were invariably polite and friendly. So my crew and I were shocked to have our exit blocked by industrial action on our attempted return flight to New Zealand.

Industrial disputes in Tahiti are pursued vigorously. In this case the unions decided to prevent entry to and egress from the hotels in support of their claims for more money. In vain, I pleaded with the pickets at our hotel that we had nothing to do with their dispute and prevention of our flight was a pretty extreme measure. But, this was Tahiti. Nothing doing. I phoned our local manager and we decided to sit tight. The media in New Zealand and elsewhere must have had good antennae because they picked up on the situation quickly. This was pure catnip – air crew captured in this exotic location! Shades of the mutiny against Captain Bligh in the *Bounty*. Many people were affected including the families and friends of our passengers waiting in Auckland. Many of the passengers had departed from Los Angeles, so Californian news outlets were also reporting the story.

At the hotel I was told that a person who disliked the unions had brought his large motorboat alongside the hotel jetty, which was hidden from the area occupied by the strikers. I negotiated with this gentleman and reached agreement that he would convey me and my crew to the city wharves, from where we would take taxis to the airport. Quietly, I had the crew move in small groups to the craft, aware that our actions were now under the scrutiny of the strikers, who seemed to be unfazed at what we were doing. But just as the crew embarkation was complete, some of our intending passengers staying at that hotel twigged to what was going on and, grabbing their bags, ran down towards us. This was too much for the strikers, who rushed the launch, yelling and waving their arms about. I was aghast when their leader produced a flare pistol and threatened to fire a burning lump of phosphorus through the hull of the boat. The captain responded by producing a rifle, which he aimed at the striker. This was serious! I had to do something quickly before the situation became really ugly. I therefore shouted to the strikers that we were leaving the boat and returning to the hotel. Which we did. To my immense relief, the fracas died away as we straggled back to our quarters.

After this, I had a further discussion with the strikers' leader and we agreed things had got out of hand and the standoff should end. We were permitted to pass through the cordon and travel to the airport. The flight to Auckland was free of incident, but there was quite a media scrum waiting at Auckland airport. I tried to downplay the event, but some reporters managed to create dramatic stories. Eventually, I escaped by pleading that it had been a long day but as I departed was photographed leaving the terminal building. Next morning, my wife was astonished to open our copy of the *New Zealand Herald* to find my image splashed right across the front page, with the story of the dramatic flight.

Never again, thank goodness, did I excite media attention in flying B747s.

Years passed, hours accumulated in my flying logbook, and I gained more and more experience.

I enjoyed every flight I made in this magnificent steed from the Boeing stable. It was always satisfying to be able to maintain a calm atmosphere in which the passengers remained relaxed and able to enjoy their flights with us. Air New Zealand crews are efficient and confident, so my task was pretty easy. But some flights could be demanding.

Arrivals at Christchurch often needed careful handling. The B747 had to land on the main north–south runway as there were obstructions close to the shorter north–west runway. Christchurch is frequently subjected to strong and blustery north-west winds. So, there was often a large amount of drift (sideways movement) in the approach, and this always had to be corrected prior to touchdown.

People looking for a bite often suggested we pilots had it pretty easy, what with automatic landings and the like, with the equipment performing all the manoeuvres for us. It's instructive to learn that the crosswind limit for automatic landings is 5 knots, whereas the human pilot is expected to cope with 30 knots. When the going gets tough, pilot skills are required. At Christchurch the crosswind at 100 feet can be 40 to 45 knots but it invariably slackens off to below 30 by touchdown. After one landing, a person occupying the jump seat (behind the captain's seat) told me that all he could see through the windscreen at 100 feet were the pine trees at the side of the approach path.

The technique for correcting for drift when landing an aeroplane is to use the rudder to bring the nose into alignment with the runway while rounding out just prior to touchdown. In strong crosswinds it is necessary to use precise movements of ailerons, rudder and elevators to counter any tendency for sideways motion downwind to develop. These simultaneous movements require the pilot flying to exhibit a high degree of coordination. In a large aircraft, the situation is complicated by the fact that the pilot is sitting a long way forward from the wheels. The turn into the wind necessary to counter drift causes the pilot to be displaced towards the edge of the runway, or even off the side of it. So, when the aircraft is ruddered straight on landing, the pilot is moved sideways from his displaced position to the centre of the runway. This movement can be quite disorientating, putting further strain on an already complicated manoeuvre. Unsurprisingly, in the 30-knot crosswinds of Christchurch, where the pilot doesn't get it perfectly right there's often the embarrassment of a rough touchdown.

A feature of Christchurch landings in the very early morning hours is that radiation fog is often forming. Radiation fog is usually caused by the thin layer of very cold air lying on the ground being stirred up by the pre-dawn air movements. The downwash from an aircraft coming in to land is sometimes sufficiently large to stir enough air to form fog. In otherwise clear air, this effect may cause fog to form in the wake of the aircraft. This fog then follows the aircraft down the runway. Early one morning on approaching the airfield I was aware that conditions were ripe for this phenomenon. I landed in relatively clear conditions but on turning off the runway was enveloped by the dense fog we'd stirred up. It was so thick that I was able to see only one taxiway light at a time and so crept along slowly and carefully. The fog spread off the runway to the terminal area. Ground crew awaiting our arrival could see the difficulties. They'd equipped themselves with powerful torches and stood in a row to lead me into the parking area. I was relieved to park the aircraft. This was before carousels were available at Christchurch and passengers descended stairs to ground level. The resourceful ground crew, aware that the passengers might get lost in the fog while making their way to the terminal building, had again formed a line of torchbearers to guide them on their way. The passengers were all quite convinced that I'd landed in these conditions, and when I made my way into the lighted customs holding area, there was a round of applause. I quite expected the media to pick this up and precipitate an inquiry from the civil aviation authorities, but this didn't happen.

I always particularly enjoyed arrival at Hong Kong's Kai Tak airport. Being able to put the big craft down smoothly in tricky crosswind conditions after that approach was always satisfying. In the 747, it's easy to strike one of the outer engine pods on the ground in gusty crosswinds, causing expensive damage and delays to schedules.

Aircraft manufacturers devote much effort to anticipating possible problems and devising appropriate procedures to correct them. As a result, operations and emergency manuals are hefty publications. Crews regularly passing their 180-day checks are inclined to think they'll always have everything under control. But aviation can spring surprises on everyone no matter how much they have played the 'What If' game of anticipation of emergencies.

A B747 flight involving a wheel well fire is a sobering example. For many years the drill for handling a wheel well fire was based on the assumption that it would have been caused by an overheated tyre. The drill was to slow to maximum speed for landing gear operation, warn the passengers so they weren't frightened by the sudden noise and turbulence caused by the wheels going down, leave the gear down for several minutes so the airflow would blow out the fire then retract the gear and carry on to destination. This drill had worked successfully on all wheel well fires experienced to that date. But on the flight in question, as the aircraft touched down at its planned destination, fire burst through the cabin wall into the cabin. Several passengers were injured in the subsequent emergency evacuation.

Investigators worked hard to puzzle out what had happened. It turned out that a 400-volt electrical cable in the wheel well had become detached at one end and was swinging about. As the loose end came in contact with various parts of the airframe, an electric spark flashed. The cable contacted a pressurised hydraulic pipe and drilled a pinhole in the pipe. A highly combustible mist sprayed out and was ignited by the next spark. The fire then activated the wheel well fire warning light in the cockpit and the crew correctly executed the emergency drill. Believing the fire to be out, they continued with the planned flight. In fact, the fire had been blown out as planned, but when the gear was retracted into the wheel well, the loose cable continued sparking, the pipe remained pressurised and the fire was reignited. Unfortunately, the initial fire had destroyed the fire warning system and so the crew were not alerted to the danger of the new fire. It was lucky the airframe contained the blaze until the aircraft touched down at destination.

A new drill was immediately determined and promulgated worldwide to all B747 operators. Everyone was shocked to think that a solution to an emergency that had been in use for many years had proved to be deficient and that a serious accident had been only narrowly avoided.

These experiences, which happened to me or which I learned about from others, all added to my knowledge and increased my awareness that one should never take anything for granted in aviation. No one can afford to be complacent in the cockpit of an airliner. Too often, if a component fails, its warning device may simultaneously fail. Older pilots are wary in the air.

After my Tahiti experience, I never again came to the attention of the media, which is the way airline pilots like it. It's said that if on retirement your airline managers hardly know who you are, then you've had a successful career.

18

A DAY AT THE OFFICE

A flight from London to Los Angeles is a good example of a day in the office for an Air New Zealand pilot.

The days starts – probably in the evening – with the flight and cabin crew members assembling in the lobby of the departure hotel in London. After the compulsory rest period, everyone is looking refreshed and alert. All the flight attendants look groomed with not so much as a hair out of place. The animated conversations are about the way the last few days' layover were spent in London. Some would like to stay in the big city; others look forward to soon reaching home. Transport arrives on time and we're off through the clogged London roads to Gatwick airport. Crew members slide through the crowds with a minimum of human contact to drop off baggage. A crew members' channel avoids a tiresome wait to be checked through security.

Pre-flight

Soon the captain and flight crew are assembled in the operations room for briefing while the cabin crew board the aircraft to see that all is spick and span for the arrival of the hundreds of passengers.

The operations staff present a computerised flight plan. Winds at cruising levels have been analysed for various routes from London to Los Angeles and the route offering the minimum flight time has been selected. Less flight time reduces the amount of fuel required. On the day of this flight, strong westerly winds are blowing at cruising levels, which will progressively climb from 31,000 to 39,000 feet. As fuel is burnt during the flight, weight decreases. It's more economical to fly higher at lighter weights. To avoid the extra time of flight resulting from selection of a route fighting the headwinds, this flight has been planned to fly an arc across the Earth which will take it far to the north, crossing Iceland and Greenland, then on the other side of the North Atlantic turning south to cross the Arctic wastes of northern Canada and down through the mid-western states of America until abeam destination Los Angeles.

A person unschooled in navigation, looking at this route depicted on a chart (a map designed for navigation), will be astonished at the apparent huge diversion to the north. But, of course, the Earth is a sphere, and transfer of a direct track (a 'great circle track') to a flat sheet produces distortions. The situation can be appreciated if one stretches a string between London and Los Angeles on a globe.

When satisfied, the captain accepts the planned route, and the operations staff file a flight plan with air traffic control. The flight plan, a document vital to safety, notifies air traffic control in the various countries over which the aircraft will fly of the flight details. The route, times of flight between specified positions, total endurance for the fuel carried, number of people on board, safety equipment carried and communications equipment details are included in this document. If an aircraft should become overdue, search activities will be based on this document.

The fuel load for this long flight is large and, because takeoff weight will be limited by the length of the Gatwick runway in use, each kilogram of fuel not loaded increases the payload of passengers and freight by a precious kilogram. The amount of fuel required to be carried is strictly regulated. There must be sufficient for the required time of flight. Figures determined by the aircraft manufacturer allow this to be calculated accurately. Then a percentage – about four per cent – is required on top of the 'A to B' fuel, to allow for wind changes en route and minor variations in performance on individual aircraft. Fuel for a full instrument approach to destination and for landing is next added. Except in the case of isolated island airfields, where two hours' extra fuel is required, there must always be an alternative airport planned to which the aircraft can divert if unable to land at destination. Fuel sufficient to fly to this airfield, make an approach and landing, with an additional 45 minutes of holding fuel, is added to make up the minimum fuel required. So, while fuel load is critical to financial performance and is exactly calculated so not a kilogram above the legal requirement is carried, an airliner is highly unlikely to have low fuel state problems in ordinary circumstances.

I recall making a second approach in heavy rain and low visibility to Rarotonga in the Cook Islands. Sensing this attempt to land would not be successful, I was mentally prepared for the diversion to Tahiti which had been planned. Busy with approach procedures I snapped a quick question to the flight engineer: 'Fuel remaining?' We both understood the answer – 10 minutes – to be the fuel left before we had to commence the diversion. The senior cabin crew member was in the cockpit area and, paling visibly, lurched back into the cabin saying, 'They've only got 10 minutes' fuel left!' We found this amusing when told about it later.

But, back to our London briefing. After checking the fuel required and signing the fuel order, it's time to look at the weather at the airports. Each airfield has a minimum level of visibility and cloud base specified for use as a destination and a higher level for use as a diversion. These minima vary depending on the equipment installed at the airfield and in the aircraft. In some cases, aircraft may land in zero–zero conditions (zero visibility and zero cloud base) and the landing may be fully automatic; that is, carried out by the autopilot. In automatic landings, everything must be constantly checked on the approach to ensure the flight path is being maintained to tight limits, so the cockpit workload is high. The aircraft must be in exactly the right position and speed arriving over the runway. Automatic landings are best suited to very low visibility, usually caused by fog, when the winds are light.

An amusing tale is told of the flight engineer asking the captain whether he'll do a manual or an automatic landing, to which the reply was, 'Manual. I'm too tired for an automatic landing tonight.'

After fuel calculations and weather forecast checks come NOTAMS (notices to airmen). These advise such things as deficiencies in navigation aids; restrictions in the use of airways; hazards to aviation, such as rockets being fired into the oceans; and issues applicable to airfields, like closed taxiways. With the absorption of this knowledge, the crew is fully prepared for the flight ahead.

Bidding adieu to the helpful operations officers, the crew traverse the long corridors of Gatwick and arrive at their aircraft. After stowing personal effects, and perhaps some duty-free alcohol to be taken home, the captain, co-pilot and flight engineer settle in to their seats and commence the long list of equipment checks. About this time, the traffic officers arrive with the fuel, passenger and freight documentation. Special note will be taken of dangerous goods to be loaded. This is cross-checked closely by both pilots satisfying themselves that no dangerous goods forbidden for passenger aircraft are included. Some items are permitted to be carried on freight aircraft only. Once in possession of this information, the crew can carry out the calculations necessary to complete the vitally important takeoff sheet. The captain will have announced his decision as to who will fly the aircraft. While every pilot wants to actually fly the leg, co-pilots must be given the experience to develop their professional abilities. We assume for our example flight that the captain is the pilot flying. It is the co-pilot, therefore, who reaches for the bulky performance manual and commences the complex takeoff calculations.

It's vitally important that these be correct. Getting several hundred tonnes of aircraft safely into the air is no mean undertaking. First, three speeds are determined. They are V1, rotate and V2 speeds. They will vary with aircraft all-up weight (greater weight, greater speeds), temperature, airfield atmospheric pressure (expressed as code QNH, this varies with airfield height above sea level and daily variations depending on the weather situation), runway length and slope (up or down) and any planned reduction in power.

For shorter runways and a set of conditions of which temperature is the most important, a maximum weight may be determined. If the actual weight is less than this, it's permissible to reduce the power. Reduction of power reduces engine wear, particularly on the critical turbine blades operating at very high temperatures and extreme mechanical loading.

The first speed calculated, V1, is the speed at which, following the sudden failure of an engine, the aircraft may be stopped on the runway remaining or may complete the takeoff with the three engines remaining. If the runway is critical (the actual weight equals the maximum permissible weight), the aircraft will pass over the end of the runway at 50 feet altitude if the takeoff is continued or stop at the very end of the runway if the takeoff is aborted. So, accurate calculation of V1 is of the highest importance. The correct and immediate application of the appropriate pilot actions at V1 is equally important. For example, if in the B747 the pilot delays the full applications of brakes and the retarding of the thrust levers (throttles) by more than three seconds, the aircraft will overrun the runway, departing the far end at about 70 knots.

Rotate speed is the speed at which the nose is raised to a pre-determined pitch angle to achieve actual takeoff. At rotate, the nose is raised but the aircraft has to accelerate further before the 16 wheels of the B747 undercarriage leave the concrete.

V2 is the speed at which the aircraft is planned to climb away. Should there be obstacles in the flight path immediately after takeoff, V2 speed is maintained until a stipulated height before the aircraft is accelerated to climb speed.

Experience has shown that a continued takeoff after engine failure at V1 is less likely to result in aircraft damage than an aborted takeoff. The latter may well result in all the tyres deflating, creating difficulty clearing the runway. When lined up on the runway ready to go, the wise pilot mentally reviews the procedures for an aborted takeoff at V1 and for the continued takeoff from V1.

Miscalculations are rare but have happened. An A340 at Melbourne struck the approach lights for the opposite runway; considerable damage occurred but no injuries. The pilot not flying had misread the aircraft weight by 10,000 kilograms and determined a power setting appropriate to that weight. That power setting was too low for the aircraft's weight. The upshot was that the crew set off down the runway at less than required power and failed to accelerate at a sufficient rate. The aircraft did become airborne but was low and impacted the approach lights. The person blamed for this wasn't the pilot who'd made the mistaken calculation; it was the pilot who checked the takeoff calculations and failed to detect the error. Personally, I would have fired both of them for failing to bring the engines up to full power when it was obvious they weren't accelerating correctly.

In London, satisfied that their calculations are correct, our crew now set the three speeds on their airspeed indicators by sliding small plastic markers to the correct position. All wait expectantly for the traffic officer to give final clearance, anxious to be on their way on the long flight. The captain will use the public-address system to briefly welcome the passengers aboard and assure them no problems are anticipated. Everyone likes an on-time departure and the airline allows only three minutes' tolerance, after which every minute of further delay must be accounted for. Nine times out of ten, it's about this time that someone like the police will alert us they're looking for a certain passenger to help them in their inquiries. Then, we'll issue an apology to all for the delay. If the person is taken off, it can be a serious delay while their bags are discovered and removed. Security considerations require that if a person fails to board after checking in, or leaves the aircraft for any reason, their baggage must be taken off.

Interruptions dealt with, it's time to be on the way and the pre-start checklist is called for. Engines four, three, two and one are started; ground power is removed; and the tug driver commences the push-back. With the tug disconnected, the crew are now on their own and call for taxi clearance.

Takeoff

On the bigger airfields of the EU, UK and USA, taxiing requires care. A turn into the wrong taxiway can result in a head-on situation with another aircraft, or the wings striking obstructions to the side. But excellent documentation is provided, and it's simply a matter of pre-study and careful adherence to taxi clearance instructions. On the way to takeoff point, the air traffic clearance is copied down and read back. UK controllers are excellent, calm and unhurried: quite different from most of their American counterparts. Los Angeles, for example, is famous for staccato clearances. A clearance is an instruction to the crew to maintain a specified flight path and a vertical profile. Except in emergency, the clearance must be adhered to at all times, unless a variation is approved by air traffic control.

At last, the long taxi is over, and our crew is poised at takeoff point. There may be a wait while other traffic lands but finally comes the long-awaited call: 'New Zealand zero two, cleared to line up'. At the time of my flights from London, the leg to Los Angeles was regarded as ultra long. We knew lots of people would come out to watch us take off as our heavy aircraft was always at the maximum permitted weight and we'd use every inch of the runway. After a final wind and temperature check to ensure our takeoff calculations remained correct, we'd be ready to go.

Nothing compares with the sheer joy of flying when one is seated in the cockpit, all preparations complete, and takes control of the four thrust levers. With a final review of the abort procedures in the mind, one listens to the thrilling skirl of the four mighty engines coming up to full power, the roar blasting out to all within earshot. Brakes off and the heavy machine starts to trundle down the runway. But being so heavy, how slowly it seems to be accelerating. One experienced flight attendant once commented that a London takeoff seems to go on forever. Slowly but surely, the speed builds till runway lights are passing in a blur. A quick glance across the instrument panel – all well, four engines producing full power. The runway rushing by now and suddenly the awaited call 'V1'! The pilot flying, who's had one hand on the thrust levers ready to execute an aborted takeoff procedure, now releases them. From now on, if an engine fails, the thrust levers will be left forward, or pushed further forward if there's power to spare. Soon comes the call, 'Rotate.' Now the pilot, flying smoothly, rotates the nose up to the exact angle required and holds it there. But the wheels are still rumbling along the ground. And then no more rumble – airborne.

The nose position is held exactly in place as the speed builds up until V2. Airspeed hold is set to have the flight guidance system maintain this speed until obstacle clearance height is reached. Then the aircraft is accelerated to climb speed to start up the long ascent to cruising altitude. Sometimes it's necessary to level off at intermediate altitudes to meet the requirements of the specified departure procedure or to ensure clearance from other traffic. As they climb away from the busy traffic of the terminal area, the crew relax and savour the joy of flying. Now is the time for an address to the passengers assuring them all is well and no problems are anticipated.

If a problem does occur and a procedure needs to be implemented that may alarm passengers, it's important to warn them. A good example is having an unlocked indication on one of the undercarriage bogeys. The corrective action calls for the undercarriage to be lowered and raised again. Speed in the climb being rather high, but below the undercarriage operating limits, the lowered wheels make a sudden loud roaring noise and marked vibration. If this happens without warning, some passengers will be badly frightened. No one wants that to happen.

The journey

Climbing out over Ireland, radio transfer is made to Oceanic Control, who confirm the cruise altitude. It is important to keep to these instructions as there is much air traffic about; going in a wrong direction or straying from the designated route, or busting through an altitude, could result in a collision with other planes. Now is the time to relax, engage the autopilot and enjoy a cup of tea served by smiling cabin crew. Time passes but all remain alert in the cockpit, checking and rechecking instruments to confirm all are reading as expected. Iceland soon appears on the radar and we fly over this fertile and pleasant land. I admire the cunning of the ancient Vikings, who named this as Iceland and the ice-covered land to the west Greenland, no doubt to lead astray any would-be invaders of their time.

And then the mass of Greenland appears. This wide land is covered by an ice sheet several thousand feet thick which, should it melt, will raise the level of the world's oceans and seas to disastrous levels. From the east, the snow-covered ice sheet rises imperceptibly to about 8000 feet. The surface is smooth and featureless. This is no problem as we pass by at 35,000 feet but in World War II an American four-engine aircraft, flying unknowingly at the height of the snowy terrain, had the most incredible accident. The pilot, cruising along normally – he thought – noticed the airspeed indicator was reading zero. Astonishingly, the aeroplane had flown onto the smooth snow surface unnoticed. The propellers dug a channel for themselves in the snow and the engines continued running as if nothing had happened. So, there they were, crashed and at a standstill on the smooth snow surface.

The western side of Greenland is a wild scene as the icefields break down to the black sea in a jumble of glaciers. It's a place just right for extreme skiers. Now we are looking down on an Arctic sea full of massive icebergs that have just broken off the ice shelf. Next appear the icy wastes of northern Canada, isolated and barren. Greenery gradually reappears as the flight progresses southward to the fertile southern provinces of Canada and then over the western states of America. And soon enough it's time to turn right across mountains under air traffic radar directions to approach the Los Angeles basin.

A sickening sight awaits. For hours we've been flying in crystal clear air with unlimited visibility but as we approach Los Angeles, a roiling mass of yellow air pollution appears, hemmed into the Los Angeles basin by the surrounding mountain ranges. Once we've descended into this muck, we're entirely reliant on instrument guidance to align ourselves with the runway in use. In the murk, it's impossible to see the runway lights, so the airfield controllers have switched on an incredibly bright array of lights mounted in a row on the extended centreline. The lights of this array flash in rapid sequence from nearest to furthest. From the cockpit, it all looks just like a rabbit bolting through the mist to its hole. When we can see the runway lights, the brightness of the approach array begins to blind the pilots, so we call the controllers, 'Kill the rabbit.' Instantly the bright reflections disappear and we can see the runway lights.

And so, on to a smooth touchdown.

Another London to Los Angeles flight has been completed.

19

ENSURING AIR CREW REMAIN COMPETENT

Just as I'm expecting the V1 call from my co-pilot, the red fire warning light flashes in front of my eyes and the strident warning light flares. 'Abort takeoff,' I order, rapidly retarding the thrust levers and applying full reverse thrust. I tread the brake pedals to the floor. Deceleration is fast, but the end of the runway seems to be coming up faster. 'Engine fire number three,' sings out the flight engineer and I respond with, 'Carry out engine fire number three drill.' The warning light is extinguished just as we stop 10 metres from the end of the concrete.

A short minute later, I'm at 35,000 feet and experience an explosive decompression. Without a break, I must go straight into this procedure.

How can this be?

I'm in the simulator. I'm doing my 180-day check.

Modern simulators are marvels. They're exact replicas of aircraft cockpits. Software reproduces visual displays that are programmed to show 3D ground and airborne views of airports and their surrounds as would be seen from the cockpit. A wide array of airports stored in the software library are available for the instructor's selection. Everything is as the pilot would see it during an approach to the runway and landing at the selected airports. Views of taxiways and buildings on the ground mirror the actual scenes. Noise effects combine with the visual representation to create in the simulator an authentic feeling that one is taxiing or flying on or over that precise spot. Weather effects can be programmed in so that the display represents what the pilot would see (or not see) in conditions of reduced visibility. Storm conditions with wind shear, for instance, require the pilot to adjust the engine power and flight paths in the simulator exactly as he would to cope with the conditions if airborne. Day or night conditions can be set and also realistic representations of approach and runway lighting systems. Everything is so realistic that one can, in the stress of carrying out emergency procedures, forget that this is a simulator, not an aircraft.

Simulators are expensive, but they allow the airlines to carry out conversion, training and check flights without flying aircraft. Cost savings are huge. Additionally, simulators allow the training of flight deck crews in exercises which, if not properly controlled in aircraft, may be risky. Historically, many accidents have occurred when training was being conducted in aircraft. Air New Zealand, for example, had two major accidents using aircraft for training before simulators were available. An Electra airliner practising a power-off approach at Whenuapai, Auckland, crashed heavily onto the runway and was wrecked. A DC8 lost control and crashed at Auckland airport while practising simulated engine failure on takeoff. In the DC8, the drill was to retard the thrust lever to simulate engine failure by moving it smartly to the rear. The lever activating reverse thrust on an engine is located on top of the thrust lever. It was accidentally operated when the instructor closed the thrust lever a little too smartly. At low speed on the runway, the rudder wasn't able to control the turning force of an engine in revere thrust, control was lost, and the aircraft crashed. If simulators had been available, these accidents would never have happened.

Every six months (180 days) each flight deck member must pass a searching medical examination and demonstrate their continued competence to perform a schedule of exercises. Failure to pass both tests results in suspension and loss of employment. The flying test is nearly always carried out in the simulator. The schedule is carefully planned to make maximum use of the allocated simulator time. The pace is hot, and the standards required high. It might be said that pilots really earn their income in the 180-day check.

Because the simulator can be reprogrammed almost instantly, the instructor can have the crew dealing with the next exercise as soon as the previous one is finished. In other words, a pilot who has just completed a stressful aborted takeoff may then find himself/herself immediately at altitude facing an explosive decompression before there's time to take a breath. The workload is high. A pass in this test isn't easy.

If a crew member doesn't display the standard expected by the instructor, any deficiencies will be discussed and there will be another chance by a repeat of that exercise. A further failure normally results in suspension and removal from the flying roster. Counselling is given, followed by further training and another test. A failure in the repeat test will normally result in dismissal.

On the bright side, failures of simulator tests are rare. Every candidate prepares properly by study and revision. Some emergency drills have initial steps which must be carried out from memory, immediately. The balance of the procedure is then carried out by reference to the appropriate checklist. No self-respecting crew member would appear for a check without being thoroughly proficient in all required memory items. It would shame them before the critical eyes of the instructor and their fellow crew members to falter in a situation which, in an aircraft, could prejudice the safety of all.

Cockpit procedures and especially emergency drills are designed to have one crew member check the actions about to be taken by another so that a mistake is prevented before it occurs. The engineer will be prevented from selecting the wrong lever and creating the perilous situation of a double engine failure. These safety precautions may seem ponderous, but they're necessary. The history of aviation is littered with wrecks that resulted from crew members taking the wrong action, or the right action on the wrong control, in the stress of handling an in-flight emergency.

While these training exercises are going on in the simulator, the trainee can expect to be questioned on standard operating procedures and company policies to ensure he or she fully understands the operator's requirements. The trainee should also be knowledgeable about aircraft systems and technical details.

In the past, when aircraft were much simpler, air crew were expected to know practically everything about the technical details of an aircraft. But modern thinking is to have the crew member learn only those details that directly concern the flight crew. But what is needed to be known must be known thoroughly.

It's instructive to look at some of the more demanding exercises practised in the simulator.

After starting engines and handling correctly some of the problems that may occur, the first test in the 180-day check is invariably an engine failure on takeoff. If the failure is before V1 speed, the takeoff will be aborted by the pilot flying immediately closing the thrust levers while applying full brakes and then bringing the engines to full reverse thrust power. Properly executed, this procedure will stop the aircraft on the runway. Bringing several tonnes of aircraft to a stop on the runway remaining after the failure puts tremendous strain on the braking system and the tyres.

The next simulated problem, after the engine shutdown drill is completed, is thus likely to be brake fires or tyre deflation. The brake fire, like any fire, is cause for emergency evacuation off the aircraft and so this emergency drill must be immediately commenced. The workload on the crew is high and errors are not acceptable.

Alternatively, the instructor may delay the engine failure, or fire, until after V1 speed, a precalculated speed that is called out by the pilot not flying. After V1, the aircraft won't be able to stop in the remaining runway distance (except for very long runways or lightly laden aircraft) so the takeoff is continued. The pilot flying must apply full rudder to counter the turning effect (or yaw) of asymmetric power (one live engine not being balanced by the failed engine) and keep the aircraft on the runway centreline. As there's less power after the engine failure, acceleration is reduced, so it often seems like a long time before the rotate speed call comes from the pilot not flying. On this speed being reached, the pilot flying must smoothly and accurately raise the nose to the pre-calculated takeoff pitch angle. Raising the nose doesn't cause the aircraft to leave the ground, but after further acceleration the speed becomes sufficient to generate enough lift to fly.

There isn't much to spare. Even in the simulator, this can be pretty exciting. The pilot flying now awaits the V2 call to adjust the nose attitude to the angle required to commence the initial climb.

If there are any obstacles in the takeoff area, V2 speed will be held until these are cleared, when the nose will be pitched down to allow the aircraft to accelerate to en route climb speed. At this point, the simulator exercise is terminated by the instructor and the crew under training brace themselves for what's likely coming next.

All three crewmembers are simultaneously tested to see they carry out their actions correctly.

With a few deft movements at the control console, the instructor repositions the simulator to a cruise altitude, perhaps 35,000 feet and, without giving the trainees a breather, sets up an explosive decompression. There is a bang and a rumble as the effect of, say, a failure of a cargo bay door is fed into the simulator program. In a real-life explosive decompression, the time of useful consciousness is brief so it's imperative the flight deck crew don their oxygen masks instantly. The life-giving oxygen enables them to continue the procedure to carry out an emergency dive to a safe altitude, usually taken as 10,000 feet, where all aboard may safely continue to live without an oxygen supply. From 35,000 to 10,000 feet is a long way, and maximum rate of descent is needed. The aircraft is therefore pitched over smartly to a steep nose-down attitude and the airbrakes are deployed. Air brakes are large surfaces at the rear of the wing that spring up at right angles to the airflow and create drag, which accelerates the rate of descent. They make quite a noise and also cause vibration. In real life these effects, plus the appearance of oxygen masks in front of their faces, is most alarming to passengers. But the cold thin air at 35,000 feet isn't a good place to be without oxygen and the steep descent must be carried out. Our crew in the simulator are then relieved to level out at 10,000 feet and remove their masks and stow them while they await the instructor's next move, perhaps a fire somewhere or a cracked windscreen. Perhaps the engineer might be tested with several failures of hydraulic systems or runaway pressurisation to confirm satisfactory knowledge of technical systems and standard operating procedures.

After about an hour of full-on testing, the instructor usually calls for an approach procedure to be set up, often at an airport where there are special difficulties, such as Kai Tak airport in Hong Kong (before it was closed) or Wellington. Problems such as a flapless landing, partial failure of instruments or brakes failure will complicate these approaches. The ability to cope while still observing all air traffic control requirements must be demonstrated for holding patterns based on ground navigation installations, for descents and for establishment onto the Instrument Landing System. At least one baulked landing, requiring go around drills and usually from a very low altitude, can be expected.

The instructor has the ability to alter weather conditions apparent in the simulator. This facility is used particularly on the approach to a landing portion of the flight where, in real life, the majority of accidents caused by weather have occurred.

The visibility can be reduced to any desired level, including zero. For each approach the minimum visibility required to commence that approach will have been specified by the national authority controlling the airport. Not all aircraft have the sophisticated equipment necessary to operate to lower minimums, such as a half or a quarter of a nautical mile. However, most modern large airliners are cleared to zero–zero. Certainly, the crews must have been trained to fly to these limits and must demonstrate continuing competence. In a zero–zero landing, the cockpit workload is very high, instruments being constantly scanned to ensure the aircraft arrives over the end of the runway at exactly the correct height, speed and direction. This landing is one of the more important exercises in a normal 180-day check. In real life the technique is used mostly for landing in radiation fog conditions, when winds will be very light, as the crosswind limit for the equipment is of the order of only 5 knots.

At some time in the check, a two-engine landing (in four-engine aircraft – or single-engine landing in two-engine aircraft) will be called for. This usually comes in the sequence after a go-around has been executed with one engine failed for the approach. After an engine failure, a minimum speed must be maintained to ensure the rudder is able to counter the asymmetric force exerted by the remaining live engine (balanced flight). Obviously, if two engines are failed on one side, the minimum control speed is much higher than for a single failure. In applying power for a go-around, the pilot has to be careful to ensure rudder is fed in at the rate demanded by the power application. It isn't a time to bring the remaining engines up to full power rapidly; if too much power is fed in too quickly, the aircraft will enter a spiral dive. The two-engine circuit is flown with plenty of room for corrections. In actual flight, radar is usually requested to guide the aircraft to an intercept of the extended centreline of the runway at about 10 miles. This allows the crew plenty of time to have everything set up exactly as it should be for this demanding approach. The last thing the pilot wants is to get low on a two-engined approach and have to feed in large amounts of power to regain his correct vertical profile; this can result in quite a struggle to control all that power and prevent a spiral descent starting.

Sadly, many aircraft have crashed on attempting a landing in adverse weather conditions. Clearly, crews have to be taught to handle such conditions as wind gusts, low or zero visibility, downdrafts and turbulence at touchdown. These conditions usually occur when there is a large cumulonimbus cloud sitting over the airfield. Cumulus (heaped) cloud of black appearance (nimbus) which has many thousands of feet of development (towering cumulonimbus) creates the dangers that pilots must always be alert for. Cumulus clouds consist of several cells of air that move in relation to each other. These may be of several miles in extent. If one cell is forced higher, then its temperature will drop, and it will become more dense and heavier than surrounding cells. It may then accelerate downwards until striking the ground, when it will flow outwards. This outward flow is commonly accompanied by turbulence, lightning, icing and low visibility caused by heavy rain. The boundary between the descending column of air and the outflow is a bad place for an approaching aircraft. The aircraft on instrument approach will receive its first warning when the airspeed increases due to the outflow. To lessen his workload, the pilot will usually have engaged speed control mode on the autopilot. On detecting a sudden increase in speed, this mode will reduce the engine power to idle. Engine acceleration from idle is relatively slow. When the flight enters the downflow, it will lose the headwind, which may be of the order of 60–80 knots, just when it becomes affected by entry to a sharp descent caused by the downflow. Loss of airspeed, high rate of descent, low power in rain and turbulence – recover if you can!

Unexpected wind changes and gusts over the runway itself are hazards that remain even after a successful approach.

Of course, the first rule for handling severe wind shear is to avoid it – detect the radar picture indicating the presence of cumulonimbus activity and break off the approach and wait for the storm to move on or divert to another airfield. Usually the control tower staff will assist by being alert to the conditions and issue a warning to pilots, but not always. For example, I recall taxiing out for takeoff in a B747 at Sydney one night and observing on the aircraft radar an active cell just off the end of the duty runway. Nothing was said by the airfield controller. I radioed that I wasn't happy with the conditions and would wait till the weather improved. It was rather flattering when a following British Airways pilot advised the tower that if it was good enough for Air New Zealand to delay takeoff, it was good enough for him, too.

In the simulator, the instructor can program wind shear conditions that are demanding and, if mishandled, cause a crash. I found the answer to wind shear conditions was to apply full power at the first sign of trouble and immediately execute a go-around. With the worst of the programs, failure to act immediately caused entry to a downdraft in which there wasn't enough power to recover. Even in the safe environment of the simulator, it's dismaying, after everything is cleaned up and full power is applied, to see the runway lights rising up the windshield as, powerless, you sink down to ground impact. This is most excellent training and the lesson of a mistake leading to a 'crash' is never forgotten.

In actual life, there are wind shear conditions from which the most powerful of aircraft and the most skilled of pilots cannot escape. The solution? Avoidance.

After all of these tests, it's satisfying to walk away with good grades and the plaudits of the instructor ringing in your ears. The public can indeed have confidence in an industry that goes to such lengths to ensure its staff acquire and maintain competence.

20

SINGAPORE AIRLINES

Over my working life with Air New Zealand, I passed numerous 180-day checks and added thousands more hours to my logbook. In 1989, around came my 55th birthday – the then compulsory retiring age for Air New Zealand pilots. After organising my superannuation scheme, I applied to Singapore Airlines for a job as a B747 captain – as had many before me – and was promptly accepted.

Singapore was, and is, a delightfully modern and go-ahead country that used to be ruled by the iron hand of a true statesman, Mr Lee Kuan Yew. Mr Lee steered his people through the difficult separation from Malaysia and set them on course to become one of the world's wealthiest societies. He went to enormous lengths to root out the corruption previously endemic to Chinese society and insisted on discipline in the financial community. He achieved the notable feat of stopping the Chinese from spitting. He was forceful in his addresses to his community and the world and had a biting sense of humour. An example of his clever wit occurred on a visit to New Zealand at the time the American war effort in Vietnam collapsed. Asked if the Vietnamese were suffering, he rounded on his questioner, 'Don't you think the Vietnamese can cry,' he asked, 'or do you think they are like the inscrutable Americans?'

Singapore International Airline (SIA) was a wonderful company to work for. The pilot force, like the rest of the company, included people from a multitude of nations. The air crew trainers were well versed in converting to the Singapore way crew members from most of the airlines in the world. Once they knew my background they immediately laid down all the things I, an ex-Air New Zealand B747 captain had to study and those I could rely on Air New Zealand training to know. They were absolutely correct, too.

One quickly learned to avoid saying, 'This is the way we used to do this in …' The Singapore way was the only way of interest. SIA benefited from the Singapore Government policies of subsidising training costs. One example was a massive swimming pool, where dinghy boarding drills and other mandatory exercises were practised. The pool had an impressive wave generator and we students had to cope with quite rough water conditions. Small Asian women, anxious to qualify for their jobs, found the tasks of towing large European air crew through the turbulent waters very difficult and daunting. We helped them as much as we could.

I made a lot of friends in SIA. These included many ethnically Chinese pilots, for whom I had the greatest respect. Some of these had been military pilots who'd been required by their government to serve a minimum period in the Singapore Air Force. Their quid pro quo was immediate command on joining SIA. It was interesting to learn there were many similarities between the Asian and European cultures. For example, one culture says new wealth lasts only three generations; the other says gutter to gutter in three generations – different words but same thinking.

But there are deep differences too. For instance, one Chinese captain, a sophisticated and educated man, recounted his experiences on the night in the year when Chinese believe ghosts move about returning those who died abroad to their motherland (on this night you don't look into the eyes of fellow travellers lest you become the host to a ghost). My friend was driving to Malaysia and was going up a hill at the top of which was an ancient cemetery. Suddenly, he realised two columns of ghosts were streaming down the hill, one on each side of his car. He was so frightened that he wet himself. Another puzzling story is about the original Hyatt Hotel in Singapore. For some years after its opening, the hotel lost money. A feng shui practitioner was called in. Feng shui (which literally translates into English as 'wind, water') is a Chinese philosophical system of harmonising everyone with the environment. The man's finding was that money was flowing out the front doors, then conventionally mounted. So the doors were reset to a 45-degree angle to impede this money flow. Ever since, the hotel has been profitable.

One facet of Asian culture was not to the advantage of aviation. Asian people are loath to criticise their superiors. In the cockpit, this tends to make the co-pilot reluctant to speak out when he should do so. Aircraft safety is built on the principle that the actions of each member of the cockpit crew are constantly monitored by the other crew members. If the captain is about to make a mistake, then the co-pilot must speak up and continue to speak up until satisfied that safe flight is being achieved. Many potential accidents have been avoided because of a timely challenge from non-flying crew members. I recall once upon approaching Wellington airport and receiving notice that the visibility was below the minimum required for the planned instrument approach. I politely gave my opinion to the captain that we weren't permitted to commence the approach under these circumstances. The captain considered this, thanked me for my input and said he didn't believe I was correct. Subsequent to the flight, the captain took the trouble to ring ATC and ask their opinion, which was that the captain was correct. He was. I was highly impressed that the captain discussed this with me and praised me for speaking up, even though I was in the wrong, and urged me never to hesitate to caution him if I wasn't entirely satisfied. This was fine leadership and I learned from it. The more co-pilots learn to act in a similar manner, the safer aviation becomes. And if captains sometimes find the interruptions irritating, they should discipline themselves to show appreciation of the monitoring.

Somewhat more difficult to handle is the Asian trait of freezing up if they feel they have lost face. During a flight from Singapore to Sydney, a NOTAM (notice to airmen) had been issued changing certain radio position reporting procedures. It was soon obvious to me that my young Singaporean co-pilot hadn't read it. When I politely suggested he report in the new way required, he asserted positively that his procedure was correct. When I corrected him by showing him a copy of the NOTAM which I'd brought along, he obviously felt that he had lost face in misadvising his captain. Despite my best efforts, for the remainder of the flight the young man was withdrawn, to the extent he was of little assistance. Quite often on layovers, I found myself in friendly discussion of the 'Asian' way versus the 'European' way of approaching cockpit duties. Local pilots would say, 'If you want our money, do it our way.' The response was, 'If you design an aircraft to fly safely with single pilot only, that may be all right. But nobody was building such aircraft.' I hasten to add that SIA's procedures were impeccable.

For long the world's most profitable airline, SIA was a very well-run company that looked after its people with care. At

Singapore Airlines

frequent intervals, invitations to an excellent dinner and update on the company's affairs were issued to pilots who happened to be in Singapore. Attendance was expected. These affairs were a good opportunity to meet some very smart people who ran everything. SIA was much admired worldwide, and start-up airlines would scramble to hire its experienced staff if they could get them.

Flying SIA's worldwide routes was incredibly interesting. At one stage, before the latest versions of the B747 arrived, I was flying to 27 different countries. The routes included some tricky airports – apart from Kai Tak, Hong Kong – on which to land a very large aircraft such as the B747. Singapore airport itself was rightly regarded as fabulous and handled extremely heavy traffic at times. Throughout our route structure, ATC was of excellent quality except for a few pockets such as Afghanistan and perhaps some areas of southern Russia and Iran.

Air traffic control cleverly plan a long way ahead to get the aircraft arriving at an airport at precisely the right intervals. Often an aircraft is just about to land as the preceding traffic is turning off the runway, thus making full use of the runway or runways available. One may start getting fitted into the landing pattern perhaps 200 miles out by speed control or routing instructions. On one occasion, I was number 18 in the approach sequence to Singapore. I was flying a B747 and each of the aircraft ahead was a B747. All of this traffic was handled effortlessly by the several terminals. Singaporeans are great planners.

One place which was interesting to fly into and to visit was Male, in the Maldives. This group of islands and atolls lie to the west of the south-western corner of India. The people have a mixture of Indian and Arab blood. For centuries Arab divers in their dhows have gone to the adjacent Indian coast during the calm weather before and after the monsoons. The Maldives were a stepping stone along the way and naturally the two races intermingled. Many world-famed diving areas are scattered throughout these islands. The government is Islamic and strictly observes laws such as the prohibition of alcohol, except for certain islands catering for tourists, where there is tolerance for western ways. Local laws prohibit the taking of fish from the better known lagoons, which contain amazing numbers and varieties of fish life.

The islands are small and the one on which the runway has been constructed is almost wholly covered by the runway. There is just sufficient additional room for the terminal building and a few facilities. Landing a B747 means an approach over the sea onto what resembles an aircraft carrier. Although an instrument landing system now gives precision track and vertical descent profile guidance to the pilot, in my first visits there this aid wasn't installed. If one happened to arrive when there was a large cumulonimbus cloud sitting over the field with typical heavy rain and vigorous wind changes, the approach required caution and skill on the part of the pilot.

Layovers, often of two or three days, were very pleasant with cool enough temperatures and crystal-clear waters filled with healthy corals and fish. Usually, a local boat and crew were hired for an evening's fishing in authorised areas and customarily the whole crew went along. On one occasion, after an epic struggle, I hauled up a hammerhead shark on my handline. My Australian co-pilot and I eyed this and decided we would bring it aboard. Realising this, the Singapore hostesses screamed with fright and took to the roof, except for one who prowled about with a large knife – I don't think she'd ever seen such a lot of fresh fish in her life before. The Australian managed to get a line round the shark's tail and there was much splashing, shouting, screaming and pulling of lines. In the midst of all the excitement, the local boatmen came up and discreetly cut our lines, releasing the fish. I thought something strange was happening so said nothing. Next morning, we discovered the local people view sharks as the embodiment of their ancestors. Goodness knows what the consequences might have been had we brought this fish in. Riots have started in Indian circles for lesser causes. I was thankful to the boatmen.

Further west in the Indian Ocean is the island of Mauritius, which has a particularly demanding airport. There is an instrument landing system but a hillock late in the approach requires the aircraft to be deviated from the glide path, obviously to the upper side. This is exactly what one tries to avoid on a normal approach, as it destabilises the approach just when you want to be in the groove, rounding out for landing. Then the runway itself rises to a hump quite sharply (for a runway) in its first 200 yards, so the round-out after recovering from the deviation above the glide path becomes critical. A slight misjudgment will see you still airborne after passing the hump where the runway is now descending quite sharply. As the runway is short for a B747, being airborne over the hump dictates an immediate go-around. Even a perfectly flown approach requires heavy braking. There is a brake average temperature indication on the flight engineer's panel and it's customary to warn the pilots if it enters the red range. Every landing at Mauritius sees the brake temperature indicator in the red.

European operations

Flying in Europe is fascinating. Traffic is heavy and airspace limited, so the rules are complex. SIA route-check requirements are to check out new pilots on only two of the considerable list of airfields to which the airline flies. So, an arrival at some of the busiest airfields is likely to be the first time one has been there. This is, in fact, a quite safe practice because exemplary documents cover every facet of operation into and around that airfield. All one has to do is read, but concentrated study is necessary. A colleague made his first arrival in a freighter aircraft at 4 am at Basel, on the Swiss border, but didn't see a note in the documents, 'Taxiway Zulu not available for B747 aircraft'. Being a little behind schedule, he set off down taxiway Zulu at a smart clip and collided in the dark with a parked aircraft, leaving a Friendship tail and his wingtip lying on the ground. On return to Singapore, he was smart – he apologised profusely to the SIA chief pilot for his stupidity and for bringing the airline into disrepute. He was forgiven and allowed another chance.

I well remember my first arrival at Schiphol, the international airport serving Amsterdam. This very large airport is always busy. Even finding one's way on the ground is demanding and requires constant reference to the aviation guide books. I'd recently completed my Europe check-out and was in command of this flight. We were arriving from the south. The Dutch airport authorities instructed me to position to the north for a landing on the southerly runway and asked for maximum speed to assist traffic sequencing. So, I was bowling along at high speed about 10 miles east of Schiphol when suddenly the controller said I was to land to the west. At once, I pulled the power off completely, of course, but didn't think I could possibly slow down to landing speed in the short distance I'd have if turning immediately to the airport. I told the controller I didn't think I could make it but confidently he said, 'Yes, you can.' Well, one does not argue with Dutch ATC and I turned for the runway.

The best technique in a B747 for losing excess speed/altitude is to slow up as quickly as possible to get the undercarriage and full flap out, which I did by pulling up the nose and climbing quite steeply to reduce to the limiting speeds. I seemed to be looking down almost vertically onto the runway threshold! But, 'dirtied up', that champion aeroplane came down like a lift, and with the merest touch of power just before rounding out, I flew beautifully onto the runway. The Dutch controller had known exactly what he was doing and I have had the greatest respect for Dutch controllers ever since.

However, they weren't so nice to German pilots. I heard one screamed at because he missed a turn from one taxiway to another. He was told not to return until he'd read the rules properly.

European arrival and departure procedures are often complex and lengthy. The southern departure from Schiphol requires passage of a certain point at a height between 27,000 and 28,000 feet. The climb requires careful handling to achieve the 27,000 feet, and it's sobering to arrive there and observe an aircraft pass just 1000 feet below.

The communities surrounding airports are noise sensitive – and who can blame them? – so special flight profiles are flown to reduce noise nuisance off most runways. Noise-measuring devices are installed on the ground underneath the departure course. An allowable noise level at this point is specified and exceeding it is called 'ringing the bells'. This misdemeanour is duly reported to the airline with a 'please explain' notice. The authorities were tough on SIA aircraft, which usually took off at very heavy weights carrying a fuel load for long-haul flights to Asia. Local European flights were invariably much lighter with fuel for short-haul sectors, and the bells tended to be set at levels appropriate to them.

It's interesting to compare styles of air traffic control in Europe with those of the United States. Europeans generally speak in measured tones and get their message across without seeming hurried; London controllers are especially good. In the United States, staccato clearances are often delivered like machine-gun bursts at the busiest airports. It's advisable to review the expected clearance before calling for it or else it's almost impossible to read it back at speed. Departure clearance at Los Angeles is an especially busy frequency and several pilots are usually waiting with their fingers on the microphone button if any chance offers. I, and no doubt many other pilots, was hugely amused one evening when a Texan aircraft was read its clearance rapidly. Silence – especially rare on that frequency – followed. Then a slow Texan drawl advised Los Angeles departures, 'This is the speed at which ah talks and this is the speed at which ah listens so please say again mah clearance slowly.' To everyone's astonishment, the operator complied.

The busiest flight I know is departure from Paris Charles de Gaulle Airport (also known as Roissy Airport) to Brussels in a north-easterly wind. The departure, specified by the French authorities, involves repeated heading and altitude changes which must be complied with exactly, climbing to about 14,000 feet. Then it's power off and immediate entry to an even more complex flight path, specified by the Belgian authorities. All this happens in about 20 minutes. I used to tell my co-pilots that if they could cope with that, they could cope with anything.

Some areas had rather alarming standards of control. The preferred route on the heavily travelled Asia to Europe sector was through India and Pakistan then westwards through Iranian airspace. Usually, about the time of entering Iranian airspace, sufficient fuel has been burned to allow a climb of 4000 feet to a more economic level. A call to Iran control – 'Singapore XZ request climb to 37,000 feet', for example – was likely to be answered by a guttural 'Yes.'

'Yes, you can do it', 'Yes, we heard you', 'Yes, I'm thinking about it' – what did this 'Yes' mean? Given the absolute necessity that there be not the slightest misunderstanding between pilots and ATC, it was necessary in such circumstances to persist with the controller until an unambiguous understanding of the clearance was achieved.

Flying the dedicated B747 freight aircraft was usually fairly relaxed without passengers to be concerned about. On my rest period, I'd often walk through the freight hold to assure myself all was well and to see some of the load we were carrying. On one flight from Singapore to London via Bangkok, we carried a heavy box labelled as containing a deadly snake, a green mamba. I know that green mambas are one of three snakes that will aggressively track human beings: the other two are the king cobra and the Australian taipan. On arrival at London, I mentioned to the company handling agent that I had brought him some interesting cargo, the mamba. I then returned to Singapore and a few days later flew back into London, where I was met by the same agent. 'Tom,' he said, 'you remember the green mamba in the box you brought in? Well, when it was opened, there was just the box but no mamba!'

Hmmm. Had it escaped and hidden somewhere in the aircraft? Back in Singapore once again, I put a notice on the operations room board advising pilots to look carefully before putting their legs into the rudder channels on this aircraft. As Bangkok is a world centre for snake venom and lots of snakes are traded, it's likely the green mamba was stolen there.

I had many SIA flights where my wife and children would come up from New Zealand and accompany me. We were given first-class travel when available and have many happy memories of these little holidays. On one trip we had three days off in Singapore. We took a ferry to a small Indonesian island. In our amusing hotel, built over the water on stilts, we found an old newspaper written in English as she is spoke. We marvelled at the story of a local citizen. Apparently, this worthy was attending to the needs of nature in the jungle when a rat ran between his legs. Instantly, he realised what was up – cobras track rats by their heat trail and this clever rat realised it had been given a decoy, a steaming pile. Sure enough, the cobra arrived before there was time to do anything and sank its fangs into the man's testicles. Once engaged, cobras often cannot be made to let go. The poor man had to stagger off in search of help. He didn't make it. I hope when it's my turn to go, I won't be taken that way.

Australian friends in SIA, accustomed to some lethal creatures in their home country, gave me good advice which I've never forgotten. In crocodile country, never stand with your back to the water! Crocodiles can burst out doing 30 kilometres per hour. You need to be quick to escape. The friend who told me this described visiting an old school friend who ran a crocodile farm. The owner entertained my associate by giving him a tour of the farm in a Land Rover equipped with heavy bull bars at the front. A large old male crocodile wandered across their path and, as it went by, swung its heavy tail, giving the bull bars a mighty blow. The Land Rover was driven about 6 metres backwards. 'Ah, time to shoot him again,' said the owner. Asked what he meant by that, the owner said about every three months, the old croc forgot who was boss and had to be shot in the head with a shotgun to recall his manners.

My most embarrassing moment

Scheduled to operate Singapore to Delhi, after briefing at Flight Operations, I entered the departure area and took my place in the queue for security search. When the captain of a flight appears, all eyes are upon him and this day was no different. This is a natural reaction as everyone wants a good look at the person who's taking them up into the air. One becomes inured to being stared at. The key is to find a friendly face and smile. A young Indian security officer came up to me. 'Captain,' he said, 'your fly is undone.'

Bangkok delay and other interesting places

One night, I was departing Bangkok for London and was pleased to record an 'off blocks' time exactly on schedule. As we were pushed back by the tug we started all four engines and were completing checklists when a flight attendant rushed up to the flight deck and announced that two passengers were crying inconsolably. This was unusual. I stopped, parked the brakes and gave her my complete attention.

'Oh, what are they crying about?'

She replied, 'They've left their children behind in the terminal building.'

'What? People don't leave their children behind.'

Well, these parents had. Inexplicably, they'd boarded expecting their children to follow. No doubt the immigration authorities had stopped the children from boarding unaccompanied. Well, I thought about this situation. It would be a real pain at the start of a long night's flying to stop all the engines, get the tug back, return to the boarding gate, get the children and go through the start-up process on four engines all over again. But then I pictured the headlines: 'Children Left Behind By Callous Airline.' I knew SIA wouldn't like that. Back we went. The parents sent me a heartfelt note of thanks. I'm sure they'd never get separated from their children again while travelling.

SIA management were experts at keeping any bad news quiet. When a new version of the B747s arrived, it had sufficient additional range to be able to fly direct from Singapore to London, a capability long desired. When the second new aircraft arrived, it was despatched to London with much hoopla, full of VIPs. Unfortunately, passing over the wild area of Afghanistan a cargo fire warning light was activated in the cockpit. Correctly the captain decided to divert to the nearest airport. This happened to be Dushanbe, a rather primitive town just across the Russian border. We may be sure there wasn't an excess of first-class hotel rooms for the distinguished passengers.

There was consternation in Singapore. A brand new aircraft, just arrived, was hurriedly prepared and despatched to Dushanbe. But when it landed, it promptly went unserviceable. Ultimately, the celebs were left cooling their heels for three days before finally arriving in London. The amazing thing about this incident is that not a single mention of it appeared in the press, which shows the mastery of the media SIA management could produce when called upon.

In that part of the world, a tribe living in the mountains of Afghanistan has an interesting history. It's still revered as the only community anywhere that managed to fight off a full-scale attack by the Mongol hordes.

Civil aircraft flew across this war-torn country at altitudes well above any danger level. Quite heavy traffic used the route transiting from Asia to Europe. No one expected too much from the local air traffic control in the troubled regions of this part of the world. One night, passing over Afghanistan, I was surprised to be called by the Afghan radar controller. We'd developed an error in the navigation systems and the controller said we were 15 miles off track. I managed to fly overhead a navigation aid shortly after this call and update our system, and indeed he was exactly right. I think that was the only time I found that radar service operating.

Another regular destination was Johannesburg, South Africa. On layovers, this was a place requiring vigilance. The gaols have such a tough reputation that some criminals would rather fight to the death than be incarcerated. On a free Sunday afternoon, I went walking for some fresh air and exercise and came across a convent. A noticeboard announced, 'Little Sisters of the Poor' and underneath 'Please ring the bell' and underneath that again 'IMMEDIATE ARMED RESPONSE'. *Wow,* I thought, *if the Little Sisters carry AK-47s, this is one tough town. Be careful.*

An acquaintance told me of a mature lady of this city who, unwisely, stopped at a red traffic light. A dark-skinned gentleman with a knife ripped open the door, leaped in and indicated she should drive on, which, wisely, she did. The man pulled his cellphone out of his pocket and started a discussion in Swahili. He then paused and, quite politely, asked her the year and model of her car, which was a fairly elderly model. This information was relayed in Swahili. After a pause, the man then said, 'Madam, would you please let me out at the next traffic light. My people aren't interested in your car.' What an insult; wouldn't you feel like slapping the guy's face! Well, perhaps not if he had a knife. Indeed, Joburg is a tough town.

Another interesting port of call was Cairo. The taxiways are immensely long and it took ages to get to the terminal building. Customs and immigration officers were quite polite and efficient. Our hotel was built on the site of an ancient palace: the central portion being modelled on the palace, with accommodation wings tacked on. Coffee was served with great ceremony in tiny cups. The coffee is so thick the spoon can be stood up in it and it's served with a glass of water to slake the thirst before enjoying the beverage. I went for an early morning run and immediately outside this palace of luxury found a woman, three small children and a dog all fast asleep on the pavement. I left them a few dollars.

The Cairo cemetery is immense and has quite a population of living people camped among the tombstones. Locals told me that it's one of the most dangerous places in the world, so dangerous that even the people who live there daren't move about at night. At the other end of the scale are the renowned museums, which display incredible amounts of gold, much of it originating from the pyramids.

One Christmas Eve

The details of a Christmas Eve flight from Singapore to Brisbane remain etched in my mind. The B747 was full to the gunwales with 378 passengers and crew and maximum freight. Departing Singapore on track for Australia involved a difficult climb with a heavy aircraft. The requirement was to reach 28,000 altitude by the end of Singapore controlled airspace; this was at the limit of a heavily laden 747's performance but it wasn't possible to get a waiver from air traffic control. The penalty for failing to reach the altitude by the specified distance was to fly a fuel-wasting, time-consuming circle to gain the required level. My Asian first officer and I nursed the aircraft carefully all the way up the climb at exactly the most efficient speeds and were relieved to make the stipulated altitude within the required distance. With the autopilot and altitude hold mode engaged, we accelerated to cruise speed. We were in cloud and the night was very dark.

Suddenly, *thump!* We exchanged looks of alarm. That bump wasn't atmospheric turbulence – it was the unmistakable mark of the slipstream of an aircraft that had passed immediately ahead of us. We'd narrowly avoided a mid-air collision. Nothing had been visible in the dark cloudy night, no navigation lights or sight of another aircraft. No warning of air traffic in our vicinity had been issued.

It was generally believed that certain military aircraft flew clandestine missions in that area, unlit and without notification to air traffic authorities.

A close-run thing there but it was the only near miss I experienced in 25 years of airline flying.

Collision avoidance systems

The avoidance of collisions is a concern of the utmost importance to everyone connected to aviation. Since about the 1980s, some clever innovations have been developed and installed in large aircraft. TCAS (traffic collision avoidance system) is designed to warn crews of traffic that may be a threat and to give instruction on action to be taken to avoid collision if a risk is developing. The expression ACAS-equipped aircraft means that aircraft has an airborne collision avoidance system. The device operates independently of ground-based systems and of air traffic control. The equipment commonly installed in airliners uses interchange of information between the two aircraft approaching one another. A device called a transponder receives a radar signal and then transmits a beefed-up response to the interrogator. This overcomes the problem that radar responses fade rapidly with increasing distance and significantly increases the range at which radar detects a target. The crew involved in a developing collision situation receives a variety of warnings, which increase in stridency as the risk grows. Typically, one pilot might be ordered to 'climb, climb, climb' and the other to 'dive, dive, dive' in a cockpit broadcast of high volume in an imperative tone, usually female – this is not something to be ignored! Naturally, some situations develop quickly and there's often no time to consult ATC. Since all air traffic is normally required to strictly maintain the flight path specified by the ATC clearance issued for that flight, a vast amount of legal work had to be done by all the countries in the world. It was necessary to legally require pilots to follow the TCAS instruction in emergency situations, even when the change to flight path would cause departure from the flight clearance without authorisation from ATC.

I've explained these systems at some length to assure readers that today, with near universal fitment of these safety devices, there is very little chance of two aircraft remaining on a collision course or of a near miss such as on my Brisbane flight.

My happy days with SIA continued. Sometimes the duty was to fly the freighter around the world. A common route was Singapore–Korea–Anchorage–Los Angeles. Often, we carried cattle from Los Angeles to Korea. If they started scouring, the smell permeating everything on the aircraft was just awful. After one such load, my crew and I were told by the Anchorage Hotel receptionist that we stank of cattle – two hours after we'd vacated the aircraft. However, there is a worse smell, which I discovered flying 50,000 three-day-old chicks from Amsterdam to Dubai.

Anchorage is known as the flyingest place in the world. There seem to be dozens of light aircraft landing fields and seaplane bases. A large number of migratory birds also fly through the area. We didn't want to tangle with gaggles of birds or light aircraft so stuck to the centre of the airways reserved for us. This is where I had my first encounter with ice fog. It has the disconcerting habits of draping the runway lights with ice masses and the sudden formation of dense fog on the runway.

21

BOYS AND GIRLS

Pilots and flight attendants tend to appreciate each other Both have been subjected to rigorous selection processes. They share good hotels, sometimes in exotic locations and are provided with generous allowances.

It wouldn't be human nature if liaisons didn't occur. Some people would stow their wedding rings until returning to home base. But promiscuity isn't so widespread as commonly supposed. Individuals who always respected their marriage vows were regarded with approval.

One captain who was regarded as a lady killer placed a device in his uniform pocket and foolishly forgot to remove it. His wife, eyes blazing with fury, placed it in front of him at the dinner table one night. This gentleman was a quick thinker. He burst out laughing. 'Bloody Tully,' he chortled. 'He got me at last. That's the third time he's put one of those in my pocket but I found the first two.' Tully was a flight engineer who loved to play jokes on people. The good lady apologised profusely for misjudging her husband. I often wonder if she was pretty dim or very smart.

I used to think the Asian flight attendants were quiet and demure. But after an overnight stop in Melbourne, I changed my mind. The cabin crew on that trip consisted of 15 women, one of whom was celebrating her birthday. We three flight deck crew members were invited to attend. I suggested that, as we were in Australia she should try an Aussie pub. Everyone agreed so I booked a table for 18 at a renowned hostelry, the Duke of Marlborough. Bottles of brandy were produced and the corks thrown away. I watched in amazement as T-bone steaks disappeared down the throats of snake-waisted beauties. The noise level rose and rose. Some young Australian men tried to muscle in, but there was no way they were going to get up to speed with this party so they retired abashed. What a riot! Next day, several of the women said it was such a good party, would I please organise another one.

Crews often socialised by getting together for dinner. One night in Los Angeles, there was a large party at a restaurant on Wilshire Boulevard. The custom was for one person to agree with the management on the bill and then collect cash from each diner. So, a large pool of cash was soon sitting on the table. The proprietor came up smiling and said he hoped we'd all enjoyed the meal. Yes, we said, it was excellent. The proprietor discreetly gathered up the cash and quietly disappeared. We all finished our coffee and prepared to go back to our hotel. Then another gentleman appeared and said we hadn't paid for the meal. He turned out to be the real proprietor. The other gentleman had scammed us – one cool customer! We bargained for a settlement of 50 per cent and all went our way poorer but wiser.

I suppose that's one way to support yourself if broke in a big city.

After five years of the most interesting flying, my 60th birthday arrived, and I had to accept compulsory retirement from SIA. Reluctantly, I departed from this fine company where I'd had a terrific time flying and had made many friends from countries all over the world.

22

FLYING STILL

I finished flying for SIA on a Friday and the following Monday reported to Air New Zealand again, in Jakarta. I had a short-term contract to fly Muslims to Saudi Arabia for their annual pilgrimage, the Hajj. This Muslim pilgrimage has continued for 1,400 years. It is one of the five pillars of Islam (the others are profession of faith, prayer, fasting during the holy month of Ramadan and alms giving). In earlier centuries, the Hajj it was a perilous journey from which not all pilgrims returned. A Muslim is expected to make the Hajj at least once in his life, when he can afford it, and thereafter is known as a Hadji. The Government of Indonesia subsidises those needing assistance to make the journey. The people we carried were gentle souls, pilgrims on a holy journey who had a spiritual air about them.

During my time in Singapore, I got to know many people of the Muslim faith. A large number of flight engineers had come to SIA from Pakistan International Airlines. One of these was from a family of 13 of which six were doctors of medicine. These associates insisted that the stereotype of Muslims as warlike and aggressive people was false. They were horrified by that image and insisted that only a small and fanatic minority lived violent lives. They said the vast majority of the faithful lead humble lives submissive to the will of Allah, of God.

It was exceedingly hot in Saudi Arabia on a typical arrival at Jeddah. The desert air was usually choppy as I manoeuvred the B747 above the desolate, arid, rocky landscape approaching the sprawling Jeddah airport with its three runways. Jeddah Approach Control was always busy, with heavy traffic inbound from everywhere. Strict radio discipline was needed as the international language of aviation, English, was spoken with myriad accents, some of them hard to understand. Lined up for landing on, say, runway 34 centre, I made a practice of reminding myself to brake gently in the 47°C temperature to avoid overheating the brakes.

Saudi Arabia allocates quotas to the many nations wishing to send pilgrims and controls the massive airlift. Within the country, excellent aid is provided for accommodation, travel and medical care. I believe the King has the title 'Custodian of the Two Holy Mosques'. The visiting pilgrims are welcomed as 'The guests of Allah'. Pilgrims are set down at a special Hajj terminal at Jeddah. It's fantastic. Open-sided and airy, the building is a series of several dozen sand-coloured 'tents' – soaring structures of modern materials, designed to resemble traditional Bedouin desert dwellings.

The universality of Islam is attested by the variety among the endless throng of people passing through this terminal. There are many nations. Statuesque and graceful Africans in brilliant colours mingle with Arab men in flowing white robes and women covered from head to toe in the black burqa and veils. There are Indians, Pakistanis, Indonesians, Malaysians, Turks, occasional Europeans and many, many races here. The pious visitors are treated with extraordinary respect. No voice is raised. There is surprisingly good order. Stacks of luggage, from the latest Gucci to fibre sacks tied with string, seem to get to the right place. A spiritual serenity hovered over these polyglot peoples. I never doubted they were pleasing to God.

Visitors to Mecca like to take holy water back to their home countries for the invocation of divine intercession for the sick of the community and family. Containers of it may be seen everywhere. Holy stones from the ceremony of Stoning the Devil are also taken, and many returning pilgrims are weighed down by pockets full as they board their return flight. Airline captains worry about the weight limits as high temperatures limit engine power but at least do not have to worry about alcohol. One American aircraft full of returning pilgrims crash-landed in Jordan and the crew supervising the emergency evacuation were astonished at the speed of passengers down the slides – they had been unaware of the practice of carrying stones.

Some things I've learned about Muslims, in flying internationally, are the vast majority do lead humble and submissive lives. Their beliefs are found in the Quran, which they believe was written by Muhammad with divine inspiration. They don't believe in the divinity of Christ, but accord respect to Him and His mother. They say Muhammad is the messenger of God, but that Jesus is the soul of God, a beautiful description. Generally, Christians are respected as 'People of the Book'. It shouldn't be forgotten that the Muslim Arabs preserved the culture of the Greeks and Romans from about the eighth century, passing the torch to Europe at the Renaissance.

I am reminded of St Francis Xavier. He was captured in Egypt during one of the battles between Christians and Muslims and taken before the Caliph of Baghdad. The two discovered that they shared common values and appreciation of virtues. It's recorded that they parted as brothers as St Francis was sent peacefully on his way to the Far East.

Pity we can't seem to recapture that spirit today.

Back to New Zealand

Returning to Auckland and reunited with my wife and five sons, I said, 'That's it' as I threw a much-thumbed passport in the drawer and prepared to settle down. The next morning the phone rang – I was on my way back to the B747 cockpit.

For the next five years, I flew under contract to Air Pacific (now Fiji Airways), until my final retirement at age 65.

I was pleased to be back in the company of the cheerful Fijians, who run a good airline under the watchful eyes of Qantas. Our principal routes were to Australia and Los Angeles. One of my good friends was a big strong Fijian man. When his powerful hands told a B747 what to do, the B747 did just that.

He told me he'd visited a friend in Honiara, in the Solomons, and there heard a fishing story that's hard to beat. The sea drops sharply off the reef at Honiara. The locals have developed a technique for successfully fishing in this situation. Plenty of coconut trees hang out over the deep water and the fisherman drapes himself with his equipment and scales over one of them. From his perch, he lowers into the water a device made from two halves of a coconut connected by a short rope. Pulling sharply on the rope creates a noise like a thwack, which attracts the bigger fish – they probably think it's a creature in distress. When there are enough fish milling about, he scatters pieces of white coconut flesh into the water. This brings the small fish out from the reef to join in the feast. All is now ready. The fisherman reaches into his pocket and pulls out a hand grenade: there are a lot of these in the Solomons – relics of the war. After the explosion, a net is cast and a nice catch of the stunned fish is dragged ashore. But on the occasion of our story, the fisherman dropped the grenade after pulling out the pin and it rolled down the tree to lodge in a frond a few feet below him. Hurriedly, the man made the correct decision and leaped off the tree into the water below, which was full of expectant fish, including sharks. The exploding grenade blew the tree down on top of him. Luckily for him, he was able to clamber ashore unhurt except for a few scratches.

The Fijians were a happy lot and usually trim and fit. In their villages, practically every night they play games. On our stopovers, there was always a game of volleyball going to help keep fit.

Their greeting, *bulla*, is universally known. What isn't so well known is that *bulla* means 'you live'. In previous centuries, shipwrecked mariners ('those with salt in their eyes') were commonly slaughtered by these cannibal folk. But if a chief took a liking to one of the captives, he'd say, 'Bulla', and the sailor would be spared.

During my time with the Fijians, the crew of an Air New Zealand aircraft on turnaround at Nadi airport were interrupted in the cockpit by a rather disturbed armed person. Correctly, the crew acceded to the man's demands until the flight engineer managed to get behind him and deal him a disabling blow to the head with a bottle of duty-free liquor. What fun the media had with that and with the engineer's comment that he hadn't done anything like that since primary school!

23

MALAYSIAN AIRLINES FLIGHT 370

I think it appropriate to comment on the mysterious disappearance of Malaysia Airlines Flight 370 on 8 March 2014. I'm often asked if I've formed any opinion as to what happened. Nobody knows what befell this airliner, but there are inferences to be drawn from what's known of the flight after it lost contact with air traffic control agencies.

Radar and transponders

Analyses of the initial portion of the flight depend heavily on radar returns. Two types of radar are involved: primary and secondary. Primary radars are military installations of high power that radiate energy from their ground antennae and show contacts on their screens as reflections from the targets. Pulses from the antennae radiate outwards in the shape of a sphere, so the energy decreases as an inverse proportion of the surface of the sphere. The surface of a sphere is, mathematically, a function of the radius squared, so the radar energy reaching a target is the inverse square of the distance. For example, if the energy reaching a target at 1 kilometre is of a certain value, the energy reaching a target at 2 kilometres is a quarter of that (½ squared = ¼) and the energy reaching a target at three kilometres is one-ninth of that (1/3 squared = 1/9).

Now, once the target has been struck by the radar energy pulse, it generates a return echo, which in similar manner dissipates as an inverse function of the square of the return distance to the radar-receiving antenna. The power of the image finally received back at the radar station is a function of the fourth root of the distance to the target. If a target at 1 kilometre returns an echo of a certain strength, an echo from a target at 2 kilometres is 1/16th of that strength (1/2x2x2x2).

It's clear that military radars must therefore be of high power to generate echoes of sufficient strength to show up on a screen. These primary radar installations are expensive, use considerable amounts of electrical power and radiate emissions that can be harmful to humans. They're unsuitable to air traffic control agencies, which use a clever device called a transponder to greatly extend the range of a relatively low-powered radar.

A transponder is a device carried in an aircraft. It receives the incoming radar pulse and generates its own pulse, which is radiated back to the radar ground installation. This return pulse is generated from aircraft power supplies and is, of course, of much higher power than the reflected echo of a primary radar system. Thus, the size of the ground installation used by air traffic control agencies – the secondary radar system – is much smaller than the installation for a primary system. This smaller ground station is able to maintain radar contact with aircraft to the distances required by each air traffic controller.

The ability of the ground station of the secondary system to maintain radar contact with the aircraft is dependent on the aircraft transponder being operative. If the crew of an aircraft switch off the transponder, radar contact will be immediately lost.

Hypoxia

An understanding of hypoxia is necessary to gain a proper appreciation of events that probably occurred on flight MH370. Hypoxia is a lack of sufficient oxygen in the body (in the blood, bodily tissues and/or cells).

The most common causes of hypoxia in aviation are:

a. Prolonged flight above 10,000 feet altitude without an oxygen supply
b. A pressurisation system malfunction
c. An oxygen system fault
d. A rapid depressurisation, particularly an explosive depressurisation, where there's a sudden loss of pressurisation due to a rupture of the pressure hull; for example, loss of a door.

Two of four types of hypoxia are relevant to the MH370 investigation. They are hypoxic hypoxia, also known as altitude hypoxia, and hypemic hypoxia.

Hypoxic hypoxia occurs with a reduction in pressure of the cabin air. The proportion of oxygen doesn't alter but the molecules, being further apart, reduce the partial pressure, producing less pounds per square inch. If the pressure falls to a certain critical level lungs cease to be able to transfer oxygen to the blood to be distributed to all the body tissues.

In hypemic hypoxia, the blood has reduced ability to carry oxygen. Carbon monoxide contamination in the air is the most likely cause in an aircraft – possibly from an engine exhaust leak or as the result of a fire. Carbon monoxide has an affinity for haemoglobin, (which carries oxygen in the bloodstream) and binds to it 200 times more tightly than to oxygen.

With a gradual loss of pressure leading to hypoxic hypoxia, the onset is insidious and the victim is unlikely to recognise any symptoms. Most crew members, as part of their training in aviation medicine, receive a lesson in this dangerous progression into an hypoxic state. They are placed in a decompression chamber (hypobaric chamber) and the pressure is gradually reduced – the students being instructed have an oxygen supply so that they remain alert but the one chosen to demonstrate the hypoxic effects is without oxygen. The 'victim' will be set a task, usually writing, and as the hypoxia takes effect, performance deteriorates: the writing becomes a scrawl and ends as a line on the page as the subject slides into unconsciousness. It's evident to the observers that the subject has no appreciation of their failing abilities.

The effect of a hypoxic situation varies from individual to individual. Some, particularly those who've been educated as to the condition, may recognise the early stages in time to take remedial action. Recovery is rapid when oxygen is administered.

Time of useful consciousness

Also known as effective performance time, the time of useful consciousness (TUC) is the time in which a pilot can take effective remedial action following a decompression at various altitudes before lapsing into a state where he cannot think or perform necessary tasks. The pilot's first – and immediate – action on recognition of a decompression is to don his or her oxygen mask. Pilots have special masks immediately adjacent to their seats that have a system of levers designed to allow placement within seconds on the head, with the mask firmly positioned over the mouth. This mask is always turned on to ensure an immediate flow of oxygen when the first intake of breath is made. Special goggles are also immediately available if smoke or noxious fumes are present. Oxygen from the mask flows through the inside of these goggles to blow away the smoke or fumes to allow clear sight of the instruments.

The figures by altitude (flight level FL) of TUC published in training documents by the American Federal Aviation Authority are:

Flight level 150 (15,000 feet) – 30 minutes or more
FL180 – 20 to 30 minutes
FL220 – 5 to 10 minutes
FL250 – 3 to 6 minutes
FL280 – 2.5 to 3 minutes
FL350 – 30 to 60 seconds
FL400 – 15 to 20 seconds
FL430 – 9 to 15 seconds

At normal jetliner cruising levels (about 35,000 feet) the pilot's recovery actions must be carried out immediately. He or she must don the mask, ensure the oxygen is flowing, enter a steep descent to a safe level – normally 10,000 feet – and deploy the air brakes (large sections at the wing trailing edge which create extra drag) to accelerate the descent. Meanwhile in the cabin, automatic systems will have caused oxygen masks to drop from the ceiling in front of passengers' faces. Additional oxygen cylinders are placed around the cabin for staff walking about the cabin. These must be taken from their stowage, turned on, checked and the attached mask fitted.

Explosive decompression

A very rapid loss of cabin pressure is known as an explosive decompression. It would normally be caused by a rupture of the pressurised hull. A cause might be blowing out of a freight door or several windows. The effects of an explosive decompression are alarming for passengers and crew: usually loud noise, a drop in pressure causing bodily exhalations, formation of fog in the cabin and rapid lowering of temperature. The pilot's immediate action following explosive decompression is to don the oxygen mask before commencing an emergency descent.

It should be noted that in an explosive decompression TUC published in the table immediately above may be reduced to one-third to a half of the table values. Thus at FL350, the 30 to 60 seconds table time is reduced to 15 to 30 seconds (one-half), or to 10 to 20 seconds (one-third) Similarly at FL400 TUC reduces to 7.5 to 10 seconds or 5 to 7 seconds. At FL430 (an altitude of significance to our considerations following), TUC is reduced to 4.5 to 7.5 or 3 to 5 seconds. The reason for this is the forcing of oxygen from the lungs due to rapid expansion of the gas in an explosive decompression. Medically, the phenomenon is called reverse diffusion, or fulminating hypoxia.

In a nutshell, loss of pressurisation at extreme altitudes, resulting in TUCs down to 3 to 5 seconds, is a dangerous business.

Communications on MH370

In addition to normal radios, MH370 operated a sophisticated satellite communications system. Numerous communications and data reporting systems, which operate according to a set schedule or in response to a signal from the communications satellite, exist. For example, data from operating engines might be regularly despatched to the manufacturers; there have been instances (unrelated to the flight of MH370) where an engine manufacturer became aware of an operating fault and despatched a warning to the crew in flight. Some information on the position of an aircraft can be deduced by analysis of the signals exchanged with the satellite.

Prior to the publicity surrounding this flight, the existence of reporting systems operating independently of the flight crew was little known. It's likely that the crew of MH370 weren't aware of some of the transmissions. They would, of course, have been trained in the use of satellite communications equipment designed to be used in the cockpit.

THE HISTORY OF FLIGHT MH370

Flight details

Malaysian Airways flight MH370 was scheduled to depart from Kuala Lumpur International Airport, Malaysia, in the early morning of 8 March 2014 bound for Beijing Capital International Airport, China. The aircraft was a Boeing 777-200ER, registration 9M-MRO. Some 227 passengers and 12 crew were on board; 152 passengers were Chinese citizens and 38 were Malaysians. A party of 20 – 12 Malaysians and 8 Chinese – were employees of a company called Freescale Semiconductor.

The captain, Zaharie Ahmad Shah, was a citizen of Malaysia who came from Penang. He was a training captain on 777-200ER aircraft and had 18,365 hours flying experience. His first officer was 27-year-old Fariq Abdul Hamid, who had 2763 hours. The first officer was on his final flight training to qualify on 777 aircraft and was scheduled to be examined on his next flight.

The flight was scheduled to depart Kuala Lumpur at 00.35 MYT (Malaysian time, which is UTC plus eight hours) and arrive at Beijing 06.30 CST (China time) on 8 March, 2014. Planned flight time was 5 hours and 34 minutes. There was enough fuel – 49,100 kilograms – to keep the aircraft flying for 7 hours and 31 minutes.

The flight

At 00.42 MYT (all times hereafter are MYT), the flight was airborne. The air traffic control (ATC) facility which controlled the departure was Lumpur Radar, which cleared the flight to climb to FL350 (flight level 350, or 35,000 feet). Post-flight voice analysis showed that the first officer made the radio calls prior to flight but the captain communicated with ATC during flight. At time 01.01, the captain reported the flight had reached FL350; this information was repeated at 01.08.

Pilots regularly report position to ATC units by voice radio transmission. On this aircraft, there was also an automated position reporting system which used a system called Aircraft Communications Addressing and Reporting System (ACARS). The last automated position report was made at 01.06. This was the last ACARS transmission of the flight.

At 01.19, when the aircraft was approaching the boundary between the Malaysian ATC and Vietnamese ATC systems, Captain Shah acknowledged Lumpur Radar's instruction to report to Ho Chi Minh Air Control Centre. Captain Shah bade goodnight to the Malaysian controller. This was the last radio transmission heard from the aircraft. No attempt was made to establish contact with the Ho Chi Minh ACC. At 01.21, MH370's transponder stopped operating, and the contacts on the Lumpur Radar and Ho Chi Minh ACC radar screens disappeared. The last transmission from the transponder showed the aircraft to be at FL350.

Shortly after the loss of radar contact, the controller at Ho Chi Minh ACC asked another aircraft in the vicinity to pass a message asking MH370 to make contact. This request was transmitted to MH370 on the international distress frequency 121.5 megacycles, a radio channel that is required by law to be constantly monitored by international flights. The call established contact with MH370, but the captain of the aircraft making the call testified he heard only static and mumbling.

At the time radar contact with MH370 was lost on the secondary radar (ATC) system, the primary radar system gained radar contact on the aircraft. The Malaysian military radar observed the aircraft make an initial turn to the left, but the turn was reversed and it stabilised on a south-easterly heading, 231 degrees magnetic, during the period 01.30 to 01.35. Aircraft altitude was determined to be 35,700 feet (10,881 metres). This course took the aircraft across the Malay Peninsula, heading for the vicinity of Penang Island, which lies off the west coast of the Malay Peninsula.

At 01.52, after passing just to the south of Penang Island, the aircraft took up a north-westerly heading across the Strait of Malacca and on across the Andaman Sea. The last radar detection, near the limits of Malaysian military radar, was at 02.22, some 237 nautical miles (439 kilometres) north-west of Penang airport. After this radar return faded, there was no further primary radar contact with the aircraft.

A private radar station in Malaysia gained fleeting contact with MH370. Probably various other military radar installations also observed MH370 but didn't report their sightings. Because of the tensions in this part of the world, some countries may not have reported sightings for fear of revealing information on the capabilities of their military systems. Thai and Indonesian military radars didn't report sightings. Unfortunately, the Australian long-range 'over the horizon' system, which has a range of 3000 kilometres, wasn't operative that night.

After the 02.22 radar sighting, MH370 disappeared. Nothing further was heard by any air traffic control agency, and the automated reporting system using ACARS was disabled, probably about the same time as the secondary radar traces disappeared.

Continued satellite communications (SATCOM) with the aircraft

The satellite data unit (SDU) aboard the aircraft communicated with Satellite 3-F1, which was positioned over the Indian Ocean. The satellite simply passed on the communication, or data, to a ground station. Both satellite and ground station were owned by Inmarsat, a telecommunications company. Messages received at the ground station were passed on to appropriate destinations.

Communication on this system started with a request to log on, followed by an acknowledgment of logging on. This procedure could be initiated by either the aircraft or the ground station through the satellite. When powered up by the application of electric power, the aircraft SDU requests a log-on. When this has been acknowledged by the Inmarsat ground station, a 'handshake' has taken place. Should the aircraft remain out of communication for one hour thereafter, the ground station would send a message requesting a log-on – this procedure is called a 'ping'.

The log of contacts which occurred between the SDU and the ground station after the 02.22 loss of primary radar contact is:

02.25   first handshake log-on request initiated by the aircraft SDU

02.39   a telephone call from the ground to the aircraft was made and recorded but remained unanswered from the cockpit

03.41   second handshake, initiated by the ground station

04.41   third handshake, initiated by the ground station

05.41   fourth handshake, initiated by the ground station

06.41   fifth handshake, initiated by the ground station

07.13   another ground-to-air telephone call, which was again acknowledged by the SDU but remained unanswered

08.10   sixth handshake, initiated by the ground station

08.19   a seventh handshake, which was initiated by the aircraft. The log-on request was answered by the ground station, and this response was acknowledged by the SDU as a limited contact called a 'partial handshake'

09.15   the aircraft didn't respond to a ping.

Conclusions to be drawn from the SATCOM log

First, at the time of the last contact, 08.19, the aircraft had been airborne for seven hours after contact with air traffic control had been lost. Examination and analysis of the aircraft/satellite communications showed that it had continued at high speed. A comparison of the frequency change from transmission to reception, Doppler effect, proved the high speed had been constantly maintained.

Secondly, at 08.19 the aircraft had been flying for 7 hours 36 minutes after takeoff. The fuel endurance had been calculated at 7 hours 31 minutes. Therefore, four-engine flameout must have occurred about this time.

Another conclusion to be drawn from the 08.19 communication is that altitude must have been maintained at or near MH370's planned flight levels. Jet aircraft are designed to operate most efficiently in the cold, thin air of the stratosphere where drag – the resistance of the air to the aircraft's passage – is much lower than at sea level. The engines are also designed to operate most efficiently in the stratospheric environment. Fuel consumption at sea level can be of the order of three times that at altitude. Since the fuel lasted until the expiry of the calculated endurance time, it follows that it hadn't been burnt up more rapidly than calculated for the planned flight. Therefore the aircraft had remained at cruising levels for the seven hours since loss of contact with air traffic control. It follows that at high speed at cruising levels, it must have travelled a great distance.

Thirdly, complex calculations on each transmission allow an estimate to be made of the distance on the Earth's surface that the aircraft is from the satellite. An arc centred on the satellite position can be drawn, and the aircraft's position must be somewhere on that arc. A series of positions can give a rough estimate of position and an indication of the general direction in which the aircraft is heading. The conclusion drawn from this information is that the aircraft was headed to the south Indian Ocean.

Fourthly, the fact that the last transmission, at 08.19, was initiated by the aircraft leads to certain conclusions. In the SATCOM system, it's unusual for the aircraft to initiate a handshake while in flight. One of the reasons which will cause this is an electric power interruption. Since the aircraft was approaching the limit of its fuel endurance it's likely the power was lost by flameout of all four engines as the aircraft entered its final dive to the wild ocean below. Boeing have built in to their 777-200ER fleet a back-up system, a generator powered by a ram air turbine, which supplies certain instruments and equipment, including the satellite data unit. The turbine would have extended automatically after flameout. Thus, the SDU would follow its programmed start-up sequence when the ram air turbine power supply powered it up, including the initiation of a handshake. The presumption of this sequence is reinforced by there being on previous handshakes background noises recorded by the ground station emanating from the in-flight entertainment system. Since this noise wasn't present on the 08.19 exchange, and power wasn't supplied to the entertainment system by the ram air turbine, the belief that flameout had occurred is reinforced. It is also to be noted that there was no response from the SDU to the 09.15 ping.

Lastly, since the position and track of the aircraft must have been known so that the SDU antenna was kept pointed at the satellite, the navigation systems must have remained operative.

Shortly after 08.19, the tragic flight of MH370 had ended.

The search

A search began as soon as it was confirmed that the aircraft was missing. It lasted from 8 March until 28 April. Nineteen vessels were involved and 345 sorties were flown by military aircraft with oceanic search capabilities. As information became available, the search area was constantly changed and extended. A total area of approximately 4.5 million square kilometres was searched. In the final phase of the initial search a bathymetric survey and sonar search of the sea floor was commenced. This was suspended on 17 January 2017. In January 2018, a new search by the United States company Ocean Infinity commenced. On 18 May the Norwegian ship *Seabed Constructor* joined in using eight autonomous underwater vehicles. The search continued until 9 June 2018.

Despite the massive effort, nothing was found.

Debris

A total of 20 pieces of debris believed to come from the lost aircraft were found on beaches on the western side of the Indian Ocean. Some items were positively confirmed as coming from MH370. Of particular interest was a piece of a trailing edge of the wing control surface, a flaperon. Since this was confirmed to be in the retracted position, it was concluded that the aircraft flaps weren't extended when the airframe made contact with the water. In a controlled ditching, flaps would always be extended to reduce to a minimum the speed at which impact with the ocean surface occurred.

What happened?

Theories as to the cause of the disappearance weren't long in surfacing in the international media, and later in the reports of various government agencies. The truth, however, cannot be expected to be established unless and until the wreckage of the aircraft is discovered.

Recriminations

Internationally and within Malaysia, the recriminations came thick and fast. People demanded explanations for the tragedy, but no one could provide details or the possible motives of anyone responsible.

In their public statements, Malaysian Government politicians and agencies contradicted one another. The relatives of the Chinese passengers were highly critical, accusing the Malaysian Government of failing to provide information in a timely manner. Some relatives held protest meetings in Malaysia and even accused the Malaysian Government of harbouring a murderer.

The Chinese ambassador to Malaysia complained that Western media published false news, spread rumours and generally did their best to stoke conflict.

Severe criticism was levelled at the Malaysian military for its failure to react to the passage of an unknown aircraft through its airspace. It transpired that the intrusion had passed unnoticed until radar records were examined some hours after the event. The appropriate minister's explanation was that they knew the intruder was a civilian aircraft and as they weren't going to shoot it down, there was no point in scrambling a fighter aircraft. Everyone was acutely aware that an interception and positive identification of MH370 could have shed light on the mystery and reduced the need for the vast search which eventuated.

Power outage

Much can be inferred from the performance of the SATCOM system. It operated normally from the time of pre-flight check (00.00) until the reply to the ground-to-air ACARS message, which was acknowledged at 01.07. There were further normal responses to ground-to-air ACARS messages until 02.03, when repeated SATCOM requests for acknowledgment elicited no response.

Power to the aircraft SDU can be assumed to have been lost at some time after 01.07. At 02.25, an air-to-ground request for acknowledgment was sent. That was unusual for an aircraft in flight. Of the several possible explanations for this transmission, the most likely is a restoration of power after an interruption. This was confirmed by certain characteristics of the transmission and by the timing. As the aircraft continued flying for some hours thereafter, the cause of the power outage wasn't flameout of the four engines. It is highly likely that someone manually switched off the aircraft's electrical system and subsequently restored it.

Australia Transport Safety Bureau's investigation

The ATSB suggested three alternatives: an inflight loss of control, a complete engine power loss, and a failure of the crew to respond, perhaps due to an hypoxia event. It favoured the third explanation, considering the lengthy flight afterwards, the absence of communications and the fact there were no significant deviations from a track that was most likely to have been flown on autopilot. The report noted that, had there been a flameout or autopilot disconnect about the time of loss of secondary radar contact, it's most likely that the result would be entry to a spiral dive and a crash in the ocean not far from the point where that radar contact had been lost. The flaperon wreckage in its retracted position supports the supposition of an uncontrolled crash.

Passenger involvement

Looking into the possibility of passenger involvement, United States and Malaysian authorities investigated every passenger whose name was on the passenger manifest. There were some alarms, principally the discovery that two passengers were travelling on false passports, but inquiries didn't suggest any likelihood of sabotage.

Wilder media speculation had it that murky spooks had done away with the technical party of 20 Chinese and Malaysians to conceal sinister intelligence. Afterwards they hi-jacked the aircraft and flew it to an unspecified Asian destination, where the persons on board remain in captivity. The ideas never gained much traction. Any flight to the politically unsettled regions to the north of the Indian Ocean would have been certain to excite hostile interest and reports from military radar agencies at the very least.

In the absence of any information to the contrary, it seems reasonable to conclude that no passengers were involved.

Cargo

The 221 kilograms of lithium-ion batteries in the hold attracted speculation, as did a consignment of fruit. The batteries been packed in accordance with the International Air Transport Association (IATA) standards and weren't classed as dangerous goods. Should overheating lead to ignition lithium-ion batteries burn with intense heat. Lithium-ion batteries are known to have caused the crashes of at least two air cargo aircraft. The batteries on board MH370 were packed on two pallets, one in the forward cargo hold and another in the rear cargo hold. From these positions it's entirely possible that either of the pallets caching fire could have spread noxious fumes – possibly poisonous – throughout the aircraft through the air conditioning system. It was remotely possible that both pilots could have been quickly incapacitated by the sudden inrush of poisonous fumes.

Yet that seems unlikely. Pilots are trained to handle the emergency of smoke or fumes in the cockpit and always have their emergency oxygen masks and protective goggles available when occupying their seats. At the first hint of fumes, each pilot would have immediately put on mask and goggles. In any case, if both were unexpectedly made unresponsive, that wouldn't explain the switching off of the transponder or the turns observed by Malaysian military radar. Rather, the aircraft could have been expected to maintain straight and level flight under autopilot control.

However, cargo involvement cannot be entirely ruled out. Poisonous fumes might have partially incapacitated both pilots. In a mentally confused state, they may have succeeded in turning the aircraft towards Penang airport for an emergency landing. Subsequent flight then might have been controlled by an unsupervised autopilot after the pilots collapsed.

The consignment of fruit – 4.5 tonnes of mangosteens – was of interest. An extensive police investigation of the people preparing this cargo for despatch and also the Chinese recipients conclude there was no reason to suspect them of sabotage.

It's reasonable to conclude that there's only a remote chance that cargo did cause the MH370 disaster.

Crew involvement

United States intelligence believe someone in the cockpit reprogrammed the autopilot to take the flight to the southern Indian Ocean. Suspicion has to be centred on one or both of the two pilots. No one else on board is known to have had the skills to control the flight of the aircraft.

At least one of these may have been a monster, a person prepared to commit mass murder to achieve his suicidal flight to one of the loneliest places on Earth, where all might disappear without trace. Murder is always wicked but the cold-blooded, premeditated murder of hundreds of innocent people, if that is what happened, is diabolically wicked. When those people have entrusted themselves to the care of an airline pilot, a person the public instinctively trust, to be conveyed through the hostile environment of the stratosphere, any betrayal would be an outrage. The suffering inflicted on the families and friends of the victims was terrible. They were deprived not only of their loved ones but left without knowledge of the manner of their demise or the location of their remains.

Is it plausible that anyone would decide to turn their suicide into the mass murder of everyone else on board a commercial airliner? Could such a monster plan to journey to one of the most inhospitable places on Earth to disappear forever? Could that person have accepted a crash into the cold, stormy seas of the Southern Ocean? Forensic psychologists may be able to provide an explanation if such evil occurred, but I cannot.

What is the likelihood of involvement in the crime of each of the pilots ?

The first officer was a young man aged 27 who'd progressed through the usual Malaysian Airlines aircraft sequence: Boeing 737 and Airbus 330 to the Boeing 777. He began his training on the 777 in November 2013. Following the MH370 flight he was scheduled for a type-rating final check on the next flight on his roster. As with all 12 crew members on the flight, the Malaysian police investigated him. His financial records revealed no significant transactions to have occurred or which were pending. Police general inquiries and interviews with his family didn't disclose any behavioural abnormalities. Given his age and the exciting life of a successful airline pilot before him plus his relative inexperience on the 777, it seems unlikely that he'd conceive the cold-blooded plan of murdering his passengers and fellow crew members. Among the acts involved were depressurising the aircraft to cause death by hypoxia, shutting off electrical power and deactivating the transponder and ACARS positioning reporting system. This sequence, requiring extensive knowledge of the aircraft systems, would have needed much confidence in his ability to perform the many tasks in limited time while under stress. For instance, cutting off electrical power would require the aircraft to be flown manually as the autopilot would be deactivated. Manual flight at FL350 requires care and attention. It's unlikely that a pilot still under training on type would be confident enough to trust himself to achieve this complex sequence. While nothing is known with certainty, it does seem unlikely that the first officer planned and executed a mass murder of all others aboard MH370.

It's almost beyond belief that the two pilots colluded with each other to commit this awful crime. They would have to have agreed to a mutual suicide pact. This leaves only the captain to be investigated.

Captain Shah was 'a Penang boy' (*Straits Times*, 8 March 2014) and had been with Malaysian Airlines for 33 years, having joined as a cadet pilot in 1981. He'd been promoted to captain in 1991. His initial command was on a Boeing 737. This was followed by command of an Airbus 330 in 1996 and of the Boeing 777 in 1998. At the time of the MH370 flight, he was 53 and had been a captain of the 777 for 16 years. He'd been a type-rating instructor and type-rating examiner for seven years, so his knowledge of the Boeing 777-200 aircraft must have been deep and extensive. If anyone had the technical capability to perform the sequence of actions required to execute everyone on board and hide the subsequent route from air traffic control and military radars, it was Captain Shah.

The Malaysian police examination of Captain Shah's financial records and behaviour discovered nothing of significance.

However he possessed a computer that he used as a home flight simulator. A Reuters report dated 9 March 2014 described him as 'an aviation tech geek'. The computer was seized and in due course examined by the United States FBI. Their experts were able to reconstruct entries that had been deleted from the computer. They discovered that Captain Shah had set up a simulated route which was described as 'closely matching the flight of MH370 over the Indian Ocean'. This information, which surfaced as a media report, was subsequently confirmed by the Australian Transport Safety Board and the Malaysian Government.

At first sight, it appears to be damning evidence. But as a geek, Captain Shah must have known that skilled persons can recover everything that's ever been recorded on a computer. If he was plotting to have an aircraft disappear, he must have known law enforcement authorities would impound his computer and extract everything from it. One would suppose that if he had planned to hijack the aircraft, he'd have destroyed the computer to avoid disclosure of the suspicious planning. This factor tends to diminish the significance of his flight planning of the fatal route. I agree with the Australian Transport Safety Board that this flight planning didn't prove that Captain Shah was guilty of murder.

Overall, however, if there was human intervention in the diversion of the flight, the United States intelligence assessment that Captain Shah must be the prime suspect is obviously correct.

Yet he apparently gave no sign of unusual behaviour in his pre-flight duties or in his radio exchanges with air traffic control once airborne. Had he exhibited nervousness or discomposure, then surely the police investigation would have uncovered evidence of this. In the final exchange with air traffic control at 01.19, when he acknowledged instructions to call Ho Chi Minh Air Control Centre, he politely bade the controller good night. If he was about to commit mass murder, he must have had nerves of steel to act normally. It would be unfair to condemn Captain Shah in the absence of further proof. Such proof is unlikely to surface unless the aircraft is found.

Is it possible there was murder most foul?

Are the known details of the flight consistent with a person – the murderer – taking control of the flight after contact with air traffic control was lost?

Commonly, investigators have hypothesised that the first officer was despatched from the cockpit on some errand and then locked out of the cockpit. The cockpit door is strong and bulletproof, so the murderer would then be safe from interference. I think this assumption needs examination.

If the captain knew he was about to incapacitate everyone on board by depressurisation of the cabin and switching off the aircraft electric power, he would know that despite the cockpit door being locked after the first officer's departure, the first officer would have remained a risk to his plans. Once the aircraft electrical power was switched off, the first officer would have been alarmed. The cabin would have retained a degree of illumination as the emergency lights, powered by a standby battery source, would have come on. At FL350, his time of useful consciousness would have been 30–60 seconds. He would have had time to grab the nearest portable oxygen bottle from a number stored for the use of crew in a decompression and don the mask fitted to it.

The murderer – demonstrably capable of detailed planning – would have anticipated that the first officer would have recognised that something was afoot when the people in the cabin started lapsing into unconsciousness all around him. Thus the first officer – and any other crew member who managed to seize a portable oxygen bottle – would thereafter be a threat to the murderer. As there would have been a number of emergency bottles available in the cabin, the first officer could have remained a threat for several hours. If he had been able to regain access to the cockpit the first officer would have fought the captain in a desperate struggle for survival. The captain would in the ensuing hours of flight remain dependent on the locked cabin door to guard against what would be a fight to the death.

It seems more likely that the murderer would have incapacitated the first officer. A weapon could have been smuggled aboard and hidden.

It's also conceivable that both pilots could have been overcome by a person unknown who had flying experience.

Meanwhile, in the cockpit, confident that he would remain undisturbed, the murderer would have been on task. After turning off the transponder to disguise his actions from air traffic control, he would have had all the time in the world to go about depressurising the cabin and switching off electric power.

In the cabin, now illuminated only by emergency lights, oxygen masks would have deployed and probably been used by the passengers. But the oxygen supply to the passengers' masks, designed to support the passengers only during a dive to a safe altitude, would have been exhausted in about 15 minutes. All occupants of the cabin except those on an emergency bottle supply would then succumb to hypoxia and expire. Whether or not these actions were actually carried out will never be known for sure unless the wreckage is discovered.

The last automated position report was receipted at 01.06, so the system was switched off after this time. At 01.21 the transponder became inoperative and secondary radar contact was lost. Assuming murder was intended, dealing with the pilot(s) is likely to have been the first action in the murderer's plan, to be followed by switching off the transponder. Any person disabling both pilots and transponder must have been familiar with the aircraft systems.

It was significant that the loss of signal occurred as the aircraft approached the boundary between Malaysian and Vietnamese airspace. The aircraft then turned to a south-east course and more or less followed the boundary between the two jurisdictions. This action seems designed to create confusion as Lumpur Radar and Ho Chi Minh control queried one another as to MH370's whereabouts. The actions indicate the diversion was due to human interference rather than as a result of the crew being struck down by noxious gases.

Another aircraft attempted to call MH370 on the international distress frequency but the call – which records indicated appeared to have been received by MH370 – was answered only by mumbling and static. Something unusual had occurred.

If the murderer then began depressurising the cabin to render all therein unconscious due to hypoxia, he would have donned his emergency oxygen mask to avoid becoming hypoxic himself. The bottle supplying oxygen to his mask also supplied the first officer's mask. It would have lasted several hours, especially if it was being used by only one person.

After switching off the aircraft electrical power, which would fail the automatic pilot, the murderer would have had to fly the aircraft manually. Manual flying requires care and attention at high altitudes. The person would have been busy indeed as he went about the depressurisation. It should be noted that there is radio communication built in to the oxygen mask, but transmissions tend to be indistinct, as they are affected by the oxygen flow. Perhaps this goes some way to explaining the mumbling heard by the other aircraft in the vicinity.

Exactly how the cabin was depressurised will never be known. It could have been a slow process so that people would slide into unconsciousness without alarming themselves or their neighbours. Or it could have been effected rapidly by the captain opening wide the pressurisation control valve. It couldn't have been an explosive decompression initiated from the cockpit. Whatever method was used, the victims would almost certainly have lost consciousness peacefully and painlessly. Death would have followed soon after.

Although there doesn't appear to be any mention of it in the various reports issued after the event, I can distinctly remember there were media reports in 2014 that the aircraft had climbed to FL430. If this climb did occur, it's a significant indication of intent to murder, to accelerate termination of 238 lives. Since time of useful consciousness at FL430 is only nine to 15 seconds, death would come quickly.

A climb to F430 in a Boeing 777-200 would sandwich the aircraft between two limits: stall speed and maximum mach number. Pilots call this space 'coffin corner'. As an aircraft climbs, the air density falls. But the stall speed, as measured by the pressure of the air due to motion (the indicated airspeed), remains constant for a given weight. The thinner the air, the faster the aircraft must go to maintain the minimum indicated airspeed. But another factor comes into play: mach number, the proportion of the local speed of sound at which the aircraft is moving. At about mach 0.85, the air accelerated over the top of the wing (which creates the lift needed to keep flying) reaches mach 1.0 and forms a shockwave. In the wake of the shockwave, airflow is disturbed. The elevators on the tailplane lose effectiveness in the disturbed flow and cannot maintain control of the attitude. The aircraft can pitch wildly in this disturbed flow. When the minimum speed to avoid stall equals the maximum mach speed, you are in coffin corner with no ability to exert control.

Pilots carefully avoid getting into such situations, partly by limiting the altitude. While I don't have the performance figures for a Boeing 777-200 available, I'm sure F430 would place the aircraft close to or in coffin corner. This altitude would never be countenanced in normal flight. If the murderer did take the risk of loss of control by ascending to this level, we may be sure it was for a sinister purpose: to ensure anyone still alive in the cabin died quickly.

The person in the cockpit, presumably dressed in normal clothes, would have been subject to severe cold as the temperature in a depressurised cabin will quickly fall to near the temperature of the outside air. Temperatures at altitude vary widely and may go as low as about minus 70° Celsius. On a standard day, the temperature of the ambient air at FL350 is minus 54° Celsius. The murderer would, when satisfied all in the cabin had become unconscious, have been obliged to repressurise enough to be reasonably comfortable. While this might tend to revive hypoxic people, the murderer, impregnable behind the bulletproof cockpit door, could afford to accept any delay in the progress of hypoxia: the aircraft was going to be crashed come what may, so if someone remained alive a little longer in the cabin, they'd soon die anyway.

The aircraft electrical supply must have been restored as subsequent SATCOM transmissions proved the navigation system was working, as was the cabin entertainment system. Power had been restored at the time of the SATCOM aircraft-to-the-ground call at 02.25. This is one hour and six minutes after the last communication from Captain Shah to air traffic control. The interval of approximately one hour would seem to have been enough to have hypoxia do its deadly work – if that was what occurred.

Apart from the possible excursion to FL430, MH370's altitude fluctuated by up to 2000 feet from FL350. Excursions of this magnitude are uncommon – and dangerous, as only 1000 feet separation is provided between aircraft flying in opposite directions. Level flight is normally maintained by the autopilot being engaged in altitude hold mode, which can be expected to maintain the selected altitude exactly. The altitude excursions were an indication that MH370 was being flown abnormally.

The aircraft's track past the island of Penang may possibly be of significance. Penang was Captain Shah's home town. If he were controlling the aircraft, he might have wanted a last nostalgic look.

All the above factors indicate that there indeed was the opportunity for the mass murder of innocent passengers and crew. But whether this happened or not, and who was responsible, will probably never be known.

If a verdict were to be given as to Captain Shah's committal of the crime of murder, the legal test of 'beyond reasonable doubt' would be best answered in my opinion by the ancient Scottish verdict of 'not proven'.

A sharpening up of reporting procedures and improvements in locator equipment of missing aircraft are the only good things to have come from the sad fate of Malaysian Airways Flight MH370.

24

LOOKING BACK

I think my experiences offer lessons to pilots. Firstly, having had rather more than my fair share of emergencies in my military flying career, I can say with confidence that if you regularly and rigorously practise your emergency drills, then when an emergency occurs you can be sure that you'll correctly follow the prescribed drill. The corollary is that if you haven't practised those drills, you're likely to make an error and compound the emergency – such as, for example, shutting down number four engine when dealing with a failure of number three engine, leaving yourself in the precarious situation of a double engine failure.

Some emergencies can be quite frightening, and it's quite normal to experience fear. Fear, however, must be controlled – and it will be controlled, as you quickly execute the required actions if you have properly practised in training sessions.

I'm reminded of the motto of the Royal Air Force parachute school, 'Knowledge dispels fear'. We used to joke it was the other way round. Interestingly, in my advanced years – at the time of writing I am 84 – some of the knowledge acquired in my parachute training has come back to me recently. Twice in recent days, I've slipped and plunged straight to the ground. Observers expected me to put out my hand and break my wrist but instead I did a parachute roll. There was certainly no time to think so my brain came up in split seconds with the fall technique embedded 60-odd years ago. Remarkable!

I recommend the practice of a mental review of critical procedures immediately before you might need to execute those procedures. For example, when about to take off at maximum weight for a runway, review the abort from near V1 speed drill and also the actions for continued takeoff.

My heavy landing of the Sunderland at Funafuti Lagoon, and the experience of finding myself unexpectedly in an inverted spin at low altitude in the Harvard with my best pupil, taught me to always be ready for the unexpected. It's recognised in flight training that between 200 and 400 hours, a pilot begins to feel he knows it all and needs to be watched. After 23,000 hours, I've learned to be always cautious and wary. Aviation may have a new lesson for you just around the corner.

When first exposed to aircraft with automated systems, you tend to not trust them, but after experience you may begin to trust them too much. Don't put all your faith in an automated system — especially a navigation system — but use all other available means to cross-check on the system performance. For instance, when motoring along with a GPS system happily indicating on track, the superior pilot will be doing such things as verifying that the magnetic compass reading is what he expects, the sun, or a heavenly body like the planet Jupiter, is in the correct relative position, and that any navigation stations within range show the expected readings.

Even experienced people can make mistakes. Inexperienced crew members must speak up if they think that something is unsafe, and continue to insist if necessary. Air New Zealand's instructions to co-pilots were, and probably still are, that they were to render their advice to captains. The captain mightn't accept the advice but the co-pilots were to continue to offer it until satisfied the operation was safe. This is a wise approach. Captains should go out of their way to encourage inexperienced crew members to speak up – some accidents would have been avoided if the co-pilots hadn't been afraid to challenge a captain's actions.

Very few pilots would have had the experience of finding themselves in a vertical dive at 400 feet with an instructor frozen on the controls as I did on my first night flying. That taught me that in extremis you depend on yourself alone.

My wild ride in the Vampire taught me that you must never give up but fight every inch of the way through an emergency.

Finally, I quote a highly experienced old pilot. He said that when there's the slightest doubt, trust *no one*, check *everything*.